Another Forward

by Thornton Krell

Fill Fuller follows *Full Filler*. *Fill Fuller* is highly allusive and will have special meaning to those who have read *Full Filler*. For those yet to read *Full Filler*, here's a summary of Full to catch you up for Fill etc.

Full Filler gathers 103 prize winning essays/stories/poems that establish a technical foundation and a generational tone plus backstory narrative indulgences along with the recognition of reality amidst sudden unexpected outbursts into pseudo philosophic frenzy; mashes those together with complex syncopations, over lapping characterizations, stylistic paragraphing and iffy punctuation....what emerges is an unforeseen story that rises above chronological plot construction.

When Ice discovered that he had prostate cancer, Ice decided to describe the journey wherever it may lead. It led to the past, the present and the future in random order. It led to untapped imagination beyond the restrictions of time. It led to a confluence of life journeys both external and internal. When organized, they came to resemble a story with beginnings, middles and conclusions.

Fiction and faction collide and produce autobiographical blarney. Is it a surrealistic autobiography, a novel, a collection of essays and poems that can be read in any order?

Yes..Yes and yes.

Let's face it, autobiography tends to address itself to qualified victories over the past and putting those events into something that resembles order creates a narrative made up of short incidents and impulses. Many of the incidents within Full Filler are short enough to qualify as allegorical in nature so keep that in mind as Full Filler continues that momentum.

So that's the ketchup on *Full Filler*, now we'll move on to the meat of *Fill Fuller*.

Full Filler was published in January of 2020 just before the onset of the "new normal". Ice continued to write his way through the pandemic. In those 30 months Ice composed another 103 prize winning essays published in London of all places and shared around the world by 350,000 readers. During the entirety of its composition, we addressed and continue to address the contagion of literal disease with the added figurative disease of disinformation. As we confronted and confront that two headed snake, our individual mortality has become more in focus as well as the survivability of our nation.

If I had to sum up Full Filler in100 words or less here's what I would choose:

Desire to survive, Pursue pleasure, Avoid pain, Playful Reflection, Companionship,

Lure of Comfort, Imagination, Purposeful Reflection, Tasting freedom, Responsibility,

Romance, Emergence of self, Synch with reality, Collision with ideals

Collision with reality, Fear, Humor, Infinite Perspective,Creative Transformation

Concern, Passion,Commitment, Suffering, Divine Recognition, Self annihilation,

Guilt before the divine, Paradox, Affirmation, Faith,Willing loss of continuity.

Fulfilment, Fill Fuller, Life etc.

Fill Fuller is a continuation of *Full Filler;* same 100 words.

It takes Rivers 700-800 pages to illustrate those words in his own way.

At this point, you can either skip both book(s) now that you know what they're about or decide to read. In case you decide to read keep these things in mind. Reading is about decision making, skill and strategy. If you've already decided to read this book(s) then persistence becomes a factor. You undoubtably have the skill because Ice is no genius even though he'll throw in the occasional vocabularic flourish. Strategy is simple but complex. You can just read the whole thing at once taking maybe 8-12 hours of your time. You can read it one story at a time once a day which will take you a couple months.

You can read it from back to front. You can just open it up anywhere, read a story and put it down. You can leave it on your shelf for the next five years and pick it up someday in the future when you've truly got nuthin' better to do and be surprised at how it comes alive and makes you wonder why the hell it took you so long in the first place. You can just figure out the am I a turtle question without reading the book and answer correctly if anybody ever asks you that question,

I trust that you will misunderstand. I already have, which is a good thing.

As it coalesced, Ice realized that *Fill Fuller* could be divided into three parts with the first and third parts acting as fun house mirror reflections of each other with the middle part dealing with Covid and serving as the mirror itself. Once again it can be read in any order.

The cover artwork and book design were done by Mary Ryan. It depicts the ancient paradox of two snakes devouring each other. The snakes are the same size, they have seized upon each other at the same time and are digesting at the same speed. What is the ultimate outcome?

Are two heads better than none?

And the essential question, are YOU a turtle? Ask yourself that now and then again after you've finished the book.

The cover art also represents the current situation in the USA as we continue to devour each other in the name of a democracy in which the future is as puzzling as the riddle of the two snakes.

Meanwhile, Putin is trying to devour Ukraine. Major League Baseball is also devouring itself in the name of billionaire greed.

Let's take a more pleasant journey. The chapters are short and there are pictures

So come along with us now particularly if you like reading, baseball, photography, aardvarks, Richard Boone, turtles, penguins, eagles,Wild Bill,

Secretariat, Zimmerman, Stingray, Daffy Duck, jazz, Ovid and Julia, Crystal Beach and a whole lot of other stuff. We're all here again. In a couple of pages the curtain will rise on Full Filler.

Hold the phone, Ice wants to get in the last words before the show like William Castle before *The Tingler* or CB Demille before the *10 Commandments* or like Richard Boone before every episode of *Have Gun Will Travel*.

A Challenge from Ice.

Thank you Thornton. I wrote the book and even I don't know exactly what you mean which is probably a good thing because it's a perfect example of exactly what I mean.

In the Police song *Don't Stand So Close to Me*, lead singer Sting alludes to "THAT book by Nabokov". Nabokov has several famous book but THAT book can only refer to *Lolita* his infamous, controversial 1958 best seller that has emerged as a classic example of literature and lesson in publishing from the mid-twentieth century. *Lolita* is hilarious, disturbing, challenging, rigorous highlighting the most insane of narrators the obsessed, brilliant, paranoid, romantic, perverse Humbert Humbert. The book itself is an allusion to a real life kidnapping that Nabokov was very aware of and inspired by...the sad case of Sally Horner.

If you don't know the book or the movie or the Sally Horner case then "that book by Nabokov" is a perfect example of unexplained allusion.

Kubrick made a movie of Lolita starring the perfectly cast James Mason as Humbert, perfectly cast Shelley Winters as Charlotte, perfectly cast Peter Sellers as Clair Quilty and imperfectly cast (thank God) Sue Lyons as Lolita. The movie begins with a full screen, worshipful pedicure which has become an inspiration for hand and foot models everywhere.

Lolita is one of those movies that when it comes on the tube, it becomes almost impossible to turn off. It shows up regularly on TCM. We've watched it at least five times and if it came on today we'd watch it again.The same is true with *Dr. Strangelove, 2001* and both *Good Fellas* and *Godfather.*

Lolita got me hooked on Kubrick and made me a huge fan of Shelley Winters who perfected the sad, naive, innocent victimized archetype in other amazing performances such as *Night of the Hunter*, *A Place in the Sun* and even *Poseidon Adventure*

But all of this is not the main point of this essay although it concurs with today's challenge. The point of today's "essay" is how much I am beginning to enjoy sub standard editions of novels as they are presented by Kindle unlimited and invite you to do the same. This enjoyment is based on my own experience with writing an e book. Our e book (free on Kindle unlimited) Full Filler was quite an awakening for me. My daughter Mary and I undertook the project with hardly any idea of what we were doing but what the hell. I had plenty of writing that I thought might entertain a wider audience while connecting with my friends, family and students. Mary is a designer. We put our efforts together and came up with a product which we submitted more or less for the hell of it. To our great surprise, the project was approved for printing, published and before we knew it, *Full Filler* e book was alive, available and loaded with the kind of blemishes that teams of proofreaders and editors eliminate from books of a more finished variety.

Someone has spotted over a hundred "errors" in the e book which might make it a great textbook to use in senior highs.... a find the errors exercise with the bonus of fresh essays. I definitely would have used it for those dual purposes.

I had never seen a book with so many zits. Maybe I was like a teenager looking into a mirror and exploding with self-consciousness at the reality of my complexion. My first cruise through our book left me kinda embarrassed.

I started looking at other self-published books. I soon realized that our effort was pretty representative of the genre. Garage rock as compared to studio rock.

Let's play *Louie, Louie* and enjoy the fact that people are dancing.

When we went to paperback format we cleaned up most of the blemishes and were unashamed of those that eluded us. We're not perfectionists. We're humans enjoying a new kind of freedom.

So how do we get back to *Lolita*.

Last week I decided to pick up a kindle version of Lolita on the cheap and was delighted to find the edition **full** of typos, spacing errors and omissions.

Here's one of my favorites.

When widower Humbert weds widow Charlotte as an excuse to get closer to his obsession, the text reads...."When the bride is a WINDOW and the groom is a widower...... I assume Nabokov intended to use the word 'widow' rather than 'window' although 'window' suggests another level of interpretation that made me pause in my reading.

Beautiful. Reading pauses are good. (Pause here if you like)

This stumble reminds me of the fact that Nabokov, he of the incredible vocabulary and immense virtuosity had once looked at a text full of errors like all of us writers do at some point before our supporting army cleans up the act.

Take the Traveling Willbury's for example. They chose their name from a common practice that all those recording artists knew when it came to errors…"don't worry about that we'll bury it in the mix."

Perfect in imperfection.

I have grown to love our e book. We created it without an army.

Now as you read THIS book, I've rewarded you close readers with at least a dozen errors. When you run across one, don't blame me. Congratulate yourself on being a person who can read for detail and consider my poor typing as a perfect example of EXACTLY what we're talking about.

We're proud of its authenticity and rough edges. Hey, check it out...it's free on Kindle.

And if you haven't read *Lolita* yet, well go ahead and try that one too.

I wonder if Sting read it. I'm sure he hasn't read *Full Filler*

I wonder how many people who have listened to *Don't Stand So Close To Me* have read *Lolita* or seen the Kubrick film. I imagine the percentage is small.

Allusion tends to work that way. Especially unexplained allusion which is one of my many bugaboos. Consider yourselves forwarded and challenged. Now let's raise the curtain and get on with the show.

Fill Fuller

Ice Rivers

Designed by Mary Ryan
Photos by Guy Conigilio, Ron Stochl, Robert Rondelli
Home Runs by Mark Texiera and Joe Lopardi
Music by Jack Neelin, Genesee Johnny, Jon Szeber

First Last Friday

Rizz didn't know the meaning of the word fear. He also didn't know the meaning of many other words which explains why he started out one grade ahead of me and finished one grade behind me at St. James.

I don't know how Rizz became acquainted with Mrs. Cole. I do know how he acquainted me with her. One Friday afternoon heading home from school, walking up Farmington towards Parsells, Rizz said, "Let's stop and see Mrs. Cole."

Since Rizz at the time was still one grade ahead of me, I trusted, agreed and followed.

Rizz walked up to the door of a pleasant, white house on the corner of Farmington and Presque. He rang the doorbell. Almost immediately a kindly looking, elderly woman appeared with a tray full of cookies.

Rizz said, "Hi, Mrs. Cole" and grabbed a couple of freshly baked chocolate chip cookies. He handed one to me as he introduced me to Mrs. Cole. She smiled her kind smile and was glad to meet me. We said, "Thank you, Mrs. Cole" and continued our trudge homeward.

We continued to make this walk for the next couple of years, always on Fridays. Mrs. Cole always had cookies and candy. She would always say, "You're good boys." when we said goodbye; good boys saying good byes.

I knew I shouldn't be taking candy from a stranger but even though I knew nothing about her, Mrs Cole could not be a stranger after a hundred or so Fridays. I guess the whole thing was supposed to be a secret. I never told my parents about Mrs. Cole. I never figured out how Rizz had discovered her. We never stepped past her doorway into her house. I never saw her husband. Mrs. Cole appeared to be a nice old woman who liked kids and liked to cook and like to share her cooking with kids on Fridays.

Kids being me and Rizz.

As far as I knew, we were the only kids who got cookies from Mrs. Cole.

Eventually, we out grew cookies. We had shortcuts that eliminated the need to walk up Farmington. We preferred cigarettes to cookies. We could smoke when we took our short cuts. Cookies were for kids. I don't remember exactly the last time that we stopped off for cookies. Rarely do we know when anything is the last time. What we do, we've done and will continue to do until we're done if that day ever comes.

I had forgotten all about Mrs. Cole until last week when I was reading a short biography of Nat King Cole at the same time I got an email from my high school pal Mike Cole. Hmmmm. Didn't I once know a lady, a nice lady named Mrs. Cole. The gentle memory returned with resonance.

Yeah, Mrs. Cole was an old woman.

Sheeyit. I'm probably 20 years older now than Mrs Cole was back then.

I'm sure that the last time we came to the door, Mrs. Cole had even less of an idea that this would be the last time than we did. We knew about the shortcuts even if we weren't taking them yet and everybody was beginning to light up. After that last Friday came the next Friday followed by three thousand twenty four more.

I wonder if Mrs. Cole was alarmed when we didn't show up on that first last Friday. Did she worry that something might have happened to us. What did she do with her cookies.

How many Fridays did she wait for us? Was she sad?

Did she stop baking?

I never heard anybody mention Mrs. Cole as if her kindness never happened.

She became less than a memory until last week.

Now she's part of a story.

A big part.

Watch out for short cuts.

Truth and Beauty and Legend

Some stories are so lovely that I hesitate to write them. Some legends are so fragile and delicate that I'm reluctant to reveal them. I'll try to do this one justice before the memories fade completely as the blur increases every day.

I remember his first day in class. He was fresh off the boat. I mean that literally. He was a boat person from Viet Nam. He was in my English class. He didn't speak a word of English. I didn't know what to do with him that first day so I somehow signaled/sent him to the main office to pick up an attendance sheet.

The secretary at the main office was expecting a student from another class named Mike. When my student arrived, whatever his name was, it wasn't Mike. Helen Fee asked my new student if his name was Mike. He didn't know what Helen was saying but he knew a question when he heard one. He nodded his head up and down. Helen said, "Here, Mike" and gave him the papers.

He returned to my classroom a few minutes later without the attendance sheet but with whatever administrivia Helen was supposed to give to "Mike". I took the paper from him. I said thanks and asked him what his name was.

He said, "Mike."

I said, "Hi, Mike."

That's how Mike got his name.

Aside from the single word "Mike"; Mike spoke no English. We were a pair, Mike and I. Mike would come into class, take his seat and listen with great patience and attention to the academic tumult engulfing him. I knew something of the concept of linguistic immersion wherein a person learns a foreign language more quickly by surrounding himself with it. I believed this was happening with Mike although I didn't know for certain. I did know that in this case English was the "foreign" language to Mike and he was surrounded.

One day after a couple of weeks, I noticed that Mike was taking "notes" of what I was saying. I couldn't imagine what Mike's notes looked like so I casually made my way to his desk to sneak a peek. Mike's "note" was a surreal and photographic drawing of a rose. As I looked at the rose, I was amazed as much by its sensitivity of rendering as I was by its virtuosity.

Near the drawing, I wrote the word "rose."

Then I said the word "rose"

I spelled the word "R..O..S..E"

Mike smiled and said "rose"

I took a risk. I had a feeling the risk would be approved by Mike.

I announced to the class. "Check this out, everybody. Mike can draw." Everybody crowded around Mike's desk. Everybody looked at the rose. Everybody flipped out. Everybody started saying, "Mike can draw" Eventually Mike got the message. He spoke his first English sentence in English class. This is what he said."Mike can draw".

That sentence contains eleven letters.

He smiled. Time stood still. I'm here to tell you.

Mike could draw.

Many scholars praise the efficient linguistic style of Julius Caesar, how much he could say with how few words. All of France is divided into three parts. Has anyone ever said more with fewer words at the beginning of his story. Perhaps the thirteen letters that Shakespeare used "to be or not to be." That's a question, isn't it?

Mike can draw. That's an answer.

Mike not only continued to draw but he also continued to listen with purpose and intention. Mike observed not only with his eyes but also with his heart and mind. Mike's vocabulary began to grow as he listened and observed; nouns first then verbs then adjectives.

Here's the story of the first adjective I can remember.

One day, I walked over to Mike's desk and noticed that he had been sketching a portrait of himself. On his portrait, I wrote a bunch of nouns with arrows like "Mike" and "nose" and "eyes" and "ears"and "head" and "neck" and "body". I pointed to each word and said it. Mike repeated the word with me. Then I added the adjective.

I wrote "famous"; drew an arrow to the picture of Mike and said the word.

Mike hesitated a second and then asked "Mike famous?"

I said "Yes, Mike will be famous,"

Mike startled me with his reply.

"No, Mike not famous. You, Mr. Rivers…you famous."

I realized that Mike's language skills were blossoming with as much beauty as his drawing skills.

From that day on, every time I saw Mike I would always say.

"Here's the famous Mike."

And Mike would always say, "Mike not famous. Mr. Rivers famous."

We would laugh.

We were connected.

Sure enough, Mike WAS becoming famous, at least in my class. He was already becoming a legend in my own mind.

I was running the school newspaper at the time. I asked Mike, still using arrows, objects and printed words to communicate, if he would draw a comic strip for the paper. He drew the strip. The school read Mike's comic. His character was a lion, The school loved it. Mike's fame grew. His audience expanded. By this time, everybody in my class knew something rare was happening with Mike and his art, kids were always crowding around his desk to see what new drawings were coming alive

I suspected that had Mike developed a crush.

I discovered this when Mike showed me a picture of a girl that he had been drawing. The girl looked like one of his classmates, a girl named Kathy. Mike was stylizing Kathy rather than photographing her with his rendering. I immediately recognized Kathy even with her stylized, over sized Disney girl eyes. I wrote "Kathy" on Mike's paper and drew an arrow. Mike blushed and smiled.

I could tell Mike wanted another word from me, an adjective perhaps so under the drawing, I wrote, "beautiful" and drew another arrow. Mike put the drawing away. His portrait of Kathy was not an image that he intended to show to the class. Not only were we connected; we had a secret.

A couple of weeks passed and Mike's language skills kept growing.

One day, he took out the picture of Kathy and showed me something new that he had added. He showed me that he knew how to change an adjective into a noun. Under my printing of "beautiful", Mike had printed a word of his own. This is the word that Mike had printed in painstaking, startling calligraphy.

"Beauty".

Beauty is truth and truth is beautiful.

I was facing a beautiful truth in my professional life as well as a crossroads. I was given the opportunity to write a grant under the auspices of the Federal Career Education Incentive Act Grant Program, the purpose of which, as the name suggests, was to help secondary education become a better link to careers.

I proposed my very first grant.

The proposal was funded for $500,000. In my proposal I visualized the creation of an intern program. The idea was radical at the time. I was chosen to be the administrator for the project. I would have to leave the classroom.

Leaving the classroom was the crossroads and a difficult factor in the decision.
When the kids heard what I had done. They were proud of me. Mike came to me and said, "Mike not famous, Mr. Rivers famous."

I left the classroom.

I left Mike in the capable hands of the Art Department particularly Larry Pace. Larry had served his country as a Marine in Viet Nam.

The day that I left, Mike showed me his private sketchbook. In his sketchbook were dozens of drawing of "Kathy". Underneath each sketch; a single printed word: Beauty.

By the time I got the Intern Program running smoothly, moving it from dream to imagination to realization, Mike was back in my life. Mike had made breathtaking progress in language and art and had begun to crystallize his dreams. Mike had grown to love classic Walt Disney cartoons and wanted to become an animator.
I had heard that fantasy from other students before and I would hear it again but with Mike...well he had a dream, spectacular discipline and dedication. I had an intern program. Uh, let's put two and two together and see if it comes out four, twenty two or five.

I contacted the only artist in town who specialized in 16 millimeter matte animation, a guy by the name of Brian. I told Brian about Mike. I told Mike about Brian. I brought the two of them together at Brian's downtown studio. With Brian's encouragement and equipment along with the ongoing help of the high school Art Dept. and the school librarian Penny Rider. Mike created his first animated cartoon.

He had even learned to play the guitar well enough to supply his own music to the animation. In Mike's cartoon one of the characters was a lion. Mike asked me, because I was "famous" to provide the voice for the lion.

Mike's cartoon was eventually selected in an extremely competitive national cartoon contest to be shown on Nickelodeon. Mike's cartoon was one of the best student cartoons in the country. Little ol' famous lion voice me was roaring on television sets across America.

Mike was only a sophomore in high school but he was already thinking about college and colleges were thinking about him. Anything was possible including truth, beauty and fame. Mike was most interested in beauty. He had discovered that the Disney studios regularly hired interns from the California Institute of the Arts. Mike knew about internships. He had completed four of them in high school. In the meantime Mike had taken all the art courses at the school plus four more at Rochester Institute of Technology and had aced them all.

Mike spoke a lovely version of the English language, the direct, clear, soft and kind version rarely used by native speakers.

Mike could draw.

Mike could talk.

Mike could write, words and music.

Mike could play the guitar.

Mike had a resume full of A's, internships, art work, awards and a cartoon that had played nationally on Nickelodeon. Mike applied to the California Institute of the Arts. We were all happy but not surprised when Mike was accepted and scholar shipped.

Mike was ready for another journey.

I was on a bit of a journey myself. My first marriage was breaking up although I didn't realize it or perhaps was denying the realization. Mike had never been to a rock concert in his life so at the end of the school year, the night after his graduation I invited Mike as our family guest to see the Moody Blues at the Canandaigua Performing Arts Center.

Mike accepted the invitation.

You'll hear more about THAT later.

After the concert, Mike left for California.

I haven't seen him since.

Here's the last few things I heard about Mike.

In college, his skill and interest continued to blossom. As an undergraduate, he applied for and completed an internship at Disney Studios. Upon graduation from college, Mike was hired as an artist/animator by Disney. His first screen credit appeared at the end of the Little Mermaid, listing Mike as an animator of Ariel, The Little Mermaid.

Apparently Disney liked Mike because his next assignment was a substantial promotion. Mike would be one of the main designers for Beauty and the Beast
Mike was helping to create Belle. By now, everybody knows WHAT Belle looks like. Only a few of us know WHO Belle looks like.

Beauty, if you will, looks exactly like the sketches of "Kathy" that Mike labored over so mightily, so beautifully, so passionately, so innocently and so truthfully during his junior high days.

Kathy is Belle.

Kathy is Beauty, at least for many of us who knew Mike back when.

Some stories are so lovely that I hesitate to write them. Some legends are so fragile and delicate that I am afraid to relate or reveal them.

Remember?

Well, I tried.

As I tried, I kept flashing back to the writers who brought us the legends of the Old west, those scribes who turned big nosed, shiftless, violent, alcoholic William Hickock into the great Wild Bill, the handsome hero who died, shot in the back while playing poker and holding the deadman's hand...a pair of aces and a pair of eight.
A cardinal rule for those writers was, according to John Ford in The Man Who Shot Liberty Valance, "if you come to a crossroads between truth and legend, write the legend."

The legend of Mike and Kathy is the loveliest local legend, I've ever personally encountered. I'm part of it; a small part but yes I was there in the very beginning.
I can vouch for everything until Mike left for California. I can vouch that Mike worked on The Iron Giant. I can vouch for the similarities between Mike's sketches of Kathy and the rendering of Beauty.

Every once in awhile, when I reminisce about my teaching days, I like to think that I was the guy who had something to do with the inspiration for the creation of Beauty.

And ya know what?

It's a beautiful feeling.
Maybe even factionally true.

Next time somebody you know mentions truth, beauty or Beauty and the Beast tell 'em this story. That's how legends grow.

Big Red and Mushingroom

T'was twenty hours before I observed a primeval, confrontational force of nature appear at precisely the right juncture in my adult development arise and abide at the perfect co-ordinates of place, event and time. Twenty hours remained before a performance so stunning in clarity that it raised the expectations of excellence of all who witnessed it. Twenty hours before time stood still. Twenty hours before I discovered what a horse actually looked like. Twenty hours before I knew the color chestnut.

It was 10 o'clock on a Friday night, not just any Friday but June 3, 1973. We were sitting in my basement listening to *Wake of the Flood*. This night and the next day would be the only time that all three of us would ever spend together. This was another last time, that we didn't see coming.

One of my friends was Avery Scoville Beer. We called him Scobey. Scobey and I taught together for a year before Scobie joined the Peace Corps. I had shown Scobie how to fold the image of George Washington on a dollar bill into a perfect mushroom. The night he left, he presented me with a frame ink etching of that mushroom that he had drawn. On the back of that work of art he had written these words   "to a true friend that I will never forget".

Scobie went to Nepal where he served for two years. In his first few months in Nepal, he tried like hell to hold on to his American culture but a few months in while riding an elephant, he couldn't hold it any longer He got off the pachyderm and fell into a swoon. When he woke up he was in a Buddhist temple staring up at a mandalla. He stopped trying to hold on to the past.

Now having just returned to the States, Scobie was being equally overwhelmed and culture shocked by America. Let's put it this way, when Scobie was driving, he had a hard time keeping the car on the street. Scobie considered the sidewalk just another yak free part of the road. I had become his unofficial guide back into America. Earlier in the week, I had taken him to a Grateful Dead concert in Buffalo where we heard *Wake of the Flood* performed live.

Also in the cellar that night was my childhood friend Johnny Crown. Crown had been out of the army for a few years by then. He had been an MP in Fort Bragg, North Carolina and in fact been one of the officers who legendarily arrested Jane Fonda in her Hanoi Jane days. Crown, on this evening, was in the early days of his "retirement" at age twenty six. Crown was finished working for a living and had decided to become a gambler. His hair was "perfect".

We were all in our mid-twenties, all single, all eligible and about as in shape and handsome as we were going to get. As we were trying to figure out what to do next, we started bragging to each other about how far we would travel to do whatever that something was. Chicago was in play, so was Cleveland, New York and Boston. We were ready to go where the action was. Nothing was holding us back.

Crown suggested that we drive to New York city and catch the Belmont Stakes. I was a sports fan and had followed the Triple Crown races that year. I was familiar with two equine stars, Sham and Secretariat who had emerged at the Kentucky Derby in Louisville and the Preakness Stakes in Maryland. Secretariat had won both races with Sham finishing a close second. Both horses had set new track and distance records in each race, the main difference was that Secretariat had two wins while Sham had two places.

In winning the Derby, Secretariat had come from last place to first place, picking off and passing every horse in the field until hooking up and passing Sham down the homestretch. During his Run for the Roses, Secretariat had raced each succeeding quarter mile faster than the one before it leaving no doubt about Secretariat's endurance.

In his Preakness victory, Secretariat had once again trailed early. The he exploded into a second quarter of 21 seconds. Having grabbed the lead, he sailed home and once again edged the fast closing Sham. With my usual underdog instinct in full gallop, I began rooting for Sham. Crown was convinced of Secretariat. Scobie was rooting for karma.

We called the argument to question. We jumped in my car and drove all night to Belmont. Upon our arrival, we stopped into a diner for breakfast. Ron Turcotte, Secretariat's jockey, stopped into the same diner and sat down near us. I didn't know Turcotte but Crown recognized him. He pointed to the short man and whispered "That's the guy. That's Secretariat's jockey." It was cool but it didn't mean much to me at the time. Ten hours later it would.

We ate breakfast, hung around for awhile and were among the first of the 80,000 who would arrive at the track that day. I got my bet on Sham down early.

We sat through the eight races as the crowd grew larger, more boisterous and more expectant at the conclusion of each race until only the Stakes remained.

I brought my camera with me so I was anxious to get some pictures. As the race approached, I made my way to the paddock near the saddling area. Most of photography is having a camera and standing in the right place. I had my camera and I was in a great place.

I had been in the paddock area at Finger Lakes, our local track, many times and had seen a lot of thoroughbreds. It became immediately obvious that the horses at this event were of a higher order of breeding. Sham came out before. I was impressed. He looked the best of the rest. He certainly looked like a winner.

Then Secretariat made his way into the paddock and I completely forgot about Sham. It was the closest I've come to animal worship; not just me, but everybody around me. A couple of people fainted. Women were having, let's just say pheremonic reactions as they swooned in the presence of Big Red as Secretariat was known. People often ask me how Secretariat looked up close. The best description I can give is he looked exactly like a horse is supposed to look. From that day forward, every horse that I saw looked a little bit less like a horse. Everything was in proportion only bigger, better and more breathtakingly real. Secretariat was the tattoo in the paddock, all others were birthmarks.

Secretariat oozed confidence. He knew he was a champion and he had come to New York to prove it once and for all. Although up to this moment he was invincible, an undeniable aura of relatability rather than snorting arrogance radiated around Secretariat. He was enjoying himself and enjoying the people who were enjoying him. Big Red was kind of an "aw shucks" good guy like most of my friends. He impressed me as a friend impresses me...a friend you can count on. If you have friend on whom you think you can rely, you are a lucky man. All of my friends look like undiscovered stars to me, this was a star who had been an undiscovered friend.

In the presence of Secretariat I felt like a lucky man.

In the presence of this fully realized horse, I felt like a more fully realized man.

People were screaming. People were in awe. My consciousness of passing time was being altered. We were all in slow motion. Gears were tumbling and clicking. Secretariat was already wearing the blue and white checkered mask that was his trademark and which made him instantly recognizable.

My camera was ready to click as well. I re-positioned myself near the tunnel where Secretariat would pass on his way to the track. He approached me. He got closer and closer. Because my camera was of the rewind variety, I kept waiting as he got closer. He was right next to me. I waited one more second. He was looking directly in my eye from under his mask and swerved even closer to my lens as the camera clicked.

I swear to God, he smiled.

Red passed me and headed into the tunnel that separates the paddock from the track. Momentary silence ensued as Secretariat entered the tunnel. In the distance, I could hear the band playing Sidewalks of New York. Then the silence was broken by a Big Apple roar as the horses exited from the tunnel and came into view of the awaiting crowd. The clamor doubled when Secretariat stepped on the track. Secretariat was the last horse in the parade to the track

I had just enough time to get to the betting window where I strengthened my wager by throwing down on Big Red. All that remained was the race.

The gate opened and immediately Sham and Secretariat left the field behind. The two rivals were racing as one, stride for stride. I asked Crown how it looked. He said that both jockeys were straight up in the stirrups. Crown told me that meant that the jockeys were letting their horses run at will and free.

Gradually, Sham's jockey started to lower himself a little to drive the horse rather than to ride the horse. Turcotte continued straight and tall. One of the jockeys was clearly pushing his horse while other jock was taking a surrealistic ride on a genius, equine rocket.

Nearing the far turn, Secretariat seemed to glance over at Sham. I imagined Secretariat smiling again. "Sham" the smile said, "you've been a great rival, maybe later someday we can have grain together but right now, I'm leavin' you. I know it's gonna break your heart. Sorry pal, I gotta go. It's legend time."

See ya.

And Secretariat hit a gear unknown to other horses. He separated from Sham. As Secretariat sped up, Sham fell back. Eventually all the other horses would catch Sham who finished last. Spirit broken, the great Sham would never race again.

Now all eyes were on Secretariat and time began to disappear as Secretariat devoured it. Shadows of the late afternoon sun painted a magical silhouette of a horse and rider galloping into legend. The crowd had screamed itself into awe struck silence or silenced itself into an ear splitting scream whichever as Secretariat came down the stretch, still running free, still increasing his lead. Now all alone, his lead stretched to twenty lengths as Turcotte glanced at the timer. The record for the race and for the distance was 2:26 and 3/5. Secretariat took a final zoom and crossed the finish line at 2 minutes and 24 seconds. The track announcer screamed "and the winner in a new track record and new world record…..Secretariat."

He won by 23 lengths.

Later that evening Scobey, Crown and I reminded ourselves about what we had just seen together. We promised to remind ourselves throughout our lives about Secretariat and each time we would recall that moment we would expect more of our existences. If we ever saw each other again we could always look back and say "well, we were together that day at Belmont."

As fate would have it, I haven't seen Scobey since that day. He had to get back to mountains. Some folks say he moved to Oregon, invented a back pack that turned into a chair and struck it rich. If he somehow walked into the door of my North Carolina home right now, I'd say "Scobe, let's take a minute and remember Secretariat.

As for George Mushingroom, I gave the precious artwork to one of my daughters, the one with the chestnut hair, when it became clear that she would be leaving home. I hoped and continue to hope that it will bring her the best of luck.

As for Crown, I called him last night and told him I was going to try and write this story. He reminded me to stay tall in the stirrups and let the words run free.

Oh and the picture...it came out a blur. Secretariat had come too close to the lens.

Heading for a Home Stretch

I don't know whether I'm coming or going.

I'm going home next week where there will be a Homecoming in my honor.

I haven't been home in three years.

Home is Rochester, New York....the flower city the home of Kodak and Xerox. The place where Rod Serling died and Louise Brooks, Frederic Douglas and Susan B Anthony lived. Suffragette City, where David Bowie was arrested for possession of weed...WHAM BAM THANK YOU MA'AM. Where the Rolling Stones caused such a disruption during their first US tour that they were banned for life from ever returning.

Photo by Guy Coniglio

Rochester has seen better days. Rochester even went so far as to win an NBA championship back in the 50's before the Rochester Royals moved to Cincinati and eventually to Sacramento, now home of the Kings.

If you're from Rochester, you should know something about photography and movies. George Eastman had the bright idea of making photography available to the common man which he did and it was and still is although we don't need film anymore. We've got great photographers in Rochester; Guy Coniglio, Ron Stochl, Bob Rondelli, Cal Brown, Montanus, Matt Wittmeyer and David Ellsworth to name just a few. (You will see some of their magical work within Fill Fuller) Speaking of film and movies, once upon a time virtually all of the film used in motion pictures was produced in Rochester. Why not, George Eastman was buds with Tommy Edison.

Rochester still has Durand Eastman Park, the Eastman House and the Eastman Theater which is home for the Rochester Philharmonic and the gifted students of the Eastman School of Music. We've got the U of R, Rochester Institute of Technology, Nazareth and St. John Fisher colleges as well as Monroe Community College and Strong Memorial Hospital. We've got a Lilac Festival and a Jazz Festival. We've got the Little Theater. We've got Oak Hill, Locust Hill and Champions Hills for top shelf golf. We've got Genesee Beer .Once upon a time, we were the sister city of Toronto which is right across from us on Lake Ontario. We may still be related but there's no comparison now. Toronto is major league. Rochester is struggling to remain Triple A. The International League which once included Toronto, Montreal and Havana has faded.

Rochester once had hundreds of thousands of residents who worked or had worked at Kodak. Many of them spent their entire careers literally in the dark. Many others were engaged in the production of cameras that didn't cost an arm and/or a leg. Cameras for the people. Photography for the people. People take pictures of each other just to prove that they really existed and to prove that they really didn't miss it (whatever "it "was). Who knew that one day people would be taking pictures with their telephones and those telephones wouldn't be made by Kodak nor would they use Kodak film nor any film at all? Rochester didn't that's for damned sure! Caught in the dark.

And Xerox is another story.

Remember a time when you would say, "make a 'Xerox' of that". Xerox figuratively meant 'copy'. We were entering an age of information. Xerox always claimed that information (not copiers) was the actual product of their business.

Information overwhelmed Xerox.

Other companies stepped in to pick up the slack.
They copied Xerox.

Xerox was left behind.

Meanwhile, the weather in Rochester continued to be cloudy. Rochester has less sunshine than any city in the United States which made it a natural place for the catacomb of darkrooms that made up Kodak processing at one time along with the high rate of bank robberies and stolen cars. Rochester can be bone chilling in January.

I finally had to leave Rochester as the future of the city looked as dismal as the weather. I was recovering from cancer at the time and my doctor encouraged the move. Doctor's orders.

The past though; that's a whole different ballgame. Wonderful, enduring friendships, bus trips downtown to the RKO Palace or Loews or The Paramount, sandlot baseball, music, education, Boy Scouts, altar boys, Dreamland Park, Jack Rabbitts, Sisters of Mercy, Knot Hole Gangs, Red Wing Opening Days, Section 5 basketball at the big house, Aquinas football, McQuaid Jesuit High and on and on.

On my return I wanted to go to see a Red Wing game. The Wings will be out of town. Last year, they didn't play a single game in Frontier because of Covid. Never Fear......I've got friends and family to welcome me.If American Airlines doesn't cancel my flight out of Charlotte. The Charlotte Airport is a hot mess at the moment. American Airlines flights are being regularly cancelled due to labor shortages within the company. We won't know for sure whether our flight will be cancelled until we get to the airport .

The Transportation Security Administration has notified American Airlines that due to very high levels of passenger activity, customers originating their travel from Charlotte Douglas International Airport (CLT) may have to wait longer than usual to clear the TSA checkpoint. Also, please note international travel may require additional check-in time due to COVID-19 documentation requirements.

I haven't travelled by myself by air in forty years. Lynn is worried about me getting lost. When we do travel, I just follow her. She has the tickets, the bag check, the passports, the cell phone. All of these items are items that I have a chance of misplacing or losing as I wander from gate to gate wondering where the hell I am.

Knowing that my trip was approaching, last month I got my first cell phone. Today, we've been practicing with it. I've texted. I've made a few calls. I've responded to texts and answered a few calls. It's cool. If I don't lose the phone, I'll be all right.

I've even taken some pictures with the phone. I used to get so pissed at people who took pictures with their cell phones in places where I as a photographer with a legitimate camera was banned from taking pictures. One such episode took place at the George Eastman house when I was prevented from using my camera to take a picture of Jeff Bridges who had come to the theater to talk about the freedom of expression known as photography and show off some his photography.

Now, I'm one of those guys with the telephone not the camera.

I've got to admit, that cell phone works very well. It works better as a camera than my Canons work as telephones.

More people are taking more pictures and the pictures are increasingly more beautiful. Quality comes from quantity. The secret to photography had always been to be the person with the camera and to be in the right place at the right time. Now everybody's got cameras and increasingly every moment is the right moment to take a picture of whatever is happening. Before, we had to be choosy because we only had 36 exposures on a role. Now, of course, you can take 36 exposures in 3 seconds and erase all of them except the one that came out best. Yeah.

I will definitely be going to beautiful Canandaigua Lake where my brother resides. My parents owned a cottage on the lake which they bought from my grandfather. I've been going to that cottage my whole life, at least the first 70 years of it. The plan was for me to buy the cottage when my parents passed away.

By the time they passed, I was looking to get out of Rochester so we sold the old cottage.

The old cottage was part of a "compound" that included two more cottages...one belonging to my cousin Moonyeen and the other belonging to my brother Deke. Moonyeen and Deke upgraded their cottages into lovely homes. I'll be visiting those homes next week if I don't lose my ticket and if the flight takes off if American Airlines can hire enough people to get the bird in the air.

Moonyeen is 80 something now and her husband Corky born on the same day as Moon in the same year in the same town is still with her at the lake and has been since they married at 18 although most of the time living in East Bloomfield, the town that expanded and swallowed swallowed the village of Holcomb. My Aunt Martha, Moonyeen's mom and her husband my Uncle Bill had moved into the cottage and made the first upgrade.

When I'm down at the lake, I'm gonna visit Crystal Beach where I learned to swim. I'm gonna take a swim and then stand in the water and look at the willow tree near the water. The willow tree that we always stand and look at when we go into the water. The willow tree that always looks the same in July regardless of the changes that have gone down in the previous fall, winter spring. The willow tree that makes time stand still and brings memories back into clear, clear focus.

I have a theory that every time I go into shallows of Crystal Beach and swim and look at the willow, I'm much handsomer and healthier when I get out.

I can't wait for that feeling.

Maybe I'll take my cell phone out into the water with me when I'm done swimming and beginning to stand there and look at the willow weeping and the way the water changes color every time that I move. Maybe I'll look away from the willow and catch a shot of a boat motoring across a golden surface.

Maybe I'll take a picture of that moment, capture it, prove that it happened. Maybe I'll make a copy of that image, turn it into a canvas. Hang that canvas in my house as a reminder of my old hometown when I get home to my new hometown in North Carolina just in case this is the last time.

Ya never know when the next time will be the last time. Plus I'm gonna check in with Crown. Probably talk about Secretariat a little and Wilt.

20 Cartoons

Once upon a time, Downtown Rochester was a wonderland. We had first run distributor theaters like the Loew's, The RKO Palace and the Paramount. We had massive department stores stores like Sibley's, McCurdy's, Neisner's, Woolworth's and Penny's. Woolworth's and Neisners were called five and dimes. If you had a nickel or a dime, you could get something. We had music stores like Levis and Midtown Records We had book stores like Scrantom's. We had a philharmonic orchestra at the George Eastman Theater. We had a YMCA a YWCA and a CYO. We had shoe stores galore. Remember Buster Brown and his dog. We even had a Mister Peanuts. We had top shelf restaurants like Eddie's Chop House. We had convenience places where you could get a quick burger or two at the White Tower. We had convenient bus routes. We had a War Memorial where we could go to see our very own Rochester Americans hockey team and rock and roll concerts. We had two daily newspapers, The Democrat and Chronicle and the Times Union. The D and C arrived in the morning the Times in the afternoon We were pretty much an American Toronto, which was our sister city across Lake Ontario.

Beautiful.

The movie houses were palaces indeed, not just the RKO. On Saturdays, they filled up with kids like me to see *I Was A Teenage Werewolf*, *The Blob*, *The House on Haunted Hill*, *The Tingler*, The Creatures with Atom Brains and From the Black Lagoon and a *Beast from 20,00 Fathoms* not to mention Hercules with Steve Reeves and the dancing slave girls.

Then, they tore down the Loew's to make room for Xerox towers and the first of its kind downtown mall...Midtown with the international clock. Around the time of the construction of Midtown, veterans using the GI Bill began moving their families into the suburbs. Shopping plazas were erupting everywhere. Downtown began to slowly suffocate/disintegrate

Prior to Midtown, I had learned how to use the bus system. We had a bus loop at the top of Parsells Avenue. All we had to do was walk up to the top of the Avenue, catch the bus and disembark DOWNTOWN.

Simple really. I was 10 years old. I knew how to use the bus. I taught everybody how to use it. Some of the kids were afraId to go at first until I explained to them how simple and safe it was. Get the bus at the stop near your house. Get off the bus at the stop next to the theater. Get off the bus. Get into the theater. Come out of the theater. Maybe stop at Critics for Cherry Phosphates. Catch the bus to your home. We all went downtown together and came home together. Rochester was at its peak and DOWNTOWN was the heart of the city.The downtown movie houses had the best movies and we could get to them easily.

On the outskirts of the city, we had smaller neighborhood movie houses. Although they were smaller, they still opened curtains before every showing. The neighborhood theater nearest to me but off the bus route was the Waring. We had to get our folks to drive us to the Waring. The Waring didn't play A movies until they were at the end of their run. The Waring played films that were often rated B by the Legion of Decency in the days when Jews made the movies, Catholics censored them and Protestants went to see them. Nuns discouraged us from going to the Waring which to them was a near occasion of sin.

The Waring had one thing that the downtown palaces didn't have. The Waring had an annual event called 20 cartoons. Cartoons used to play when the curtain first went up at the downtown theaters. They would show one cartoon before the matinee. We loved 'em.

The idea of 20 cartoons in a row was unbelievable.

The Waring distributed Warner Brother's films which means they had first crack at Warner Brothers cartoons. They would bunch 20 of them together and have their biggest kid show of the year.

I remember my friend telling me about the existence of 20 cartoons and I thought he was fibbing. Surely, no such event actually existed. Nothing could be that good, I checked the Democrat and Chronicle every day to see what movies had come to town. The downtown theaters had the biggest advertisements. One day, I noticed that the Waring was advertising 20 Cartoons. The damned thing actually existed.

I talked my parents into taking a carload of my friends to the Waring that day. Sure enough, 20 Warner brother cartoons played one after the other. Everybody was laughing and yelling for Daffy Duck, Bugs Bunny, Sylvester and Tweety and Porky Pig.

The Waring was packed.
One cartoon followed another. We were delighted.
I'll never forget that afternoon when actualization lived up to expectation.
The first cartoon was Daffy Duck.

Developmental Hell

Every night just before I fall asleep,
my inner director starts pitching ideas
to my inner producer.
Some of these ideas
have been pitched for months
but get stuck in developmental hell.
The worst kind of stuck
follows the lack of follow through
that ideas have when I describe them t
to another person orally as in
"I'm gonna write something about" and then I flesh out
the idea to the listener who usually responds :
"Oh that's a great idea"
"What have you been smoking"
"I can't wait to read that"
"You have such a vivid imagination"
"Bout time somebody wrote about that"
"That could be a movie"
"That's freaking hilarious"

I very rarely get back to any of those ideas.
The time never seems right.
The idea cools off
or more usually
something else comes along
the one that leaps through
the window of opportunity
that starts typing itself and before long
it's on paper with zero time in development
like this one here and wonders where it came from
Beneath what sea and how many fathoms deep
And mixed in metaphor
overlooking Serenity Street
And Parsells Avenue, while closing the distance

Defenestrating and floating safely to the ground
while the others linger somewhere in there
Hidden behind venetian blinds
the one where recovering Rizz
Takes his daughters to Ellison Park.
the one explaining once again the difference
 between impeachment and indictment
with Spiro Agnew as the main character
the one where Jacques LaPlumer and Bull Donlelfechski
get captured by the jungle queen and
avoid being turned into skin boats
by puncturing themselves with forks.
the one where I explain curfews in female dorms
the one that begins "all men like to be on a first name basis with their boss"
the film noir interlude between Tee and Ruth who meet in a dive
and begin their fatal dance with a hot conversation
that uses the feline line "you shouldn't be wearing legs like that"
as they pursue the legendary leopard skinned pill box hat.
The one about the ghouls
The one that is so bizarre
that if I write it and my wife sees it
she might take me for a Clive Barker
All of those are hanging around
Don't count on reading any of 'em
Their chances further diminished
by their present utterance here
reducing them to the bullshit heap
of ideas without implementation.
Rooms without windows
Truth is I don't know what's next
 I think it might have something to do
with Jezebel and Elijah
or Julis Caesar and Decimus
which leads to fake friendship,
mendacity, treachery and assassination
which leads to the last episode of the Sopranos
which I might have written about today

but instead decided to try and describe the process of development
which got in the way of the story about Julius and Tony
which means Decimus might never be captured
by me in the words I wanted to use
before I got carried away with this thing.
Who knows
Oh yeah
There's also the one about carving
Johnny Depp as Hunter Thompson

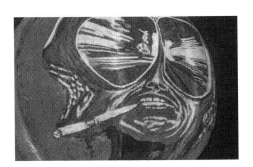

Into a gigantic Kentucky Pumpkin
There's also one about Daffy Duck
There's one about the jitters of
repressed hyper-sexual hysteria as
expressed by Charley Brown
And one about when my friend
Dogs met my friend Cat
And the son of a bitch who stole my gal
And the one comparing folks who love each other and have arguments
with the folks who love arguments and have each other
And the ongoing disinformation campaign of Merle Seton
And the fate of Thornton Krell
And the de-evolution of Mastin Thrust
And the love story of Haylen and Rebecca

All of them gleaming for a moment
Before slipping further away.
Ready to be pitched again each night
Just before dreams take over
And the window of darkness
Explodes into vivid black and white
With the voice of Robert Mitchum
Calling for children
After drowning Shelly Winters.

Top Drawer

by Thornton Krell

The old wallet died characteristically as a hero.

Ice had walked the four rows down from his VIP seats at Citi-field in order to snap a shot of Aaron Judge. Taking a great photo is all about figuring out where to stand or in this case kneel. As soon as Ice got into perfect position, not a moment sooner or later, Judge unleashed a ferocious swing. The sound of collision between bat and ball was startling. Ice, startled, snapped. The slight movement caused by the startling sound and the ferocity of the swing would cause a bit of a blur for sure.

The ball landed 450 feet later in the left field stands.

Ice lowered the camera to take a look while Aaron ran the bases. The stadium roared in awe as fans realized where the shot had landed. Ice recovered in time to get a picture of Judge getting ready to touch home plate. Aaron pointed to the heavens in gratitude as the fans pointed towards left field and released a collective "Holy Shit".

Ice retreated from the position that he had held for maybe twelve seconds. As he returned to his seat, he looked at the click and whispered "I got it". Then automatically he reached for his wallet and realized "I don't have it". The wallet was missing. In near panic, Ice sorted through the camera equipment that was now in his seat. He had gotten up in a hurry. He looked through the equipment and couldn't see the wallet.

He looked behind the seat and there was the wallet....covered in beer. The covering was the result of a fan jumping up and dropping his beer on the wallet. Beer combined with 30 plus years of service had put an end to the wallet as a functioning billfold.

Ice was relieved to find the damp thing. Everything in it was soaked.

Ice carried the wounded wallet for the next two days but realized it was time to throw in the towel.

When he got home. He took everything out of the drowned billfold. He retrieved the replacement from where it had been waiting for twenty years in the top drawer to get into the game. The replacement wallet was a Christmas gift from his mother-in-law. He left the pictures of Allan Ladd and Virginia Mayo in the new/old wallet. He added his driver's license, his library card and his Dylan ticket.

Everything else remained in the old wallet. Ice placed the old wallet in the top drawer underneath a framed picture/poem that his parents had given him many years ago.

The writing on the picture said;
"To Our First Born
We've always loved you best because you were our first miracle. You were the genesis of our marriage and the fulfillment of young love. You sustained us through the hamburger years, the first apartment (furnished in Early Poverty) and our first mode of transportation (1946 feet) and the seven inch TV set that we paid on for 36 months. You were new, had unused grandparents and enough clothes for triplets. You were the original model for a Mom and Dad who were trying to work the bugs out. You got the strained lamb, the open safety pins and the three hour naps. You were the beginning."

Underneath the writing was Ice in his white dinner jacket and bow tie smiling for this senior portrait. Next to the senior picture was a smaller picture of the family dog, a mutt named Lassie who could not have looked less like the Lassie on teevee.
Above the mutt

Love Always
Mom and Dad.

This is the stuff that was in Ice's wallet on the wallet's last day;all of them stories. Some of the stories already written others to be written. Some of this stuff was not gonna make the transfer to the new wallet and settle instead in the top drawer.

His library card.

a photo id card for radiology treatment

a photo id card from his second year year at college

a current New York state drivers license

a guest pass for Artisan Works

a ticket stub from a Bob Dylan concert at RIT

A funeral card for his mother

A laminated Buffalo Bills schedule from 2015

a laminated country club membership card

A ticket stub for the Chuvalo banquet.

A medicare registration Card

A business card for Tasty Parker

a $2 win ticket on Secretariat from Belmont Park

An amusement park photo machine photo of him and Lynn on their first date.

The last thing Ice noticed as he shut the drawer was that somehow the ticket for Bob Dylan at RIT had broken loose from the sacred discards.

Photoluminescent Effect/Affect

Eventually, we all see something that glows in the dark.

My first memory of that moment involves a plastic crucifix with a glow in the dark Jesus suffering upon it in the process of redemption.

I was in third grade.

If we sold enough Easter seals we could get that crucifix.

I got everybody in my neighborhood to buy Easter seals . My parents, aunts and uncles also bought the seals.

I got the crucifix.

I hung it up in my room.

I invited my buddies over to watch the suffering as it glowed in the dark.

Later I learned the word photoluminescent.

Soon after that I learned about "black lights".

Soon after that, we had a black light in our cellar.

And a lot of parties. Maybe you came to one or more.

I began to use the word photoluminescent with regularity.

One day, a new guy came over to the cellar and I said "Photoluminescent".

He asked, "what does that mean?"

I said "glows in the dark"

He said "why don't you just say that? It doesn't take as much time and tells me what it means as you're saying it"

I compared syllables and sure enough "glows in the dark" has two less syllables than photoluminescent.

Perhaps articulate vocabulary was a deterrent to efficiency.

After a moment of conjecture, I rallied.

"Why say four words, when you can say one?"

"Yeah but your word makes me feel stupid" he observed.

I learned several lessons that day.

1) Just cause you know a word doesn't mean that anybody else does.

2) It's possible to make people feel stupid even when you don't intend that result.

3) The language is available in many different levels and packages.

4) It's a skill to match the level of the language you that speak with the level of the language that the person that you're speaking to understands.

5) Vocabulary is destiny

6) When it comes to destiny, efficiency may or may not be an asset.

7) Some people will always use "photoluminescent" regardless

8) Some people will always use "glows in the dark" even after they learn "photoluminescent"

9) My reading was influencing my vocabulary, thus my destiny and perhaps complicating my life.

10) Not everybody wants to read nor needs to read nor seeks a complicated life.

Everything that is photoluminescent whether it be a word or a suffering Jesus, loses its glow when darkness retreats whether above or below the surface.

Rose at Shannon

My aunts and uncles were infamous for their selective, skillful flatulence. I remember one "disturbance" in particular.

We were at the Shannon airport in Ireland and only minutes away from hopping the KLM to wing back across the ocean. It was 1958. I was 12. I still can't figure out what inspired my trip to Ireland with my Aunt Rose and my Uncle Joe. Uncle Joe was my grandfather's brother so to him it was a Homecoming which he over celebrated from the get go. I think the intention was for Rose and me to visit the World's Fair in Brussels. Joe got bogged down in the pubs of Dundalk and we never made it out of Ireland. I remember Joe kept ordering Guiness which I thought looked like Coke with a foam until I snuck a sip and almost puked. Whatever it was, it damned sure wasn't Coke. Let's say I've adjusted a lot since then.

I was too young for the Ireland experience and suffered from culture shock. I couldn't wait to get home to rock and roll, baseball and Little League. I'd had enough "football" thank you.

I saw a black thorn shillelagh in the airport gift shop for sale. My aunt gave me the money to buy it.

I got in line but inadvertently got on the wrong side of the customs rope. I bought the shillelagh and headed back to my aunt who was only a few feet away when I was stopped by a customs agent who asked me if I had my passport. I didn't have it on me and the agent decided to be a prick and not let me cross to the other side of the line. A commotion started; an international dispute.

My aunt Rose began arguing with the customs guy but she wasn't getting anywhere, matter of fact things were getting worse. A small crowd began to gather.

Rose did have her secret weapon though.

She passed gas, silent but deadly.

The crowd began to react to the change in the air quality with Rose reacting most dramatically.

Rose began making faces, gagging and pointing at the customs guy, blaming him for the noxious odor. The gathering crowd, already on my side, started blaming the customs guy for the foul air. He started denying it and pointed back at Rose. Rose had done this trick many times before and she was very good at feigning innocence. She had been blaming her brother and sisters for years, eventually her classmates, her teachers, the parish priest and even her bosses at Kodak Camera Works.

The crowd believed her and started yelling at the customs guy who started yelling back at the crowd declaring his innocence. The commotion was enough to cause a distraction at which point Rose signaled me to cross over to the correct side of the customs line which I did taking my new walking stick with me.

When I got to the other side, the American customs guy asked for my passport which Rose gave to him while still hyperventilating at her creation that was now being credited to the account of the Irish customs guy. Everybody was yelling at the Irish guy including the customs guy on our side who was disgusted by the behavior of his workmate on the other side. He defended me and told the other guy to wash his underpants.

I was safe. I was headed for home. I had my souvenir.

Ten minutes later we were boarding the plane. Our fellow passengers who had witnessed and ingested the situation at the airport were cheering for us.

We were heroes.

The flight back was long. The stewardess made the mistake of giving Rose a dirty look. Rose repeated her process. She started coughing and pointing at the stewardess and the passengers in our area of the plane began to suspect the stewardess. The stewardess was as happy as we were to be getting off the plane.

Reluctant Pioneer

As I'm sure it is obvious to anyone who reads my words that stay, I spent a large part of my early childhood hoping to survive. My family was loving, forgiving and fun. My neighborhood was supportive, diverse and down to earth as a mud puddle. Yet, I was constantly afraid of two killers that persistently stalked me. Killer number one was the atomic bomb. Killer number two was polio.

I was a member of a kindergarten class that was regularly pulled from the classroom into the hall way while air raid sirens were shrieking all around us. The message was clear that f we didn't get into the hallway when we heard those sirens, we would be blown to smithereens if the bomb hit our school. Apparently St. James School in Irondequoit, New York was very high on the communist hit list.

Most of my classmates took the whole thing as a game but I took it seriously. I was much too aware that my life could end at any second and that my odds of reaching fifteen much less fifty were extremely poor. As a matter of fact, the odds of the earth lasting until I was fifteen were equally poor. But all of that is another story. My story today deals with polio.

Polio was a child killer. I knew at least three children on my block who had polio. One of the children had died. We used to talk about when (not if) we got polio, we hoped we would only be paralyzed or in an iron lung for a few years.

Also according to neighborhood mythology, everything caused polio. If somebody spit on you, you could get polio. If you ate the wrong food, you could get polio. If you got bit by a dog or even petted a dog, you could get polio. If you were "bad" you could get not only coal from Santa Claus but also polio.

Almost as terrifying as polio and atom bombs were "shots" at the doctor's office. I remember my first shot at the doctor's office. I couldn't wrap my mind around the fact that for no ascertainable reason, a stranger called a doctor was going to stick a needle into my arm. I couldn't believe it and certainly didn't believe the stranger when he said "this won't hurt." Of course it hurt. I mean this is a needle going into my flesh etc. I sure as hell wasn't gonna take another one without fight or flight. I can still recall being chased around the doctor's office by the stranger, eventually cornered, physically overpowered and punctured.

The doctor, I'm sure, hated to see me as much as I hated to see him. He made our rocky relationship very clear to my parents.

Somehow I made it to second grade, although most of my fingernails didn't get that far. I was doing great in school. The kids liked me. I was the best reader in the school, even sent up to the eighth grade to show them how to read with "expression." I was still scared of polio and atomic bombs and shots but reading and enjoying my classmates made school seem to be fun.

I considered school to be a safe place except for the occasional air raid sirens which came less frequently but even then I figured that the walls of the school were thicker than the walls in my house, plus I had my desk which I would hide under as another level of protection. Sometimes I wished my parents were in school with me because if two bombs fell, one on my house the other on my school (both still high on the commie target list) I didn't think it was right that I would be safe and my parents would be mertilized (whatever mertilized meant)

I believed in my teachers. They liked me. They thought I was smart and cute. They knew I was obedient. So one day when Sister Denise told us that we all had to go to the nurse's office, I felt pretty secure. The nurse was a nice person. I never had a fight or flight experience in her office. I kind of liked to visit her. She was like a teacher but she had a uniform. She was cool.

As we walked to the office, I asked Betsy Behr if she knew what was going on. I figured it was a hearing test. I didn't mind that because I could hear and it didn't hurt. Betsy told me that we were all gonna get a shot and she showed me the piece of paper that she had in her hand with her parents signature and the words **Polio Pioneer** on the top.

What a scene of horror.

Kids walking in a weary line toward a puncturing dungeon and calling themselves pioneers. I wanted to start running until I realized that I had an out. I didn't have one of those pieces of paper with my parent's signature on it. I was gonna escape this particular terror. One by one, the kids entered the dungeon. Nobody ran. Nobody resisted. The phrase "lambs led to slaughter" still comes to my mind when I recall that moment. Most of the lambs were indeed silent. A few people cried, somebody screamed but the procession continued. As my turn approached, I said a silent prayerful thanks to my parents for not being cruel enough to put their names on that terrible piece of paper. I got just outside the door, when I decided to make my case. I said to the Nurse, " I don't have one of those pieces of paper so I guess I can't be a pioneer." I faked disappointment. The nurse took a kindly look at me and said "don't worry, you are still a pioneer. I have the permission slip right here in my hand. Your parents brought it in earlier this week."

I said,"there must be some mistake." I firmly believed that my parents would never do such a thing. I asked to see the paper with my own eyes. The nurse showed it to me. There, on that piece of paper, was the signature of my mother AND my father.

Betrayed.

I remember walking into the puncture zone thinking "if they drop the bomb on us right now, my parents can stay at Parsells Avenue". Defeated, betrayed with the nurse cutting off my escape route, I went in got the shot and became a Piofreakineer. The shock of betrayal dulled the pitch of the puncture.

It took me a long time to trust my parents again. It took me an even longer time to trust school again. My fear of abandonment had begun.

Then I heard that this was only the first of three shots that we were going to have to get. The next two were called booster shots and would come in the near future. The boosters would be equally dreadful and complicated. I think you can fill in the dots, the futile strategies, the outsmarting, the fear and loathing, the betrayals "for my own good" etc.

Anyway, bottom line. The Salk vaccine actually worked. We arrested the serial killer. I was part of the squad that nailed polio. I was a pioneer.

A few years later, the scare started again. The scare wasn't that polio was loose again. The scare was called the Sabin vaccine which sounded even more terrifying than the Salk vaccine. By this time my brother had to get the Sabin treatment.

The Sabin treatment turned out to be an oral medication.

I was pissed that my brother didn't have to get a shot.

65 years later, we all have to get two at least according to Fauci.

Stingray Summer

As you know by now, when I was a kid I hung around at a baseball field behind my house. A core group of about 20 of us avoided juvenile delinquency by meeting every day at the field to smoke, swear, spit, play baseball and generally "chill" as the idiom goes today.

Some of the guys I hung around with were Cactus Cal, Holly Hood, Justin Sane, Mr. Crown. Hazey, Stash, Chief Chewacki, Ugg Too Much, Jock, Dogs, Bates,Mr. Moll, Rizz, Jamer, Rick, Raw, Redass, Mack, Johnny D, Johnny P, Deke, Spook, Fuzzy, Feeb, Happy Jack and Frog.

Obviously, a nicknaming process was in play big time at the field. Nicknames were based on idiosyncrasies, charisma, outrageous behavior, physical appearance, tics or general coolness. If ya hung around the field long enough, eventually somebody hung a handle on ya and like it or not, it stuck.

One day, a new kid showed up. The only guy who knew him was Justin Sane, who had Spanish class with the kid at East High. Justin recognized the guy because in Spanish class, he had given his name at what Justin approximated as "Hymay". For the first week or two the kid was known as Hymay if he were known at all.

Then one day somebody, I think it was Froggy came up with the concept that if you gave a guy a cool nickname, the guy automatically became cool. We spent an entire rainy afternoon sheltered by the shanty, debating the theory and thinking up cool nicknames. At the time the coolest car was a Stingray so we decided that would be a great nickname.

To test the idea someone, I think it was Dogs came up with the idea that we should give the coolest nickname to the uncoolest kid and see what happened. We scanned the list of uncool, bland, not yet nicknamed kids who showed up irregularly. I think it was Bates who suggested "How bout that kid Hymay?"

At first most of the guys didn't know who Hymay was because he was so non-descript and innocuous. We reminded those guys of a couple of very routine plays that Hymay had made and a few inoffensive cuss words that Hymay had uttered. Hymay came into focus. Everybody agreed. The next day Hymay would become Stingray.

So the next day when Hymay showed up at the field everybody started calling him Stingray. After about an hour of this, Hymay began to acknowledge the handle and respond to it. For the rest of the summer whenever anybody arrived at the field and yelled "awright" the next words became "Is Stingray here yet?". Stingray would eventually show up and everybody would start cheering " Hey, the Stinger has arrived."

Everybody started praising everything Stingray did. His pants didn't look like anybody else's. Everybody else had those tight jeans that were the beginning of the Levi invasion. Nobody wore shorts. One day somebody, I think it was Stash showed up with a ridiculous pair of pants and everybody started to get on him until he made the statement "Hey, these pants are just like Stinger's. The razzing of Stash ceased and turned to praise when Stingray finally showed up and it became clear that his pants did indeed look like the pants that Stash was wearing.

A couple of days later Ugg showed up with a similar pair of pants as did Feeb.

By the end of the summer, everybody had changed their style and we all looked like a school of Stingrays until one day somebody, I think it was Feeb said "Hey, ya know what, we all look like a bunch of assholes." We looked around and realized it was true.

The last day of summer arrived. Stingray showed up but by now everybody had changed style and become Anti-Stingray. Stingray told everybody that he had had a great summer, the best one of his life. He also so said, "I want everyone to know that my name is Jim."

We never saw Jim again. Every once in awhile someone who survived the field will come up with a rumor about Stingray and renew those glorious days.

Photo by Robert Rondell1 III

Willie Mays and Glory Days

If baseball is our first love, then Willie Mays was my first crush.

7 years old was I and playing baseball every day in my backyard with the barbed wire boundaries and cherry tree grandstands.

1954

Everybody was calling themselves Wille Mays. I don't think I knew for sure that Willie Mays was real. I thought he was a comic book character, a Batman or a Superman.

Then he made that over the shoulder basket catch in the World Series against Vic Wertz of the Indians and then he wheeled around and mid wheel uncorked a throw from the deepest part of centerfield back to the infield. Some said the only living person who could have made that throw was also the only living person who could have made that catch. That year the Indians set a record for most wins in a season.

They lost all four games of that World Series. The Giants were the World Champions.

Willie was 23 when he made that catch and that throw. He was beloved in New York City. The future was unlimited for Willie and for all of us as we entered a period of peace and hope. Being black on the diamond was cool beans.

Willie was the original 5 star player. He could run, field, throw, hit with power and hit for average.

He was the natural. He loved the game. He even enjoyed playing stickball with the kids in the streets of New York. Everybody loved Willie.

Wille had the luminous smile, the exuberant style and the otherwordly skills.

Oh, and about that style. Willie was the first ballplayer to have his uniform custom tailored.

Not only did he play better than everybody, he looked better.

Even the fold in the bill of his cap was perfect.

And that cap was always flying off his head at the perfect moments like when he made the catch.

The Giants won that 54 World Series with the help of characters like Dusty Rhodes, Whitey Lockman, Rochester's own pride and joy Johnny Antonelli, Leo Durocher, Monte Irvin, Hank Thompson on and on. Fantastic names. Names that rivaled names also playing in New York at the time, Yogi Berra, Phil (the Scooter) Rizzuto, Mickey Mantle, Whitey Ford, Pee Wee Reese, Roy Campanella, Duke Snider, Don Newcombe, Carl Furrillo. God how those names rolled off the tongue.

They all sounded like superheroes. They were all real. All in New York all at the same time. And at the very top as 1955 rolled around was Wille Mays at the exact same time that I began to realize that baseball was something much bigger than what we were doing in the backyard. I was in love with the game.

Eventually, the Dodgers and Giants split for the Coast breaking our hearts. Willie continued to be Willie but he never again won another World Series although he came close in his final season when he returned home to the New York Mets.

That dream was one dream too far.

Willie was of course a first ballot Hall of Famer.
Yesterday, Willie Mays turned 90 years of age.

90.

Willie Mays....the Say Hey Kid is 90.

All of the other famous New York names that were his contemporaries have passed away.

Only Willie remains. The greatest living ballplayer.

Maybe the greatest ball player of all time.

All of us old guys always feel a little younger whenever we think of Willie Mays even today when we're in our seventies. For a few moments we are back in the Polo Grounds or in our backyards or Little League fields with our first mitts and battered baseballs.

We wanna be like Willie Mays. We still wear baseball caps. We dream big dreams

And as for our playing careers well, we all went about as far as we could go before we took our last at bat and passed our glory days on to our dreams

Last Game of Numbers

Towards the end of sandlot days, we had trouble getting eighteen guys on the field for pick up baseball games. We invented a truncated baseball game called Numbers. We played Numbers with four guys on a team. A team would take the field with two infielders and two outfielders. The batting team supplied its own pitcher.

A swing and a miss counted as an out as did two foul balls. A ground ball, pop up or line drive gloved by an infielder counted as an out. Anything hit to right field was an out. Anytime an outfielder caught a ball in the air, that too was an out. Nobody ran the bases, too hot and dusty for that crap. We assigned numbers to all non-outs. A fielding error or single was one point, a double was two points, a triple three and a home run four. The numbers were judgment calls as nobody was running bases. In the field we had a way of erasing Numbers from the score. If someone made a "nice" play in the field, it subtracted a point. If someone made a "great " play it erased two points. If someone made a "sensational" play,known as a "sensay", it would erase three points and automatically bring the fielding team to the plate.

I can still see Rick Cicotta charging in from the outfield claiming "sensay,sensay" after a making a sliding diving grab in shallow left field. Of course, Frog, on the hitting team would claim "no sensay" and the game would slow down for awhile until a consensus was reached, usually without a fistfight.

We kept track of the numbers. Higher number after seven innings wins.

The only 5 point number was a ball hit against or over the fence into the cornfield. The fence was three hundred feet from home plate, guarded by an apple tree and about ten feet tall. Some of us, were able to reach the fence but no one had gone over it. If a batter hit a home run, not only did he get four points but he immediately got another at bat.

Late August heat was upon us. We had been playing baseball, not only all that summer but also what seemed like our entire boyhoods. We were tired of being boys. Baseball was beginning to slow down and wear out. Cars were appearing. We were starting to get around.

On that day, we had only one playable ball left. We had either lost or beat the life out of all the rest.

The Numbers game proceeded as usual. One side up, one side down with only the occasional arguments about a number. Precedents had been set and were referred to. "That's not a 'great' play, Feeb made a much better play than that last week and it was only 'nice' etc." As the summer grew more heated, the arguments grew less heated. We had other things on our mind and we were just trying to play the game and get off the field. We were finding new places where the kids were hip.

Efficiency was the beauty of Numbers. A seven inning game took only about an hour and a half at the most.

On that day, it was the bottom of the fourth inning when Jake came to the plate. Over the course of the summer, Jake had made the the most dramatic progress with his swing.

Jake had three nicknames besides Jake, which itself was a nickname for Jeff. Jake was called Crocodile or Crock because his nose came to a pointed snout. He was also called Cement Mixer or Mix for his mix of muscle and determination along with his complete absence of behavioral and/or linguistic subtlety. He was also called Chim..short for Chimney because he smoked like one.

Jake signaled to Big Joe, where he wanted the pitch. Joe threw it right there and Jake went yard, clearing the fence.

Everybody on both teams appreciated the shot. Jake asked for priase and he got it.

The blast broke up the momentum of the game. We had to climb the fence and search for the ball. Everbody on Jake's team lit up while my team trudged to the fence, climbed over it and searched for the ball. This took about fifteen minutes.

Dogs Drexel finally found the ball.

The game resumed.

Jake was still at bat.

He signaled. Big Joe delivered.

Jake blasted another one outta here.

Everybody oohed and aahed. We climbed the fence again. The hunt for the ball in the cornfield recommenced. More sun. More cigarettes. Another fifteen minute search

Somebody found the ball.
The game resumed.

Jake still at bat.

KEERAK

Another one.

At this point appreciation turned into irritation and irritation was approaching awareness and contempt. Everybody started yelling at Jake. Instead of praise, Jake started getting blame and venom. "You big muscle bound asshole. You're ruining the game with this shit. C'mon Mix, let's get this shit over with."

Jake was in uncharted territory and he had taken all of us with him. The suspicion started to grow that the field was too small for Jake and he could go yard at will. We were starting to get too old and too strong for Numbers.

The search for the ball took even longer this time. The game had been decided. What was the point of the search? What was the point of continuing? What was the point of hanging around every day at a baseball field?

So hot.

Sun so relentless.

Jake still at bat.

The whole afternoon was starting to feel like Hell.

Like eternity.

Finally the ball was retrieved.

As Jake dug in at the plate, everybody on both teams was swearing at him. He was a muscle bound, lame brained, crocodile faced, cement headed, goofy, walking cancer factory etc. He had ruined our afternoon. He was in the process of destroying the game of Numbers which was our last link to sandlot baseball, in many ways our last link to boyhood.

Jake didn't give two shits. Guys like Jake love pressure as much as they love pissing people off. I'll never forget watching Jake at that moment. He didn't care about anything that anybody was saying. He didn't even care about the end of boyhood or for that matter, the ash dangling from his Marlboro as he dug in at the dish. Those kind of distractions were for singles hitters like me. Power don't go there.

Big Joe was tired of lobbing the ball where Jake wanted it. This time he reared back and put all of his mustard on a fastball, inside corner. Joe had plenty of mustard. He was 16, six foot two, two hundred thirty pounds.

Jake got around on it.

I never had and never will see a ball hit that far on that field. That last shot went fify feet further back into the bushes surrounding the cornfield, into zone unknown, out of boy's town into manland. Jake's blast lost the last ball on the last pitch of the summer……..

Everybody stopped mocking Jake. We were all pals again. We gave Jake the praise he deserved but we realized the game was over.

We went home

We had changed

No one bothered to find the ball or even look for it.

We never played Numbers again.

Summer ended.

Two weeks later Dogs was driving Old Bessie, who was born in 32 but still looked so pretty.

Soon, my buddies and me would be real well known. We were going to college and/or getting drafted.

First Day At College

I got to my dorm room in Blake Hall before my other roommates. The room had a bunkbed and a single bed. I didn't know which bed to take or whether I should wait for my roomies to arrive and we'd decide together. My mother gave me her last bit of pre-college advice.

"Take the single bed". That's some great advice.

I took the single. She helped me make it.

They said goodbye.

I was on my own.

I lit up a Newport and realized nobody was going to stop me. Smoking was still a big deal in 1964. I exhaled and the smoke never looked more beautiful. I blew exquisite smoke rings and rings through rings.

Eventually, my two roomies showed up. They were both big guys. Rob was from Utica and Louie was from Auburn.

I left the room while they got unpacked. I explored the rest of the dorm. When I returned, me and my roomies began to feel each other out. They had settled in the bunkbed...Rob on top...Louie below.

Louie was a basketball player and Rob had left his girl back in Utica.

We decided to take a walk uptown, into the village and get a pizza. I had never had a pizza before in my life. First day in college, first day with new roomies and about to have my first pizza. We walked up the hill to Main Street past the fountain of the bear and made our way to Pontillo's pizza.
I was pretending that I'd done this many times.

We sat down and Rob ordered for us. While we waited for the pizza, we talked about why we chose Geneseo State and why we wanted to become teachers. We were so young and so earnest. They had a juke box in the pizza joint. I played two songs. *Pretty Woman* and *Baby I Need Your Loving*.
I told Rob that I played *Baby I Need Your Loving* out of respect for the girls we had left behind and *Pretty Woman* for the girls we would meet.

Baby I Need Your Loving came on first and it arrived as our pizza was served.

I had no idea how to eat a pizza so I watched as Rob expertly spun the pizza around and separated the pieces.

We were in semi-formal mode. We hadn't laughed or cursed at each other yet.

Rob removed the first piece of pizza and put it in his mouth just as the Four Tops were singing OOh Ooh Ooh Ooh, Oouh Ooh, Oooh.

The piece was too hot and Rob stated going "Ooh ooh ooh" in pain just as the Tops were singing Baby I need Your Loving."While he was oohing and aahing in pain a big gobby string of cheese had slipped off the pizza and was stuck to his chin all the way to the pizza which he had pulled away from his face. He looked hilarious. I tried not to laugh at his pain but couldn't help myself. He didn't mind. He laughed too and so did Louie. Louie and I decided to wait a little bit before we took our slices.

I was very careful with my first bite of my first slice of pizza.

I've eaten a lot of pizza since then and not always as carefully.

Soon I would meet a pretty woman but that's another story.

Whenever I hear either of those songs, I think of that day and that pizza.

Amazingly, as I go to publish on Feb. 3rd, I located Rob. I hadn't seen or heard from him in 40 years. He had a picture of us uptown with Doreen Aguglia a few weeks after that first pizza. Rob went on to a stellar career in education. That's Rob in the fake stash with Doreen between us.

Orbiting

I had been in my Blake Hall dormitory for about a month when I got a visit from Vin. We walked around the quad. In order to walk around the quad, the walker had to turn right outside my dorm... walk to and past the college center... turn left.... walk past the Wadsworth building.... turn left walk past the library turn left past the administration and then take a ralph past more dorms until the walk ended at the entrance to Blake Hall, about half a mile altogether.

This was in October of 1964, almost exactly 58 years ago.

At that time the moon was not a documented magnificent desolation but more of a benevolent mystery. Astronauts were learning how to maneuver in space while satelites like Telstar were orbiting the planet for the first time.Vin observed that the quad walk "would make a beautiful orbit".

I didn't know what the hell he was talking about and asked for an explanation."Here's what you do, get a bunch of guys from your dorm. Send out one guy at a time to run around the quad. Time the run. Call every timed run an orbit. When one man completes his "orbit" have another guy take over relay style. Maybe make an aluminum ball that one orbiter can pass to the next orbiter. While in orbit, if the orbiter passes anyone they are required to say "beep beep" while passing. If you get the right guys, you might be able to keep that orbit going for a long time: hours, days, nights, weeks, months maybe until we land on the moon. You and the orbiters might make this quad famous if the media gets a hold of the story."

I liked the idea and told Vin that I would get an "orbit" going soon.

Over the next couple of weeks, I talked up the idea of the orbit to the guys in my dorm. I set a time and a date for the "launch". At launch time, we had the aluminum ball ready to go and an orbiter on the launching pad which was really the front steps outside Blake Hall. We had gathered the usual 10 guys who counted down the launch. The first man in orbit was Butsh. Cat Miller did the actual countdown At the call of "ignition", Butsh took off. Everybody had a clear view of the launch and commented "it's a beauty" and how "all systems were go" etc. Up near the administration building, trees blocked the porch view of the orbiter. We all knew that blockage was coming so we had called it the dark side. I remember when Butsh disappeared from view. No one had ever entered the dark side while orbiting. Everyone was very relieved when Butsh emerged from the dark side and headed home for his landing. The next orbiter, Don Horner was waiting to receive the aluminum ball and begin his orbit. While Horner was in orbit half of the guys were watching his orbit and the other half were questioning Butsh who was in quarantine until Horner completed his orbit. In quarantine, Butsh was asked about the condition of the orbit. Was there a lot of debris? Did he notice any spy satelittes. How many times did he beep? And then Horner was in the dark space until he emerged to the cheers and admiration of porch monkeys and future orbiters.

The aluminum ball was passed many times but momentum began to wane after a couple of hours. Either the orbit would spread to another dorm or it would fade away. At that point a new guy entered the scene. He had been in the college center listening to the jukebox when he heard about the orbit going on. He had run cross country in high school and he thought he would be comfortable with multiple orbits until replacements could be found. He took off on his orbit when the sky darkened and the rainstorm began. Everybody ran for cover, the mission aborted except for the orbiter who to the amazement of all completed his orbit and then with lightning and thunder booming and flashing, he did the unthinkable. He went for one more orbit.

He completed that orbit. He was soaked to the bone. I met him on the porch. He handed me the aluminum ball. I saluted him and said "Mission Accomplished." I had never met this person before although I had seen him around a few times.
I asked him his name and where he was from.

He said, "Wild Bill" from West Babylon. The orbit had ended but my friendship with Wild Bill went on for days, night, semesters, years, moon landings, moons, decades, Derbies, half centuries and lifetimes.

And for the last 50 years, no Geneseo Homecoming would be complete without him.

Outta This Place

Sitting in the Merchant's Bar and Grill at last call. Dino, the bar tended, has changed his shoes and he's ready to go home which means we are as well.

I'm with my pal, Al.

Five hours from now, we'll be heading to a job that we both hate.

We're working for the Grounds Department of the City School District.

We'll arrive at the shack on Jay Street in a dirty old part of the city. Some old fart will tell us what tools we need and how much fertilizer, mulch or whatever we had to load on the truck in fifty pound bags. Everything we loaded, we knew we'd have to unload. It was like picking out the whip that somebody was going to beat you with.

Then we got in the dump truck, in the back, with the fertilizer.

Usually, the bosses would stop off at a bar and grab a couple of shots of whiskey before taking us to the worksite.

The level of the work depended on the mood of the field boss who was usually in fear of the master of the work domain who we used to call the janitor but now we called the custodian and he/they didn't like us because they suspected we were college kids/lazy long haired assholes.

We worked all day with a couple of breaks. One time we took a break and went down to the beach where Richard lost his shoes. Richard was one of those deprived kids whom the city tried to help by giving him a shitty job that he despised. It did not go well with Richard when we returned to work. Old Joe was our boss that day and he hated Richard. Richard tried to get out of work on the basis of having no shoes. Old Joe wouldn't have anything to do with that. He went deep into a shed and came out with a gigantic pair of ancient galoshes and some twine. He made Richard twine the galoshes onto his feet and get on with the job. Richard said that he wasn't going to wear those "fookin things."

Richard went and disappeared somewhere and he took his spade with him.

Nobody knew where he was until suddenly he emerged, staggering at galosh speed, whooping and brandishing his spade like a spear. He was chasing a giant rat and sure enough, he launched the spade into the air ahead of the rat who ran into it with its face and then ran eyeless and noseless into some bushes. When we got to the spade, imbedded in the mud, it was full of ratface.

Eventually, our work was finished and we got back in the truck and drove to the dump. Going to the dump was the highlight of the day because it meant our work was more or less over.

From the dump we went back to the shed, where we told the story of the galoshes and the ratface spade. We went home and cleaned up. Went back to the Merch where Dino would always say "Two fer you?" when we walked in knowing that we weren't going to get just one draft at a time, we were going to order two which we did and before long we started to dread the next day and hope that our bosses for the next day would be the black guys who instead of stopping off at the bar for a whiskey, took the truck into the ghetto and used the equipment on the lawns of their neighbors. When that happened we would sit in the dump truck and sleep it off as best we could.

Then it would be back at the Merch. Sometimes we'd put a buck in the jukebox and play "We Gotta Get Outta This Place" ten times in a row.

Eventually, somehow, we did.

Don't know what happened to Richard but I don't think that he made it out.

Sky Catch

We played catch constantly on the Avenue and in the field.

If you're gonna play baseball, you've got to be able to catch the ball.

We all loved our mitts. My favorite mitt was a Rawling's six fingered, Eddie Matthews model. Partly because of that glove, I earned another nickname. They called me Raw, short for Rawlings. Catch came in many varieties.

At first, we just tossed the ball back and forth, over and over again. This of course required a partner. When we were alone, we learned to throw the ball against porch steps and catch it when it bounced back. We played in the street.

Eventually, when we had a partner, we'd play pitch and catch. In pitch and catch…one of us was the pitcher and one of us the catcher. The "pitcher" would do the full windup and throw the ball to the "catcher" who was in the crouching position. Occasionally, the catcher who was also the ump would call balls and strikes and sometimes make a clicking sound upon catching a "strike". The click meant the ball was in play. The throwback would be a pop fly or a hard hit ground ball. The pitcher had to be prepared for the click. If he fielded the ground ball, for instance, he would become a momentary infielder and fire the ball back to the catcher who had become a momentary first basemen. Every three "outs" we would change position…the pitcher would become the catcher and the catcher would become the pitcher.

Me and my buddy Al played the most pitch and catch.

Then there was "pepper" which involved a bat. Pepper was played in close range, maybe three feet apart. The fielder would underhand the ball to the guy with the bat and the batter would tap it back. Pepper was all about reflex and bat control and trust. Once again, Al was my best partner for pepper. He had great bat control so his tap backs were hard but not too hard. We weren't trying to kill each other. I trusted Al.

Two of my crazier friends, X the Known and King, invented a game called wipe catch where they would fire the ball back at each other as hard as they could while decreasing the distance between them. That game usually ended with either King or Known getting wiped out by a return throw that came in way too fast and too hard and ricocheted off their bodies.

Nobody wanted to play wipe catch with either of them. They were trying to kill each other. King eventually became a dentist and Known a bank examiner.

I kept playing baseball all the way into college. I played on a great intramural fast pitch softball team. We were great because we had the "fastest" pitcher in the league...a guy named Peterson. We called Peterson Cougar because of the word and insignia on the Zippo lighter that he always carried which had Cougar written on it. He could care less if he killed the batter or not. Nobody dug in against him. Nobody even wanted to bat against him. One guy I knew got hit in the ass by a Peterson fast pitch and didn't go to class for the next week. I'm not saying that his bruised ass was the only reason he cut all his classes but he used his ass as an excuse. It takes more than a bruised ass to earn a zero cumulative average.

My freshman year, I lived in Blake Hall which was a temporary residence while the new dorms were being built. My sophomore year, the new dorms were available. The new dorms had suites of three rooms surrounding a common room. My suite was B1d on the ground floor of spanking new Wyoming dorm.

In freshman year, we had no choice of roommates but by sophomore year, we were able to choose and be chosen. Six guys in a suite. Six all stars. My suite mates were Paul, Butsh, Cat, Beast, and Murph. All of us were ballplayers and some of us, like Paul, Butsh, Cat and Beast were varsity players in their freshman year.

All of them were great guys. Murph, Cat, Butsh and I came from Blake Hall so we were already friends. Paul and Beast were from Sturges Hall where they had been roomies. I didn't know Paul that well but I knew he was a tremendous athlete.

On moving in day, Paul and I settled in first. We had a few moments so we decided to play catch. Catch measures trust as well as skill.

It was a different kind of catch. Paul didn't have his glove so he threw and I caught. Paul had a formidable arm. He started throwing the ball high, frighteningly high, up into the air. It was wipe catch except the ball speed was based on the velocity of its descent. The first couple of throws he made got my attention. I'd never seen a guy throw a ball that high.

I was in a space between the dorms that was still scarred by construction. There wasn't a lot of room and the area that was available was loaded with ditches and rocks.

After I caught the first couple of throws, I could tell that Paul was impressed. I was getting a little nervous. I raised my index finger to signal "one more".

Paul realized this was the last throw and put everything he had into it, the highest fly of them all. I circled around trying to avoid the obstacles. I got under the ball when I stepped into a ditch and lost my balance. I fell to the ground. While on the ground, I remember thinking, "damn, I was right under that ball". An instant later I realized how "under the ball" I was as the ball, picking up speed all the way, hit me right on the top of the head with the power and precision of a giant eagle landing on a Moa.

I'm told that the ball bounced fifteen feet in the air directly off my dome.

Momentary visions of Willie Mays and the sound of eagle wings took over my brain. I must have been "out" for a few seconds.

When I regained my consciousness, I realized that most of my new suite mates had gathered just as Paul threw the ball. Everybody saw what happened and everybody froze. When I focused on them, they all had an expression of horror and humor on their faces, especially Paul.

Somebody yelled, "Are you allright, Raw."

I didn't know if I was or not but I managed to say "Yeah, I'm good." With that everybody broke out into relieved, raucous laughter.

I picked myself up and joined them at the entrance to the dorm.

I didn't know exactly what to say but I remember uttering these words: "I knew I was under it."

Photo by David Ellsworth

"Yes, you were" they all agreed while stifling their laughter.

Thus began the daze that I lived in throughout my sophomore year, a year that played out like some kind of radio dream, full of music and surprise.

Perfect Example

In my high school days, one of my best friends was nicknamed Dogs. In my college days, one of my best friends was nicknamed Cat. One fine day when Dogs came to visit me at college, I introduced the two, "Dogs, this is Cat. Cat, this is Dogs." Naturally they got along great.

Cat was the quarterback of our fraternity flag football team. He wasn't particularly big, fast, or strong armed but he had great savvy and he knew how to win.

Cat was a math major. He would quarterback math study sessions in his room before big exams. The sessions were called "Victory at Bat with Cat". Alas most victory sessions turned into all night euchre games and/or bullshit sessions so the academic victories in that particular arena were a bit sparse.

With all of this going for him, Cat loved to play tricks. You always had to be paying attention with Cat. One of his favorite tricks was "the perfect example". Here's how it went. Three people would be in a space. Let's call them Murph, Cat and Red Hot. Two of the people ....Cat and Murph...would be hip to the trick. The innocent, unknowing third person Red Hot would make an innocuous, natural gesture like checking his hair in the mirror. At that point, Cat would nod at Red and say, "See".

Murph, in on the trick would nod and go, "Uh huh, oh yeah. I see."

Then Cat would continue, "yup that's a perfect example of what I mean."

Red Hot would come off the mirror and ask, "what are you guys talking about?"

Cat would look at Murph and reply to Red Hot by saying, "See perfect example."

Murph would laugh and reply to Cat's reply to Red Hot by saying, " I see exactly what you mean." They would nod knowingly with barely suppressed grins.

Red Hot would now be growing insecure and kinda angry, the more insecure and angry the better. Red might say something like, "why don't you assholes take a shit for yourselves."

To which, Cat would respond, "See I knew it....freakin perfect."

Murph would chime in "EXACTLY what we were talking about."
And on and on and deeper it would go until Red Hot finally caught on. Catching on was the initiation point. From that point on the Red Hot in this example could become either the initiator or the chorus of a "perfect example" of his own if he had another person in on it and another Red Hot out of it.

Perfect examples spread around the campus like wildfire. The process kept repeating itself like a virus.until eventually a third of the student body living on campus was affected. At that point, perfect examples were being indicated of professors, campus cops, bartenders, girlfriends, boyfriends. The same process...initiation and then collaboration. Some folks never "got" it and grew increasingly more insecure and angry as the persons pointing out each of their moves every day grew and they never knew why. A lot of those people went on to become bad teachers, so bad in fact that they went on to be college professors.

Then as the sixties took their dark turn, the news and the newspapers and the war and the draft became further perfect examples of perfect fookin examples of exactly what we meant. Of course, when we made that transition into reality rather than trickery, nobody really knew what the "fook" anything or anybody meant.

Johnson would come on teevee and talk about sending more troops to Nam.

We'd sit around the tube and say, "Perfect."

Even to this day, I still carry around a load of that insecurity, dark humor and anger around with me wondering if all this can actually be true and not some kind of joke. This story is a perfect "f**king example of it.

Forever Endeavor

Andy and his brother Pete heard the word through telegraph, a modern marvel in 1898.

The final flock of carrier pigeons, 250,000 of them were approaching. The flock was called Endeavor.

Andy, who knew a lot more but said a lot less than younger brother Pete, had already witnessed and assisted in one major devastation. He had already spent an entire September day among the dead, they dying and the mangled; picking up perforated pigeons and heaping them into piles. Andy had watched eagles, hawks and vultures arrive to share in the spoil of pigeon piles. Only a comparative few of those scavengers were shot for their carrion on but the pigeon corpses were everywhere.

Andy gathered and stashed five lifetime's worth of pigeon feathers, bones and birdmeat and drove a horse drawn carriage full of dead passengers home to his hogs.

At one time, a single flock of passenger pigeons contained more than 2 billion birds. As the most common bird in America, many flocks and colonies existed. The passenger population appeared not only inexhaustible and invulnerable but also territorially threatening. One flocking colony known in Wisconsin as Endeavor, spread over 750 square miles.

Endeavor could and did obscure the sun.

People of Wisconsin, future Cheeseheads, were not about to surrender that much tundra neither frozen nor thawed. Andy and Pete were riflemen in the gaggle of hunter/soldier/patriots about to converge on that flocking colony from below.

As the targets approached, Andy could feel a surprising current of air. He heard a sound that reminded him of a tempest at sea. The passengers were overhead. The sky was dark. The brothers and the gang of hunters opened fire, reloaded and opened fire again and again and again and again.

The not clay pigeons dropped from the sky like bleeding, bleating hailstones. Children on the ground, fortified with poles and clubs were waiting. Andy was in such a frenzy that he didn't hear the cursing and thudding that surrounded him. Andy barely noticed the dozen passengers that fell on him while he was pulling and reloading. He didn't hear the thousands of gun reports coming from each side. Each unheard report bore mute witness to a load of scatter shot that could and did take down as many as ten passengers per blast.

A certain amount of time passed although the exact amount of minutes/ hours is unclear.

Some have speculated that it took a bit longer than did the massacre at Little Big Horn with each blast the equivalent of ten arrows.

And then the flock passed.

And then there was silence.

Andy, with gun barrel still smoking, turned to Pete and said "that telegraph's a pretty damn good idea."

Ten thousand of a quarter million passengers flew away.

Twenty years later only ONE passenger pigeon, a bird named Martha, remained alive.

When Martha finally died, her body was suspended in a tank of water then freeze framed into a three hundred pound block of ice and sent to the Smithsonian Institute. Martha's carcass.

Martha's carcass is still around.

Andy and Pete are long gone now but their great, great grandsons hold season tickets on the frozen tundra of Lambeau Field. They wear cheeseheads and feathers as they back the Pack.

Right before the kickoff of the opening game at Lambeau Field, a tremendous roar emerges from the crowd. Dozens of people in the crowd, including all those related to Andy or Pete always turn to each other and remark that the roar sounds like "a thunderstorm of bloody passengers". Great, great, grandson Andrew didn't have a clue where that odd expression originated only that it had been in his family for more than a century.

We have a tendency to forget or minimize big deals. Let's make a vow never to forget Covid.

Aardvark at the Ball Park

A bunch of us started comparing what we carried in our wallets. A lot happens when men bare their wallets. Jack Stafford won the competition that day. For some reason Jack carried a picture of an aardvark in his wallet. He had been carrying it for decades. In the course of the ensuing years, I would often ask Jack if he still had the aardvark picture in his wallet. He always did.

One night at Frontier Field, I was talking to George Fern when Jack came over. I told George that Jack carried a picture of an aardvark in his wallet. George wanted to see it. Jack took out his wallet and showed George. Fern, a born contrarian whose week consisted of six Mondays and one out of control Friday said, "that's not an aardvark, that's an anteater."

Jack took great offense to this characterization. An anteater in a wallet is a whole different ball game from an aardvark in a wallet. Jack went all out Nicholson

"Hey, It's an aardvark for God's sake. Don't start calling it an anteater just because it eats ants. It eats termites too. If you called it a termite eater that wouldn't be that bad because it sounds kinda like terminator but it's still not as good as aardvark. An anteater is a whole different mammal. Okay ,they both got long snouts so I'm surprised y'all didn't just call 'em nose sniffers and put em in the same swamp."

The "conversation" paused. Meanwhile on the field, Joe Lopardi put the home team ahead leading off the inning. As so often happens Joe had made a sensational leaping grab of a hot liner headed for extra bases to keep the game even until he put us ahead. We all started cheering and slapping each other on the back

Jack began again

"You're not gonna find an aardvark's ass in a swamp, brother. They don't chill around water. They dig the woods, man. Plus, they hang out at night in the woods not during the day in a swamp down by the river. He's an aardvark goddamned it. He's got teeth. You wanna see his teeth? Here check 'em out."

Fern took a closer look at Jack's picture and noticed the teeth.

"Now go find an anteater somewhere on some other continent and see if that son of a bitch has any teeth. He doesn't have any...never had any...he's a godamned anteater. Anteaters don't have teeth....aardvarks do. Aardvark is a beautiful name. Always right up there at the top of the alphabet when people are in an animal naming contest. Most people don't have any idea what they look like until somebody confuses them with anteater and then they get stereotyped with those assholes."

Jack took a long swig from his beer and continued

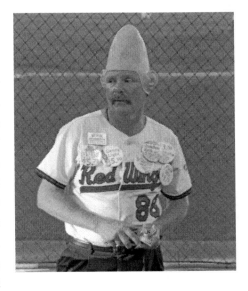

"Oh yeah, one other thing, take another look. See the jungle in the background? See the moon. That's Africa for Christ sake. Aardvarks live in Africa..anteaters live in South America. They live above the ground. Aardvarks live below the ground. They only come up at night. If you think you see one in the daylight, then you're in South America in a goddamned swamp somewhere and you're looking at an anteater. Meanwhile, an aardvark is in its in burrow, chilling out and getting ready for the night life. So let's not make that mistake again. Let me simplify this for you.This is an an AARDVARK and he lives in the dark, and his teeth leave a mark. Got it? Good. You wanna beer ? How bout you, Ice?"

On the diamond, Joe Lopardi made a sensational lead saving play at third base and then as so often happens, Joe blasted a four bagger as the home team took the lead for good.

Conehead came by and Jack bought the three of us beers as the ballgame continued.

Back on the field Sal Timpani Jr. came in and closed the door on the Texarkana Treemen.

A lot happens when a man bares his wallet.

Flower Guy

Twenty years ago I persevered through one of my favorite rituals, the annual Valentine's Day masculinity panic. As of 2:50 PM on that fabled Feb fourteen, I still had not confronted Valentine's Day "responsibilities"

I was teaching Cinematic Literacy to a group of film lovers and we were watching Charley Chaplin's City Lights where the Little Tramp falls in love with the blind flower girl, which took director Chaplin over 500 takes to get right. This romantic situation inspired one of my students to ask, "Mr. Rivers, did you get your wife some nice flowers for Valentine's Day?"

Most of the class was surprised when I confidently and proudly stated that I hadn't bought anything "yet."

I added that I wasn't worried because I knew where the flower guy was on West Henrietta Road. I was pleasantly surprised that several of the males in the class also knew where the flower guy was and were planning to visit him after school. For the ones who didn't, we smartened them up as there would always be another February…another opportunity to panic.

The flower guy was a merchant who sold flowers out of his truck. I had been going to the flower guy for years, not just on Valentine's Day but on those numerous occasions when I feel overwhelmed with gratitude for being married to the wonderful woman that I am married to and stop and pick up some flowers as a tiny token of my admiration for her beauty, integrity, patience, uh wisdom, uh reliability, uh responsibility, uh loss of two pounds last month, uh new haircut, uh savor faire, uh joie de vivre, uh etc.

By the time I got to the flower guy, a small line had already formed. I took my place in line and bonded with the testosterone surrounding me, all of us immediately recognizing that we were in the same circumstantial basket and proud of the fact that we knew the flower guy and our asses were safe. Most of the guys in line looked as if they considered their bodies more as taverns than as temples, but I did notice one guy who looked as if he not only did the cooking but also the cleaning in his crib. His fastidious appearance stood out in this particular line which featured beer guts, baseball hats, jeans, cigars and Carhart jackets. I blended as if I were invisible.

Usually the flower guy had a bunch of arrangements ready and would say, "this one's five, this one's eight, this one's ten, you can have two of these for twelve etc." On that day, the flower guy had been so overwhelmed before my line began that he was making up the arrangements as he went along which added to the length of time we spent in line which added to the bonding thing which added to the disparaging discourse about Valentine's day as a "chick thing" or a "marketing gimmick" or a "fake love camouflage."

By the time I got to the flower guy, he was pretty frantic and barely recognized me although I had been the only person in line on many previous Fridays.

I said, "Long time customer"

He said, "I recognize you brother."

"How far does ten bucks fly today brother", I asked.

"Flies this far", he answered and handed me an arrangement with four red roses and six white carnations.

Normally, I would have expected the flower guy to cut me a special deal but I could see he was overwhelmed. The line and the grumbling down the line was growing fast. The cops would be arriving soon and then everybody would be shit out of luck until or if the cop got a good buy on the flowers he was gonna need.

I paid the bucks, grabbed the arrangement, said "so long boys" to the guys in line and made my way to Wegman's for part two: The Card.

Rochester used to be famous for Kodak and then for Xerox.....both companies were fading fast and Rochester was now becoming famous for Wegman's, the super duper market that was beginning its indomitable spread across the country. I made my way to the nearest Wegman's with the perception that I could walk right in, pick out a great card, walk right out and be back home in ten minutes.

I made my way over to the card area and found a big red section called Valentine's Day. I noticed the section was filled with men. I grabbed a few cards and realized this was going to be more complicated than I had imagined. All of the cards were of the My Dear wife, I love you so much that my tender heart breaks with the overwhelming joy of your radiant kindness on this our romantic day of days with hearts and angels and all of that crap.

In a panic, I looked at card after card. They were all the same, the kinds of cards that men hate to give and women hate to get because they SCREAM last minute.

I couldn't help but speak out loud.
"Man. these cards suck."
I immediately got responses from all the guys in the section who were having the same problem and realization.
"Right on."
"Damned straight"
"Word"
"You got that right, man."

Once again I could feel the bonding at this annual ritual. Then one guy pointed out an entire empty section of cards. Somebody figured out, "that's where all the good ones were." Naturally, all the good ones were long gone. We all paused for a moment to visualize wonderful guys buying witty, sexy cards two weeks ago and normally priced flowers two days ago. We all vowed to be that guy next year. I started talking to the guy who had said "Word". He said he couldn't find a card and he didn't even have flowers yet. I explained the flower guy. The Word guy said he was going there but he only had a half hour. We estimated the time that it would take him to drive to the flower guy, wait in line, buy the flowers and still be on time so he wouldn't get home late and have his ass chewed off by his furious wife.

He came to the conclusion he wasn't going to risk it. He would pay the wildly overpriced flowers at Wegman's, even though he was "broke" and wanted a beer.

I told him to pick up two of those cards that you stick in a flower arrangement, one for him and one for me which he did. I wrote, "here's something simple" on the card that he gave to me. Also, since he had saved me money on the card, I gave him enough to buy a 24 ounce Labbatt's Blue Light which he now had plenty of time to drink in the parking lot.

I got home on time, gave Lynn her flowers. She read the note. It worked. She liked the presentation because it was "simple" not a big goofy attempt to gild a rose unlike my usual tendency to "make a big deal out of everything." Simple indeed.

Twenty years later, it's even simpler. I buy her some daisies a week before Valentine's day and truly love her all year long.

But just in case, Wegman's opened a super center in North Carolina a year before we moved here.

I don't know where the flower guy is but I wish ya well, brother.Black Rock

Black rock glistens in the rain.

When I was a child, I learned to swim in Crystal Beach at Canandaigua Lake. The bottom of Crystal Beach is full of thousands if not millions of rocks. As a result, on a calm day, the water is crystal clear, hence the name for the beach.

My father as well as my grandfather learned to swim here as did my brother and sister as well as my children. We all dove for rocks.

Forty yards from the shore, the water is over my head. I remember hearing the warning "don't go out over your head". I took that warning seriously. I'd spent most of my life at a safe depth, thirty yards from the beach.

When I learned to swim, I realized that it didn't matter how much water was beneath me as I was safe on the surface. I began to venture over my head.
I've been over my head a lot since then.

I heard of a rock pile that once you reached it, you could stand on the rocks and keep your head above water. If you stepped off the pile, the water was deep and not as clear as near the shore. Ten feet from the rock pile, a black rock stood out from all the rest. Black rock was the North Star. When you came to the black rock, that meant that the water was over your head and yet the rock pile rock pile was very near.

Safety and momentary security

All of the other rocks surrounding black rock appeared brownish barely indistinguishable one from the other. They had remained in place for God knows how long. Decades...centuries.

The first swim of the year was always a great moment. Before you went in, you'd always ask "how's the water today and the answer was always the same...."It's cold until you get used to it...then it's beautiful."

As I taught my kids to swim, I told them about the rock pile and the black rock. Eventually, they found both. Standing on the rock pile was an achievement, a step towards daring, a sign of growth, a symbol of eternal summer. Swimming in from the rock pile, we always passed black rock. always in the same place.

My children grew.

We moved.

I took what I imagined was my last swim at Crystal Beach.

I decided to take black rock with me.

I lifted the rock from its resting place and brought it into the shore. On the shore, drying out...black rock lost some of its mystique. It kinda looked like just another rock.

We built our house.

I placed black rock in the garden.

It's been many years now. We've moved several times. We always take black rock with us.

Whenever my kids come to visit, they always look in our gardens to find black rock and when they do, we all flash back to family days when we were all together. The summer of our lives

Black rock shimmers when it rains.

It takes on its original ebony and stands out from every delicacy in every garden...standing watch. Strong, exceptional, still showing the way home.

When it rains as its doing today, I tend to look at the garden wherever we might be.

Always there, black as night.

Black rock, ancient and adaptive.

Glistening.

Hooray for Mrs. Leary

I'm an ex-teacher so I'm kind of an attention freak. I encouraged attention in my classes. I didn't demand it but was sensitive to it. I encouraged it. The kids who paid the most attention got a lot of my attention in my return plus they probably understood what I was talking about or demonstrating. I didn't mind kids doodling in my classes because I'm a doodler too. I understand that doodling is a combination of intuition and feeling. I'm not going to discourage that product.

Often I would reward it.

Let me tell you a story about an attentive teacher who paid attention to an inattentive student.

George wasn't doing well in his second grade class which means that he was having trouble with reading. The bluebirds were getting all the attention. George didn't like school. He thought he was "dumb".

George slipped into a habit of doodling. He was always afraid that he would get caught by his teacher. Sure enough one afternoon his teacher decided to challenge youg George on his attentiveness. She knew that he was doodling. George knew he was busted. He tried to slip his doodle into his desk but it was too late. The teacher demanded that George show her what he had been doing. Let's call the teacher Mrs. Leary.

George felt afraid and humiliated but being a good boy, he dutifully handed the doodle to Mrs. Leary. Mrs. Leary took the doodle from George. She brought it to the front of the class and asked George to explain what he had drawn. The doodle was full of "cowboys and Indians". George felt his humiliation slipping away being replaced by a new feeling...a feeling of confidence. George explained his story to the class. Everybody in the class paid attention to what George was saying, most of all Mrs. Leary.

The story was very imaginative and the images in the doodle matched the story perfectly. At the conclusion of his story, the entire class applauded as did Mrs. Leary.

Mrs. Leary said "George, every Tuesday afternoon, I m going to let you draw your doodle on the blackboard and you can describe your doodle to us with another story but only if you pay closer attention during the rest of the week. Is that a deal?

George said, "Yes, Mrs. Leary."

George paid closer attention during the week and made great progress in his reading which added to his confidence. Every Tuesday he went to the board and drew a story. He became a top student and a popular kid. Everybody looked forward to Tuesday afternoons.

George's last name was/is Lucas.

George has since claimed that if he had been humiliated that day "everything might have turned out different. Everything."

Where would we be without *Star Wars*?
Where would we be without the great teachers Yoda and Obi Wan?
Where would we be without the Force.
Where would we be without Industrial Light and Magic.
Where would we be without great teachers like Mrs. Leary and the force and the light and the magic that they bring.

Hooray for Mrs. Leary and for attentive, kind teachers everywhere.

Here are a few of the Mrs. Leary's I have known including Mrs. Leary herself....Mrs. Sachs, Ms. Rider, Mrs. Kimmell, Mrs. Scarborough, Mrs. Dewhurst, Mrs. Mertel, Mrs. Amstey, Mrs. Miller, Mrs. Lazeroff, Mrs. Brown, Mrs. Dewald, Sister Denise, Sister Matthias, Ms. Hogan, Ms. Morgan, Miss Holzer, Mrs. Seelman, Mrs. D, Mrs D'Imperio, Mrs. Barr, Ms. Milhouse, Mrs. Prescott, Mrs. K, Ms. Cappelippo, Mrs. Aryonde, Ms. Clark, Ms. Nolan, Mrs. Matthews De Sant, Ms. Loftus, Ms. Underwood, Mrs. Loeffler, Ms. Kleintop, Ms. Bodak, Ms. Nelson, Ms. Nesbitt, Ms. Abraham, Mrs. Sturtevant, Ms.

Zeiner, Ms. Agnello, Ms. Tassey, Ms. Nuss, Mrs. Fazio, Mrs. Blier-Mervis, Ms. Guenther, Mrs. Breese-Sykela, Ms Kellar, Mrs White, Mrs Wilson, Ms. Kellar, Ms. Botting and many others.

Prodigious Piles of Penguin Poop

Is this a change? Yes, yes it is. This IS a change if you don't believe in recurring cycles.

This is the first time I've put a title on an essay before writing the essay. In the past I have put hundreds of titles on hundred of "posts" and called them "essays" or "stories" or "opinions" or "obscure art" or "poems".

That recurring cycle is known as "writing".

So the fact that this "essay" is title driven is not so much a change as it is a cyclical recurrence.

I am currently interested in another little know cyclical recurrence, namely, that every dozen years or so, way up North and in New Zealand, unexpected piles of penguin poop suddenly appear. The piles are concentrated in a circular area and they have been puzzling poopoligists for a while now since they have not yet been identified as part of a cycle rather than a random series of evacuations.

My conjecture is that every dozen years for the past few centuries, what with the global warming and all, penguins have realized that they need to fly because pretty soon the ice will be gone and things will get mighty awkward or heaven forbid even might become aukward like the extinction of the once great auk.

Word

So every dozen years, the penguins gather around in a circle and try like hell to start flying. They just stand there and strain their minds to imagine themselves flying and the strain mimics the strain of bowel movement which produces the prodigious piles as the penguins will stand in one spot for a couple of days, straining, imagining, willing, and pooping.

To the objective observer, (of which there aren't any as this effort is always made in secret and in fact will not even be attempted unless complete absolute privacy is assured) it would appear that the penguins are just standing there pooping but my conjecture is that much more is happening.

Penguins, through imagination, are attempting to speed up the evolutionary process.

Whenever a non-flying organism is trying to will itself into flight, that organism typically has the appearance of just standing there or just sitting there in a private lotus position; Mike Love for example before Beach Boy concerts in the seventies. Unfortunately for Love, however, his concentration and privacy were regularly interrupted pre-flight by the sudden, cursing, drunken appearance of band mate Dennis Wilson who seemed to take delight in the act of vomiting on the head of Love when Love was at the height of astral concentration. This violation left Love as earthbound as a pooping penguin.

After about a week or so of straining, the penguins give up and banish the thought of flying from their minds entirely and focus on the hope of being captured and taken to zoos where they are in great demand simply because they are the rare birds that can not fly away and escape.

Eventually, penguins must learn to fly or become extinct. Thus is the nature of cycles and the constant need for change. The effort becomes more and more urgent thus the even more prodigious piles. Like the change in the appearance of this post what with the title and all.

But it's not just the appearance of the title that marks the change.

Usually when I write, the title is the last thing that I come up with as it is a way of pretending that I had a controlling concept to begin the piece rather than just a flow of ideas that when completed I need to read to grasp and when read suggests a "concept" which can be fortified by taking a few words from the discovered "concept" and putting those words at the top of the piece and calling those words a "title".

In this case, the title, an actual controlling thought, came first and everything else has strainlessly evolved from that thought and will lead to the precise, alliterative, feathery ending which will be missed by some readers because they shook their heads and stopped reading a few paragraphs back but not by you the truly intelligent, patient and charming few who have read this far and only have thirty four words to go.

Thank you for getting this far with this post and I hope that these paragraphs have been worth your attention and are not merely

Prodigious piles of penguin poop.

A Human Response

In my very first year of teaching back in '68, I was shutting a classroom window when somehow I cut my hand. I didn't want to look at my wound because I was afraid that I might be bleeding. In all of my years of learning, I had never seen a teacher bleed.

Trying to be non-chalant, trying to ignore the obvious, I pulled my hand back from the window and started walking towards the front of the room, much like Gene Wilder when in Y*oung Frankenstein* he slammed a scalpel into his thigh and never changed facial expression while he dismissed his astonished class. My class had just begun, so dismissal was out of the question. I took just a couple steps when Elma, (I still remember her name after all these years) a student in the window row near the front of the class sort of whispered to me, "Uh hey, Mr. Rivers, you're bleeding". I noticed actual caring and concern in her voice.

I was only five years older than the 'kids' in my class.

I grabbed my handkerchief and wrapped it around my hand but too late. All the kids noticed that there was some blood on the floor. I had to excuse myself. I asked a hall monitor to watch my class for a 'few minutes' while I made my way to the nurse's office. Mrs. Hindmarch, the school nurse, bandaged me up. I went back to the classroom, thanked the monitor and for a moment tried again to pretend that nothing had happened.

A teacher for less than a semester and I had already revealed my vulnerability, my humanity in a way that I had never seen before. I remember hoping that the principal wouldn't find out….maybe I'd get in trouble.

When I got back to the front of the class all bandaged up with some of my blood still on the floor and while waiting for the custodian, we had a little talk, my students and I. It was as if I had suddenly turned real and could stop pretending to be a person pretending to be a teacher. I had suddenly turned real.

We connected that day.

So much of teaching and learning has to do with connection. Spontaneously, unpredictably, magically, individually we become real to one another; imperfect beings of spirit, thought, energy, struggle, hopes, dreams, flesh, blood, spirit, syrup and saliva.

We teachers are not attention seeking vampires who live in a classroom coffin springing to life at the sight of students. We are, for the most part, intelligent, educated, civilized citizens hoping to make a mark on the future by professionally, skillfully and thoughtfully attending to the present.,

We have our style. Frequently our teaching style comes in conflict with the learning style of a student. If connection is to be made, something's got to give. The longer that I taught, the more able I became to operate within different styles in order to activate my students' pre-existing body of knowledge and wealth of experience. It was my hope to model adaptability rather than lecture about it.

Sometimes, we encourage the student to temporarily depart their learning style and immerse within another which sometimes feels like drowning but more often serves as a familiar form of irritation. When connected teachers irritate students, that irritation is only one side of a coin. The flip side of that coin is awareness. We irritate in order to invigorate. Invigorated lessons require the most struggle but once accomplished they last the longest.

Before I cut myself on the window that day, I was fooling with the Venetian blinds. We all have Venetian blinds around our working memories/intuitions If we decide to keep the blinds closed, no light can enter our consciousness. When we consciously decide to open the blinds, we're usually amazed to find a teacher next to us in the sunlight celebrating the brand new day.

Elma went on to the local community college. Then she got a law degree from Syracuse and helped me through my divorce. Later she became a judge and rose to the level of State Supreme Court Judge.

Elma died at 63.

She was my student and my teacher.

That's the way it works when it works, except for Elma's way too early passing.

The picture below was taken on my very first day of teaching. I was approaching Carlton Webster when I noticed a bunch of guys hanging around in front of the school. I said, "hi guys."

The kid on the right who I'm pretty sure had just put out a cigarette asked me "who the heck are you." I said "I'm a teacher." This picture is a click taking a few seconds after that introduction. I don't think the photographer knew who the hell I was either.

All of these guys ended up in my class. They also had a great influence on my career.

The kid on the right is Jim Harter. Today, Jim is 68.

None of us are kids anymore.

Nickname for Blue Eyed Twin

Isabel has playful brown eyes and long brown hair.
William has sparkling blue eyes and short blonde hair.
William and Isabel are twins.
Twins don't have to look alike.
They live in a big house in Duxbury.
They have an older sister named Eva.
Eva is beautiful and a little bit shy.
They have an older brother named Oliver.
Oliver is younger than Eva.
Oliver has brown eyes and brown hair.
Oliver loves all sports and is good at them.
Everybody has brown eyes and brown hair
Even the youngest brother Hamish.
Everybody except Will.
Hamish likes to help his Dad
When they work around the house.
Hamish loves to hug his Mom.
Hamish knows a card trick.
The children have a chicken coop.
They collect eggs every morning.
Isabelle has a nickname.
Everybody calls her Belma.
Belma loves to read and write.
Grandma sends her books to read.
She wrote an alphabet book
A is for apple. B is for banana.
William doesn't have a nickname
Except for Will rather than Bill.
Will loves video games.
Will loves to sing and dance.
He knows all the songs from Hamilton
And all the words to all of the songs.
Grandpa thought that Will needed a nickname.
On Thanksgiving, Grandpa whispered to Will

"I have a nickname for you"

"What is it?" Will whispered back.

"I'm gonna call you Riff from now on."

Will thought Grandpa had said something else.

"You're gonna call me Rick?"

Grandpa whispered again

"Not Rick.. I'm gonna call you Riff."

"Riff?" whispered Will.

"Riff "whispered Grandpa.

"Riff," whispered Will.

"That's right, Riff"

"Who's Riff" asked Will.

"To me you are" said Grandpa.

"Okay." said Will.

Grandpa knew that someday, somewhere

When the time was right.

Will would watch West Side Story

And find out who Riff is.

And he will sing and dance.

His way to stardom

Maybe even Hollywood Blvd>

A Crime Between Stars

It was my first walk on Hollywood Boulevard as I passed Grauman's Chinese Theater. *Enter the Dragon* was on the marquee. I remember thinking how appropriate it was that Bruce Lee who was already a superstar in China would be on that marquee on that theater on that morning in LA.

Yeah as Ray Davies said, you CAN "see all the stars as you walk down Hollywood Boulevard, some you can recognize some that you've barely even heard of, all of whom suffered and struggled for fame, some who succeeded and some who struggled in vain."

My traveling companion JJ Gleason and I were on our way to Disneyland but decided to take a quick detour and check out the Boulevard. We had about a half hour to kill before Disneyland opened for the day.

JJ wasn't as interested in the stars as I was so he stopped into a coffee shop across the street while I walked and looked down at the stars, their names written in concrete. I was young. I was single. I was on a road trip. I had visited in at least 20 states for the first time in the past sixteen days. I had driven down Route 1, the long and challenging California highway with the ocean on one side and the mountains on the other. Look at the mountains and you almost drive over the cliff into the ocean. Look at the ocean and you drive into a mountain. I was on my way to Disneyland and then San Diego and then Mexico then back up through Arizona past the Grand Canyon and home again.

Yeah, I had a beard and handmade vest and cut offs and a battered hat on my head. Road clothes yeah. The best. The most comfortable.

Yeah.

So I continued down Hollywood Boulevard rarely looking up and putting distance between me and Bruce Lee. Every once in a while the stars would disappear and I would realize that I was coming to a side street. Then on the next corner the stars would appear again and I would continue my walk.

You ever have one of those days where you're the only person on the golf course or the only person in the lake or the only person walking down 42nd street and it seems like you own the whole area.? That's how I was feeling. I couldn't believe that I owned Hollywood Boulevard.

Then, suddenly I didn't.

A cop had materialized from somewhere behind me and he was telling me to "stop."

I stopped on a dime as innocent as a child.

The cop told me to "turn around"

I turned around. I said, "Hi, how're ya doin' this morning."

He asked if I had any identification.

I asked him why he was asking.

He repeated the question. I knew enough to obey.

I showed him my driver's license. He looked it over carefully and began writing something before he handed it back to me.

I asked him why he wanted the wallet and what was he writing.

He said that he was writing me a ticket.

I asked him how could I get a ticket, I was just walking down the street.

He said, "That's the offense. You jaywalked."

Remember aside from me and the cop there was not a soul on Hollywood Boulevard this morning.

It is possible that I crossed one of the side streets while a do not cross sign was flashing. I don't know. I was looking at the stars and there were zero cars.The street was empty.

I explained to the guy that I was in LA for this day only and was on this Boulevard for only a few minutes and that we were on our way to Disneyland and then out of LA forever. Why are you bothering to write up this "ticket."

Again his answer was simple "You jaywalked."

I said "okay, write up the ticket but I'll tell you right now I'm never gonna pay it. I'm gonna throw it out the window somewhere between here and Mexico."

His response was simple "shut your mouth."

I shut my mouth. He finished writing the citation and handed it to me.

I said, "Thanks for nuthin. And nuthin is what I'm gonna pay for this ticket."

"Oh yeah?," he said, well maybe I should just take you down to the station right now. Would you prefer that?
Once again I asked "what the hell for? For jaywalking?. You're gonna arrest me and take me to the station for jaywalking?

"No I'm taking you there for resisting arrest. Now do you want this ticket or not?"

Meanwhile I noticed JJ. He was heading towards us to see what the commotion was and he was legitimately jaywalking (literally and figuratively) as he approached. Somehow I signaled him to go back to the car before we became a two man gang of Mansons from New York resisting arrest in California. I said, "I'll take the ticket."Before he handed it to me he asked "Is it your intention to pay this citation."

I lied.

I crossed the street. Got into my car and the left the stars and the badges of Hollywood Boulevard behind me forever.

Looking back today on the experience with the ghost of George Floyd haunting all media, I consider myself very fortunate.

If I had been a black man walking down Hollywood Boulevard that very day and had reacted in the very same way, perhaps I would still be in jail today if not shot or clubbed or kneed to death.

We've all been discriminated against and we need to keep a fresh memory of that pain and humiliation and injustice as we hurdle into the new normal of understanding, empathy, reform and freedom.

Two Men In Texas

Shelley Seton was expecting, expecting. Shelley Seton was expecting twins. Why wouldn't she be?

Shelley had an identical twin named Kelley. Kelley and Shelley grew up dressing alike. They were so identical that nobody even bothered to try and tell them apart. They were known individually and collectively as Kelleyandshelley or, depending upon the suspicion, Shelleyandkelley. Or the Macdonald twins.

One fine day, Kelleyand shelley met Ronaldandonald. Ronaldandonald or Donaldandronald, depending upon the suspicion, were the Seton twins.

The attraction was immediate, intense and opposite. The only difference between Kelley and Shelley was that Shelley was left handed and Kelley right. The only difference between Ronald and Donald is that Donald was right handed and Ronald left.

The twins began double dating and in so doing gave new dimension to the term double dating; doubles dating doubles while dating. Opposites do tend to attract. Left handed Shelley was attracted to right handed Donald. Right handed Kelley fell in love with left handed Ronald. World War two was raging.

All over the country, young couples were getting hitched just before the males were shipped overseas. Ronald was drafted and headed for war after boot camp in Texas.

The two couples decided to get married.

They gave new dimension to the term double marriage.

They got married in Texarkana. Before the marriage, the couples thought how neat it would be if they were to take the girl's last names. Then the boys could be Donaldandronald Macdonald or Ronaldandonald Macdonald based upon suspicion. After a few laughs, the couples decided to stick with tradition. Shelley MacDonald became Shelley Seton.

After the marriage, the boys went over to the line separating Texas from Arkansas. They got into position like two centers ready to hike two footballs with the line of scrimmage being the state line. Shelley snapped the picture.

Two men in Texas, two asses in Arkansas.

A year before the two asses squatted in Arkansas, Shelleyandkelley and Donaldandronald realized that they had a problem. The old twin switcheroo.

Except this time, the possibility existed for the almost impossible to comprehend double twin switcheroo. Vertently or inadvertently, it was possible on any given night for left handed Shelley to wind up with left handed Ronald and/or for right handed Donald to end up with right handed Kelley.

The couples decided that one way to prevent this problem was a sign-in sheet. The sets of twins could and should demand a writing sample before every date and even during some of those dates, particularly the double dates, before moments of intimacy, after arguments at any time of doubt or joy, of hope or faith.

A request for a writing sample, it was agreed should never be turned down. Obviously, it wasn't the content of the note that was important, it was the hand that was used to write the note. If anybody was ambidextrous, he/she kept it a secret.

Donald would make sure that the twin from whom he was getting a writing sample was writing with her left hand and that would prove it was Shelley. Then Shelley in turn would make sure that the guy writing the note to her was writing the note with his right hand and was indeed Donald. Even though the content of the note wasn't critical, the foursome decided to come up with a note that would unite them while simultaneously dividing them. The note had to be long enough to test writing skills but short enough to not take up much time particularly before moments of passion. This is the note they decided on.

Ronaldanddonald would write: "i am who i am and that's all that i am, I'm Ronald (or Donald) the Seton twin".

Shelleyandkelley would write: "I am who I am and that's all that I am, I'm Shelley (or Kelley) the Mackdee twin".

Let's hope it worked because as mentioned earlier, Shelly was preggers.

Shelley had the names picked out for the twins she was expecting, expecting.

If they were girls they would be Helen and Ellen in honor of Shelley's mother Ellen and her identical, dress alike sister Helen, formerly the Tower Twins Helenandellen or Ellenandhelen Tower.

If the expected twins were boys they would be named Merle and Earl in honor of Donald's father Merle and Merle's identical dress alike twin brother, Uncle Earl, formerly Merleandearl or Earlandmerle Seton.

If they were a boy and a girl, the twins would be named Merle and Pearl in honor of Donald's father Merle and his wife, Donald's mother, Pearl.His parents were known as merlandperl.

Around the sixth week of her pregnancy, Shelley experienced some unusually heavy bleeding without much pain or cramping and was alarmed until she visited her obstetrician and was assured that the pregnancy was still viable. The heavy bleeding was nothing out of the ordinary at that stage of pregnancy according to Dr. Rudolph.

This was way back in 1946, well before the advent of sonograms, ultrasound and amnios No one knew then what we know now.

This is what we know now.

Women have always carried twins with far greater frequency than imagined. In the old days, those twins were never captured on sonogram so most women never knew they were carrying twins and when they experienced heavy bleeding around the sixth week of their pregnancy, they were unaware that they were actually miscarrying one of the twins. They would go to the doctor the next day and the doctor would say what Doctor Rudolph said to Shelley. "This is nothing out of the ordinary" Which was true.

Sorta.

So the expectant mother would go home assured that her unborn child was still developing according to plan and totally unaware that one half of the in utero twins had already left the building with very little fanfare.

Earl was gone and forgotten not only as a has been but a never was and never even had been.

Merle went full term and was born alone. The only evidence that Earl existed in the first place is the evidence that Merle brought with him. Surviving twin babies have one consistent characteristic. They are overwhelmingly left handed.

As was Merle.
Six years later, half-twin Merle Seton Fell out of the bunk bed.

Bunk beds had quite a history In the Seton family. Merle's mother and her twin sister had both slept in bunk beds As had Merle's father and his twin brother. Merle's grandmothers and grandfathers had also slept in bunk beds. All four of 'em, always two per bed.

None of them had ever fallen out of a bunk bed before.

Of course, all of them had lived in Dubuque.

Merle and his Mom and Dad were sleeping in Nevada.

His Dad had done his war time stint working on the Manhattan Project. The Manhattan project was only the beginning. The experimenting continued.The war was over but the Reds weren't.They were all over the place. Some were in Nevada. "Spying", Merle's Dad said.

Merle's Dad never said much else 'bout his work even the morning after the night That Merle fell out of the bunk bed. The top bunk of the bunk bed. Thank God, it was a low top.

Merle Seton was a dreamin' bout sittin' on a dock three feet above soft rocks that were covered with warm Lake Water. Merle slipped gently off the dock, feet headed for the rocks but found only air and instead of warm crystal clear water his bare feet found nuthin but floor beneath his six year old soles.

Somehow he landed on his legs before he fell on his ass which was the cause of the crash which woke Merle up uninjured. Merle climbed back up the ladder, no wiser and no sadder, to the bunk not the dock. He took a look at the clock which was pointing to midnight. He fell asleep in atomic fright Feeling kinda sore and sad. Where the heck were Mom and Dad?

See, the Setons lived in Nevada as close as anybody to the atomic bomb testing grounds and were in the forefront of American fifties families who learned to love the bomb. Merle's father was involved emotionally and economically with the atomic arming of the Cold war. His great triumph occurred with his contribution to the Manhattan Project which probably saved the life of his twin brother who was stationed in Manila and warming up to be cannon fodder during the inevitable horrific invasion of Japan that would make Iwo Jima look like Ding-Dong school but then we dropped the bomb on 'em and all the living brothers came home.

Since then Merle's Dad had labored on various side trips, brilliant defense measures that ended up being expensive dead ends. These dead ends included the nuclear bazooka, the F3H jet, the atomic artillery shell and the various pills and nostrums the atomic alchemists devised to cure radiation poisoning including what would become LSD. Yeah, Merle's Dad was convinced that the bomb was his friend and the guardian of his family.

Shelley had her doubts but had learned how to be married as the forties turned into the fifties. and the Kramden kings were in their castles. She kept her big trap shut.
The Setons were used to seeing flashes and minutes later feeling their house

rock. Shelley heard the crash from the bunk room. She opened her trap, nudged her husband and whispered, "what's that" Merle's father, worn out from a hard day's night at the plant sleepily replied "Jezzuz, go back to sleep, it's only an atomic bomb . I gotta be at work early tomorrow."

Before shutting her trap and settling back in bed, Shelley whispered to her husband "All right. I was afraid that maybe Merle had fallen out of the bunk".

Copperhead and Cut Throat

The first book that I ever took out from a library was a book about snakes by Herbert S Zim. My next two books were also written by Zim. One was about dinosaurs and the other about whales.

I loved the names of the snakes in Zim's book. I was fascinated by the idea that they were fanged and poisonous, especially the ones with the coolest names; cobra, rattler, diamond back, copper head and the best name of all...water moccasin.

I also loved the names of ones that were huge and could squeeze ya to death; boa constrictor, python, anaconda.

I was relieved and yet disappointed that none of these snakes lived in New York so we made 'em up. It Didn't matter much that they weren't around when we were playing " run through the jungle" which was always full of pythons or " lost in the swamp " which was always full of water moccasins.

In New York, we did have a snake that looked poisonous....the king snake. A king snake resembles a coral snake, one of the deadliest. I always hoped to see a king snake which became my favorite snake because not only was he the king of snakes but also a good guy who wouldn't hurt you.

Still, I kinda wished that we lived somewhere else so I might see one of the deadly snakes. As a boy scout, I learned how to apply first aid to a snake bite. Cross cut between the punctures, suck out the venom, apply a tourniquet and get to the doctor ASAP.

When we moved to North Carolina a couple years ago, I wondered if I might see one of the poisonous snakes. Around our neighborhood, there were rumors of copperheads in the woods.

Whenever we walk through the woods around here, we're always a little wary that we might step on one and it might strike back.

Yesterday, we were on our daily walk around the neighborhood. We were nowhere near the woods. We were walking on the sidewalk. I noticed what appeared to be a very long worm at rest on the sidewalk. When I got closer, I realized that I was looking at a baby snake. When I got closer still, I realized that I was looking at a copperhead.

The copperhead was in our territory and therefore was in much more danger from us than we were from it. When I was in Montana, I heard a story about a little girl who had played with what she thought were biting worms but were in fact baby copperheads. She had been bitten a few times while she played with them and almost died from the tiny bites until her parents figured things out and got her to the doctor just in time.

The little girl's name was Claudia. When she grew up, she loved the mountains and the mountains, in their savage way, loved her back.

I got up close to the copperhead to check out the copper on the head. Lynn warned me to stay away fearing, supposing that the worm would jump up and attach it to my face. I was pretty sure that snakes didn't jump so I took a good look from a safe distance just to make sure.

Yup, it was a copperhead.

Also it was December and it was 76 degrees.

Strange things are happening.

I realized that if I wanted to I could just stomp down on the reptile's head and that would be it for this neighborhood terror. This beautiful worm, after all was on our turf catching some unexpected warmth and didn't belong there. It was gonna be a long crawl back to the woods from whence it had emerged and it might run into a kid along the way who wanted to play with the cute worm.

Live and let live is one of my mottoes. We walked past that copperhead. I was reminded of Herbert S Zim and my first trip to the library.

And once again remembered Montana, mountain goats, buffalo jumps and cutthroat trouts.

I'm no fisherman but I have a fish story.

The story takes place in the mountains of Montana, the last of the big time splendors.

My companions were Bruce and Claudia. Bruce and I had driven cross country from New York for the express purpose of going for a hike with Claudia into the mountains. The previous year, Claudia and I were camp mates on a week long hike into the Grizzly Mountains. Since that time, I had talked so much and wondrously about Montana, the mountains the streams and Claudia that Bruce just had to come and see for himself.

We arrived in Bozeman. Claudia was waiting for us. We went for our walk.

I am an indoors man by nature but I had been to the mountains and hiked with Claudia.

Bruce was more of an outdoorsman than I but he had never been into the mountains, hadn't even met Claudia.

Claudia was from Montana. Her relatives had come from the Alps. She was an outdoors woman. She was the same height as Bruce and I which made her a tall woman. She was lithe and lissome. Broad shouldered, long arms and legs. Naturally blonde. Nordic. She loved the mountains. The mountains loved her. The higher we got in the mountains, the more beautiful Claudia became. She was a total natural.

Claudia knew a lot of trails. She chose for us one of her favorite trails, a trail rarely taken by anyone other than a person who knows the mountains. She had figured out our measure. The trail she had chosen would meet and push that measure without overwhelming it.

We walked and talked as we climbed. Bruce and Claudia hit it off great. Claudia and I meshed again as we had the year before. It was if no time had passed.

They have a saying in the mountains...."the higher you get....the higher you get". The three of us were getting plenty high when we came to our first stream crossing. Claudia bounded from rock to rock and was over the stream in a flash. Bruce tried to match her gamine grace but that didn't work. He lost his balance and tumbled into the stream with a huge splash, He quickly climbed out but he was soaking wet. He came back to my side of the stream. Claudia recrossed the stream and joined us.

It was mountain time for a break as we had been going for about three hours.

While Bruce dried off, I went back to the stream to take a better look into the water. It was loaded with fish.

Loaded.

I watched the fish swim around for awhile as if they owned the place. I said that if ever I was a fisherman, this would be the place that I would fish. Unbeknownst to me, Bruce had brought a fishing pole. The three of us returned to the stream. Even Claudia was impressed by the gathering of the fish in the crystal clear, ice cold stream.

All of our attention was focused on a huge fish that was hanging around, treading water and minding it's own business. I almost got the feeling that the fish was looking at us like we were looking at it and wondering "what the hell". Bruce dropped his line into the water right in front of the fish. The unsuspecting fish went right ahead and took a bite off the hook and the next thing that I knew, this beautiful natural creature so full of life was emerging from the stream dangling at the end of a line.

Bruce pulled the fish out of the water like a silver and ruby diamond of truth.The fish flopped off the hook and landed on a rock. This was most definitely a first time experience not only for me but also for the fish.

I didn't know what do or to say. I was stupefied by the struggle of the magnificent fish on the rock. We watched it as it tried in vain to regain its grace and dignity.

That's when Claudia said, "we either eat it or we put it back. It's your fish Bruce."

Bruce hesitated in his answer. Claudia made the decision.

She picked up the fish and before my astonished eyes, she smashed that fish head first into a rock. The struggle ended there.

She found a place near the rocks to start a fire.

She cleaned the fish.

She said it was a cut throat trout.

She cooked the fish.

We ate it.

I'm not a big fish eating guy. Fish fries and tuna fish sandwiches are about as far as I go. Not on that day. As we were eating the fish, we filled our canteens up with stream water. To this day, I swear there is something hallucinogenic about that magical water that flows in the streams high in the mountains. Ya gotta taste it to believe it. I had told Bruce about the effect of drinking that water. Claudia knew all about it. We ate and drank heartily.

We crossed the stream and got even higher in the next two hours.

As we continued our walk, we talked about the fish. How in a matter of minutes it had gone from its natural kingdom, onto a rock and into our stomachs.

It was a Montana afternoon. Splendiferous sky. Crystal clear water. Mountain breeze. Infinite panorama. Three friends walking and talking as if forever...

Freedom to Fly

Last night, I dreamt that I could fly sorta. When I hit the sheets, I was the opposite of hungry.

My flying was more like walking on air, very pleasant. Some folks call this phenomena astral projection. Most of us, I'm lookin at you Steve Miller, think romantically about flying especially when we observe and contemplate the soaring of a bald eagle.

Photo by David Ellsworth

Few of us consider the flight of the eagle to be what it is, a life long search for food.

That search becomes intensified after the birth of an eaglet. The eaglet receives incubation from the mother for the first three days of its life before it is joined by at least one and sometimes two eaglets with mouth(s) to feed. Thus begins a nearly unprecedented sibling rivalry for survival.

The first born has a huge advantage. First off, he is more fully incubated which means he's bigger and stronger and better adapted to the nest than his rivals. When the parental eagle returns to the nest, they drop off the food and the eaglets compete for it with no holds barred and no referee. The eldest of the eaglets usually wins this competition and grows stronger while his brethren starve and grow weaker. As they grow, the eaglets continue to fight for ring room even as the nest is growing smaller because they are getting bigger especially the eldest. By now the weaker brethren is not only starving but being pecked to death by his nest mates even as the nest if filling up with eagle excreta.

After five or six weeks, the adult eagles leave the nest and find another place to   chill, an aerie away from thespian in the ass eaglets, only one of whom is doing alright. They don't bother with child care. They leave the kids to battle it out

At this point the weakest of the three is killed by its brothers as the parents look on without interfering. If the surviving weaker of the eaglets makes it to eight weeks, that eaglet is trying like hell to get outta this place too soon and away from the constant pecking and poking and bullying. Here is where many eaglets attempt to fly for the first time without proper preparation and usually fall to the ground while experiencing premature elevation if not pushed out of the nest by bro bro. An eagle out of the nest becomes prey for foxes, coyotes, mountain lions and other predators. The parent eagles don't even bother to try to take the fallen eaglet back into the nest although they will bring it food if they find enough in their flights.

Meanwhile back in the nest, the surviving eaglet has learned to crap outside of the nest. Nobody teaches him how to do that, he just figures it out, same with flying itself. There is no instruction from parents

Upon reaching 8 weeks of age or more, the eaglets start start flapping their wings to develop muscle strength. They flap their wings in place and perform jumps on the nest. Then they start learning how to take-off and land skills by bounding from branch to branch branch to branch. This is the period where most eaglets miss a landing and fall to the ground. Whoops.

The eagle parents do not teach the eagle babies how to fly. When the time to fledge approaches, the parents may encourage them to get the hell outta the nest the nest by flying around the nest while vocalizing the avian version of GTFO.

Field observations indicate that up to half of bald eagle fledglings end up on the ground.

The one that survives imitates the parents in flight and learns all about drafting. He follows his parents everywhere and for the first five weeks, they will continue to feed him until everybody gets sick of the dependence and the eagle survives on its own.

Next time or if ever you see an eagle in flight; remember he didn't get there while waiting for a bus. Through struggle, starvation, parental neglect and sibling rivalry; he's earned his wings and his freedom to fly.

Hombre Dinosaur

Thornton Krell was a huge fan of Richard Boone due to Boone's portrayal of Paladin in the adult Western *Have Gun Will Travel* which was the lead in to *Gunsmoke* on Saturday night teevee. The influence of Krell led me to become a fan and student of Boone.

Boone had a significant career in movies and teevee, playing both heroes and villains villains against the likes of Paul Newman, John Wayne and Marlon Brando. His villainous stint in *Hombre* opposite Paul Newman is particularly nasty and has one of my favorite lines in all of moviedom. He plays a character named Grimes who's a classic bully and criminal. It seems that Grimes has Newman's characters trapped on a mountain ledge. To further add to his sadistic villainy, Grimes/Boone has captured one of the women in Newman's group and tied her to a rock in the broiling sun. After a couple of days, the begging of the dehydrated, blistering woman for water is becoming too much for everybody. Grimes decides this is a good time to bargain. He constructs a white flag and walks within yelling distance. Grimes describes the situation to Newman's character John Russell.. You have no water. You have no food. You're all gonna be screaming like that poor suffering soul tied to the rock.There's only one way down from the hill. Grimes and his scumbag henchmen will be waiting at the bottom of the hill with their rifles ready. They also have the delirious woman in their rifle sights just in case anybody gets any ideas about rescuing her. Boone makes a great case for Newman to turn over the money and everybody will go free. Boone ends up his presentation with "any questions".

Blue eyed half-breed Hombre Newman yells back, "Just one, how are you gonna get back down the mountain?" at which point he shoots the astonished Boone. I try to remember this moment whenever I start to get cocky.

By 1977, however, Boone was pretty much washed up. He headed for Japan to make one last movie. That movie turned out to be *The Last Dinosaur,* shot for television in the Japanese Alps.

Boone plays a gazillionaire named Mastin Thrust who has invented a rocket ship that fires INTO the earth, penetrating deeper than any previous penetration searching for oil.. Thrust will do that for your penetration.

We're gonna try to avoid the psychiatric analysis of this film which almost always leads to sexual implication while we pretend that some times a penetrative borer driven by thrust into mother earth is really just a penetrative borer driven by thrust into mother earth.

Eventually Boone chooses four crew mates and decides to ride the Polar Borer into the earth himself where it is rumored that a prehistoric jungle had been discovered on a previous "voyage". This film has become my number one guilty pleasure when it comes to golden turkeys that I am compelled to watch over and over again.

The female member of the crew is played by Joan Van Ark who later will go on to fame in the teevee series Knot's Landing and eventually will be cast as Imma Cumming in one of her bottom of the barrel roles. In *Last Dinosaur* she plays Frankie, a "modern" woman who is shocked, dismayed, and disgusted by Mastin's way over the top chauvinistic behavior until she finally begins to fall madly in love with him.

The movie opens with a bombastic theme song sung by Nancy Wilson called of course *"The Last Dinosaur."* The songs is a fantastic rip off of the Goldfinger song and tells the story of Mastin in the most hyperbolic and testosteronic of lyrics.

The other characters are: a guy named Chuck, A Masai warrior and tracker named Bunta and a Japanese scientist named Dr. Kawamoto. Thrust holds a press conference that must be seen to be believed where he introduces Bunta and Kawamoto. ("His name is Bunta") Right from the get go, these two characters Bunta and Kawamoto are obvious dinosaur food.

After the Polar Borer has penetrated the virginal core of Earth, sure enough the explorers come upon a land unknown full of pterodactyls, stegosaurus, cave people and needless to say a totally, fake T-rex who of course has to battle another dinosaur and rip that rubber thing apart with his jaws and claws producing kegs of syrupy fake blood. When the Trex finishes dismantling his prehistoric enemy, he comes across the Polar Borer and kicks the crap out of it leaving the survivors with no direction home. In addition, the Trex has gained an appetite for human meat after devouring Kawamoto.

This pisses off Thrust who pledges to kill the dinosaur, even though he is armed with only a primitive bow and arrow which is used to fight off cave people and attracts a Yoko Ono cave woman to Thrust. Thrust is repulsed by the woman who gets the name "Hazel". The atavistic survivors find shelter in a cave as weeks go by and Thrust continues to exhibit ultra masculinity, chauvinistic aggression and contemptuous disregard for the advances of both Frankie and Hazel.

Eventually, Thrust and Bunta construct a primitive catapult from which they will hurl a gigantic fake rock at the rubber dinosaur when Trex comes looking for another meal. In one of the greatest moments in shit movie history, the Trex comes stomping through the jungle, they launch the gigantic bogus boulder and it hits the fake dinosaur in his fake noggin which leaves a goofy dent.

The survivors ask Thrust..."did we get him?"

Thrust replies " I don't know."
(" I don't know" is one of the more infamous quotes from the film. Lynn, who rightly hates the film has to hear me say "I don't know" in Boone voice when she asks me a question that I really don't know or don't feel like answering or selected not to hear which of course irritates her.)

It turns out that the fake boulder didn't kill Trex so Trex eventually makes a meal of Bunta before lumbering off into the phony jungle.

Meanwhile Chuck and Frankie have found the Polar Borer, fixed it up and are prepared at last to pull out. Frankie brings the news to Mastin who says that he ain't goin anywhere. He's gonna kill that Trex.

Frankie says "How can you kill that. It's the last dinosaur to which Thrust replies "No, it isn't. I am.", as the music swells to indicate profound metaphorical irony.

With that the Boner er Borer departs, leaving Thrust alone on his final hunt accompanied only by the fake Yoko Ono who worships him.

The voice of Nancy Wilson returns. "He is the Last dinosaur."

Yes, I've given you many spoilers but it doesn't matter. You're gonna know exactly what's gonna happen by the time Thrust has his press conference at the onset of the film. It's not the story that counts although the story perfectly matches the tragically comedic execution of the story. Thrust is a long, long way from Brando, Newman and Paladin.

Somehow Van Ark's career rebounded and she became a teevee star.

The entire film is available on youtube.

I dare you to watch it.

But be careful, you just might have to watch it again and again and again and again as guilt turns once again into masochistic pleasure.

Night of Champions

One of the first lessons of Education 101 is this "Don't have favorites."

This is one of the first rules that I was determined to break.

I decided to make every one of my students a favorite.

Once I had gained enough seniority to begin offering electives, my rulebreaking went to another level. I had favorite favorites. I called them Champions. These were the students who I met in my regular classes who felt so favored that they decided to take all of my electives. Sometimes, as in the case of Creative Writing, they took an elective multiple times. One of my Champions was Mike Champion. Champion was his actual last name. Mike was in my class at least 7 times....4 for Creative Writing...2 for grade level Language arts and at least one Cinematic Lit.

Mike and I would write and talk about a wide variety of subjects yet we kept returning to the subject of professional wrestling. Joining us in this topic was another Champion, Scott Lemmer. Scott was about twice the size of Mike but was graceful and co-ordinated enough to play on the varsity hockey team. For all his size and speed, Scott's outstanding characteristic was his gentleness.

Upon their graduation both Scott and Mike joined the labor force. As a second or third job, they took up wrestling. Like all wrestlers, they paid their dues learning to sell, work the microphone and take bumps. Like almost all beginning wrestlers, they were being paid with pain for the love for their art.

We all considered wrestling as performance art. Even before Vince McMahon defined wrestling as sports entertainment, we were smartened up while still remaining marks. We endured the taunts of those close minded folks who insisted that "wrestling is fake."

Most wrestlers perform in tiny organizations at bars and high schools. Even though the risks are the same if not greater than in the big time, these wrestlers pursue their art before tens or hundreds of fans.

Mike was not only a wrestler but he was a manager and promoter. He was part of a promotion of upstate New York wrestlers known as Kayfabe.

A couple of dropkicks above bars and high schools in status level was the Henrietta Dome, a facility that was part of the local fairgrounds. I heard that there was going to be a wrestling show at the Dome. I contacted Mike. Mike was part of the promotion and through him, I got permission to photograph the show. This wouldn't be my first time as a ring side photographer. I had been a correspondent for Ring magazine, the boxing bible. I had also snapped lenses for Rocky Fratto when Rocky was a middleweight champ not to mention my freelance work at Ali-Frazier 2.

Naturally, I was grateful for the opportunity even more grateful when Mike told me that AJ Styles was gonna be on the card as well as "The Big Cat" Scott Lemmer. I asked Mike not to tell Scott that I was working the card.

The crowd in the Dome that night was small but large by Kayfabe standards. Big Cat, working as a heel, was in the second to the last match of the evening. By this time, the crowd had been worked into a fever pitch, cheering for the faces and cursing the heels.

Amidst the tumult and the shouting, the announcer said " From Rochester, New York at 325 pounds....The Big Cat."

Scott emerged fro the dressing room in black tights, bandana and a black teeshirt emblazoned with a screaming skull. God damned he was intimidating.

He was playing the heel that night and the crowd responded in kind...hating him with passion and poison prejudice which Scott returned in kind with stiffarms and bellows.

As he made his way to the ring, this gigantic marauder was surprised to see me. Amidst the bedlam, Scott gave me a secret look and softly whispered " Mr. Rivers. Wow. Thanks for showing up." For a split second we were back in the classroom where we had often imagined just such a moment.

I flashed back fifty years further when I had gone under the ring at the War Memorial and fetched the robe of Baron Gattoni. Once again, I was struck by the complexities of art and the thrill of performance.

I can't remember the outcome of Big Cat's match. I had a curfew of my own so I couldn't stick around for the post promotion party. I thanked Mike for his help in making this night of Champions possible.

Post Script

I just heard from Mike that he has opened up the Flower CityWrestling Academy at Marketplace Mall. The Academy will offer courses in Pro Wrestling Fundamentals, Character Development and conditioning.

According to Mike......

You know that 'where do you see yourself in 20 years' thing they make you do in high school? I feel like with this new school/ pro wrestling arena at

marketplace mall, a son named after Stone cold Steve Austin, and an alcohol
problem that I hit it right on the head

Many dreams imagined in high school come true. They weren't really dreams in the first place. They are visions of the future that are being constructed while we imagine and on a day in the future when our imagination has turned into imagicnaction, it presents itself to us as a realty successfully projected.

Oh and for you close readers, imagicnation is not a spelling error. It's a word I invented to describe the moment when action makes dreams come true.

etc.

No More Rootin' for Seymour

One of my students was taking a typing class. His assignment was to record and transcribe a story told by another person. He asked me if he could record one of my stories. I agreed and the next day, I told my class this story when we had some filler time. This is approximately how many of my "story" classes sounded.......

Me and the first wife, we bought ourselves a little piglet. We brought it back to our place. We put the piglet in a horse stall.

We went up to the house and left a little time for the pig to hang out and make hisself comfortable.

Ya know.

We went up to the house. Had dinner and whatever else what we was gonna do or have. When I came back to the horse stall in the barn, the piglet he was gone.

Where in hell is the little pig? The pig's gone. Where's the little sumbuck?

MISSING PIG

Now there was a golf course not far from where we lived. I had this fear that eventually the pig was gonna find a place to live over at the golf curse.

Some day, some millionaire would be out playing the match of his life with thousands of dollars riding on every single putt. Then out of nowhere would come this outlaw four hundred pound pig snortin' slabberin', runnin' and fartin' his way on to the green, grab the ball, ruin the round, scare the beejezuz out of everybody. Cause a coronary. Lose a bet

"Who owns that pig?' the millionaire screams to his lawyer who holds up my glossy.

"Sue his ass for everything." The millionaire sneers. His lawyer nods.

I had that catastrophic fear, oh yeah.

We looked all over the pasture for the pig. No find.

A few hours passed. I got a call from a woman from her farm up the road apiece.

"Did you lose a pig?" she asked.

"Yes Ma'am I did."

She says "Well we've had a pig in our garage for a couple of hours."

I said, "sounds like my pig. I'll come and get ham."

"Come and get ham huh, that's a good one." she said before hangin up.

I came up and grabbed the little pig; brought him back to my barn.

I couldn't understand the problem.

If you know anything about pigs, you know how he got out.

What do pigs do all the time? Huh? They dig. Right. They root. This little pig had been doin' that and had rooted a route for hisself right out   the horse stall and out of the barn, up the read apiece to the woman's garage.

The first wife and me, well we didn't want that to happen again so we called a farmer from across the road. We asked Farmer John "how do you prevent pigs from diggin?" Farmer John say "you got a put rings in they nose. The rings make they nose sensitive. They root with they nose. If they got the rings through they nose, they don't root no more."

So OK says the first wife and me. Let's put rings through the pigs nose. Sure how do we do dat, I asked Farmer John.

Call da vet. Tell him to come over. He'll put rings through the pig's nose no problem.

I called the vet. He busy but he gonna send a ringman to do the job.

The vet's ringman shows up in a wink.. Ringman say "go get the pig". I went and grabbed the pig. Holdin' the pig in my hands I say "whaddya want me to do right here and right now?"

Ringman say "You want rings through that pigs nose right? OK , just hold on to that pig."

So I'm holding on to the pig. I'm no farmer. I'm no Ringman. I ain't even down the road nor across the road. I don't know what I'm doin. I'm just a guy in my long driveway who thinks he knows what he wants and he's holdin' on to a piglet who has a pretty good idea what he don't want.

Ringman comes up. He's got like this pliers with a brass ring on one tip. I'm holdin' on to the pig. Ringman walks up, confident as all hell and goes WONK and smacks that plier thing right in the pigs snout. The pig starts goin WHOOO WHOOO WHOOOO. The pig be squealing, struggling squirming, spinnin' me and itself around and WHOOO WHOOOING.

Like passing the brass ring dispenser on the Seabreeze merry go round, the ring man being the dispenser, the dispenser grabbing for me stead of me grabbin' fo it. Every time I'd finish a spin, the Ringman would go CRONK and hit the snout with another ring.

WHOOO   spinaroundCRONKWHOOOspinaroundCRONKWHOOOOspin aroundCRONK WHOO spin around.

The Ringman is cronking. Me and the pig are spinning. The pig is WHOOOOing. I can barely hold on to the little varmint. So we CRONK and WHOOO and spin around eight or nine times. Then the ringman says "All done."

The piglet had nine shiny rings in his now tenderized snortin' snout. Me and the Ringman walked to the barn where I placed the pig back into the horse stall. I asked the Ringman what brand the rings was. "Day's Seymours....Day da best."

So if y'all evah need to stop a pig from rootin'....Get Seymour nose rings. THEY ARE THE BEST. They worked for me and my pig way back int the Spring of 77. Those rings went the distance.

Later that night, we named the piglet Seymour after the rings in his nose. We built him his own pen and he grew to be a two hundred pounder and quite a good drinkin buddy before we put a bag over his head one day, painted our name on his side and left him alone one afternoon next another big pig who had another name painted on his side both of them prolly thinking that this can't be good.

Seymour is a star of *Full Filler* if ya need to ketchup.

Punk Bucket

It was the season of the deactivated, the disconnected, the disinterested, the discouraged, the dissociative and the disagreeable. It was summer school in the seventies. The halls were empty. and everybody present was dealing with failure.

I loved teaching summer school. These were my peeps. I too had been a discouraged and disconnected student. One of the main reasons I went into teaching in the first place (after my typical flirtation with rock drumming) was my resentment for the teachers who failed to even attempt to connect with me. I loved catching kids doing something right and the connection that usually followed. By the seventies I had established a reputation of "being good with those kind of kids"

I was a full time teacher which meant during the summer I taught, I didn't paint houses.

That summer both Goth and Punk were making their way into the suburbs on their way to mainstream but nowhere near arriving. Styles beginning to strive with the pissed off and alienated while broadcasting that neighborhood to the more stable. Heresy was on the way to orthodoxy. Outrage was headed towards fashion.

In my class was an intimidating straight edge punk with Doc Marten boots leather jacket over flannel shirt and multiple piercings. His name was Josh. He played bass on a shitty amp which he hoped some day would become a Marshall. Josh was a mixed metaphor of attitudes. I came to understand that the day before summer school started he had gone "oi" and traded in his Mohawk for a skin head. Skinheads had yet to break into political affiliation. The movement was still apolitical, still about the music and the attitude.

During the regular school year, Josh went to class once in awhile if he had nothing better to do. He never did any homework of any kind. He didn't want to know anything about anything. He believed it when Alice Cooper said

" Don't ask me about politics. I'm a moron. That's why I'm a rock star." If it was good enough for Alice it was good enough for Josh.

Josh was big kid....6 foot three and 250 pounds. He had a beard when he was 15 but lost it recently during the same style shifting urge with which he sheared his Mohawk. With all of his regalia and bulk, Josh looked like a goon.

At the time I was running our in-school radio station WBER so I knew most of the punks in the building. The kids who dug Dead Kennedys, Violent Femmes, Betty Boo, Johnny Rotten, I Hate Myself, Livin in a Box, Buzzcocks, X, Lydia Lunch, Romeo Void, Sisters of Mercy, Roscoe Flamefart, Captain Beefheart and of course the Ramones, Metallica, the Clash and the Pistols. In other words, the only music that mattered played on WBER, the only station that mattered.

I was in the studio one day when one of my deejays played a cover of Paul Simon's *At The Zoo* by a   local band named Globdammitt that I had never heard before or after. They played the song at triple speed. After it ended I asked Glen, the deejay, what he thought of the song. Glen said "it was great" and he knew a couple of guys in Glob. I said,"it sounded too fast ". Glen said if it sounded too fast than I was "too old."

Hmmm.

A few minutes later I asked Glenn if he knew Josh.

Glenn said he did. He told me that Josh was very good on the bass but he was shy. He was afraid to perform live. He always claimed he had a shitty amp.

I took all of this into consideration as I dealt with Josh.

I thought we'd start with flexible then move towards supportive. This was my chronology of connection before we moved on to step by step and finally to challenging.

One day in the classroom I was trying to explain point of view and using my trash can as an available metaphor. That particular trash can had been one of the constants in my life. Every time I got a new room assignment, I took that trash can with me.

I tried to explain how a trash can might be viewed differently by a romanticist than by a realist. One of my college professors had used this technique and it resonated with me when he said the realist would want to write a description including function, size, volume, circumference and color while the romanticist might want to write a rags to riches/Cinderella/ detective story.

It was pretty good place to start so I did my best. After I had finished, I asked the class if anybody else could come up with a metaphor regarding the trash can. We brainstormed awhile. Josh raised his hand. I was glad to see Josh involved as he had become increasingly less isolated once he began to realize that I might be on his side and wasn't going to bury him for not doing his homework. Our task that summer was to pass the Regents exam that they had all failed. The grade would be based on the test not on the homework in preparation for the test.

I said "Yeah Josh, whaddaya got"

Other kids had come up to the board and written down their idea so nobody was surprised when Josh got up from his seat in the back and slowly walked to of the front of the classroom. There was always a lot of motion in my classroom to help the hyperactive kids who couldn't sit down. I handed Josh the chalk. He waved me off.

He went to my waste basket and kicked it against the wall.
Then he looked at me as I tried to get his meaning.
He said "Punk!"

Of course we were all stunned. It was one of those moments in a classroom where a whole bunch of gears are starting to click together. It's at moments like this that students look to teachers for interpretation.

Josh put the bucket back in its place and returned to his place while the room was still buzzing. I knew I had to do something with the moment. Josh got back in his seat. The moment had arrived. What could I teach? I walked over to the bucket, kicked it against the wall...paused for a moment and then asked "punk?" Josh hit that question out of the park with his answer which I will never forget and which has guided me through many a matter of taste and question of authenticity

Josh said, "Rip off".
I got it. Everybody got it.
Josh was the teacher.

When we teach we learn. When we learn we connect. When we connect we remember. I kept that garbage can with me throughout my career. To this day, I remember Josh.

Everybody passed the Regents.
Everybody except Josh.
He didn't show up for the test.
He really didn't care.

I hope he got his amp.

Wakening From A Steve King Nightmare

I have been institutionalized and remain institutionalized.

I have awakened from Stephen King's nightmare after reading 41 of his books. His nightmare was to be institutionalized somewhere and within the institution writing his stories that no one would read except inmates within the institution.

38 years of schedules and guards has an effect on a man even when he becomes "free".

It all began with *Carrie*. Sometimes books are donated to the institution. Donated books have the covers ripped off probably to prevent inmates from ripping off the books by swiping them and selling them as brand new. The books donated are damaged goods delivered to damaged goods. Rip offs delivered to rip off artists. Nobody had heard of King forty years so I wasn't expecting much from the novel. Instead I was amazed at all levels. Levels being coherence, rigor, authenticity, validity and engagement. I figured the writer whoever that he/she was would never be heard from again, what with the fake name and all. Steven King yeah right.....why not Johnny Crown or Lynn Sweet or Haylen DeBryan. Too bad, this was some good shit.

So I was astonished a few months later when *Salem's Lot* showed up in the institution. I'm not a big vampire guy as I'm surrounded by them but once again I couldn't put the book down. Best vampire story evah. Who the hell is this King guy?

Next came *The Stand* and this one was even better than the first two as it included a wider range of characters, a deathly plague, an unnerving evacuation, a charming villain who might be the devil, a series of massive journeys and a final show down between good and evil.

I thought I was the only person in America who was reading this guy. I raved about him within the walls but nobody ever heard of him. I told the inmates to read the books but no-one ever did. Rarely, does anyone in or out of the institution pay much attention to raving.

Next was the effort that I consider and still consider the culmination of them all, *The Shining*. Jack Torrance is suffering from alcoholism and suffocating writer's block. He believes that isolation will help him to confront his demons so he institutionalizes himself and goes crazy. Believe me, institutionalized isolation will do that to a man. What people tend to forget is the unhappy consequence of demon confrontation.

Shortly after I read "The Shining" a counselor named Haylen approached me and noticed that I had the book in my cell. She asked me if I enjoyed the book. I began to rave about the book, about isolation, about institutionalization. She told me to "shut up and listen for a goddamned minute."

It turns out that she had been listening to my raving all along and had read all four of the books. She agreed with me on their quality. She couldn't wait for the next one to come out and when it did, she would purchase it and get it to me.

It came out. She purchased it. She gave it to me. I read it and gave it back.

This happened again and again and again and again and again. *Firestarter*, *Cujo*, *Dead Zone*, *Christine*, *Pet Semetary* and on and on and on and on

Meanwhile I continued to write my own stuff. Haylen started to read it. She thought it was good, too bad that no one would ever read it outside the institution.

Demystifying the Exorcist (urban legend)

Our youngest daughter Mary lives in Boston. Way up North and not too far from Salem and the ghosts of witches past. I miss her every day but most of all on holidays or whatever Halloween is. I texted her this afternoon. I told her that I was missing her and I was having writer's block.

She suggested that I write something about Halloween.

I told her that was the problem. I had been assigning myself the task of writing something about Halloween. When I assign myself a task, it seems like work and my natural streak of lazy kicks in and blocks me.

She replied "that's the story of my life".

I said that I needed a spark.

She suggested that I write about a scary movie or an experience from the old days of Halloween. "Why don't you write about the guy who came to the Halloween Party bound and gagged and tied to a chair. I love that story." I love that story too but it's long and I've told it so many times that telling it again plus typing it feels too much like work.
Mary knows many of my stories so I started fishing for one that she didn't know.
I asked her if she knew how two of my friends were irresponsibly responsible for an urban myth surrounding *The Exorcist*. She said she didn't know that one but it sounded hilarious so I began to text it to her.

Two of my friends, Jim and Keith had somehow managed to get involved in a double blind date. Jim was the kind of guy who customarily wore a tee shirt that said, "I have an idea". Jim had some bad ideas particularly one he painfully realized earlier in the week. He had flunked out of community college but decided before he left to drop some acid and try out for the wrestling team. Let's just say that didn't work out well. Jim had never wrestled in his life but on that day, it seemed like a good idea.

Keith liked to wear a tee shirt that said, "hold my beer and watch this..." As you might imagine, many people had watched Keith do many things...many of them insanely funny with an edge of alarming.

I guess it was Jim's sister who got the bad idea of fixing up a couple of her friends with Jim and Keith. The plan was to go see the opening of *The Exorcist*. The guys were not real good with "dates" but pressured by Jim's sister, they managed to put on shirts and pants and sweaters and shoes and to their amazement, they cleaned up pretty good.
They climbed into Keith's piece of shit car which he had cleared out of beer cans, joints and sprayed with Right Guard. Before picking up the girls, Jim had an idea.....let's go get smashed...which they did in order to calm down and not be "uptight".

They picked up the girls... Betsy and Deb... and the fearsome foursome made their way to the theater. According to plan, they arrived for the very first local showing of the film. There was a line to get in and the double blind daters were near the front of it.
Mission accomplished. They became part of the first *Exorcist* audience in Rochester.
After an awkward attempt at small talk, tensions were relieved when the movie started. After an hour, and under the guise of going for popcorn, Keith had to make a deposit of the beer that he had rented prior to the show.

After relieving himself, Keith headed towards the popcorn stand but halfway there he spotted a couch. and figured rest might help the situation. He reclined on the couch and promptly passed out for the next hour.

Meanwhile his date Deb, who didn't give two shits about Keith in the first place was into the movie and barely noticed that he was gone. Jim had another idea. He decided to attempt to "make out" with Betsy who had another idea that did not include making out with a total, drunken stranger while watching *The Exorcist*. She opted to watch the movie and made that option clear to Jim who with nothing better to do began to watch the movie himself.

Nobody cared that Keith was gone.

Keith remained in the lobby for the entire duration of the movie. The line outside the box office noticed him on the couch. The word began to spread that *The Exorcist* was causing people to faint from the intensity of the movie and Keith was "proof". When the movie ended and the new crowd came in, everybody took a cautionary look at Keith on the couch and prayed that they would not end up like him, petrified to unconsciousness because of film fright.

Meanwhile, the threesome in the movie figured that Keith had bailed out on the blind date and that's why he didn't come back when they finally noticed that something was missing while they headed to the lobby.

As they walked through the lobby, they saw Keith on the couch. Jim, who was not unfamiliar with Keithian situations like this, went over and woke Keith up with an ungentle tap on the forehead.

They got into the piece of shit car and drove the relieved girls home. The guys, relieved in their own twisted way, decided to go out drinking.

The next day, the local critic wrote about the guy he saw in the lobby who had passed out from fright. The legend began. People were passing out from seeing the Exorcist.

The next day after reading the review, I went to see the film. While waiting in line everybody was talking and hoping they wouldn't pass out. One of the people in my group was a kid under eighteen. The ticket taker, now fearful of people passing out, informed us that we couldn't get in because the kid couldn't prove that he was eighteen. A minor pissing contest began as I claimed to be the kid's guardian and he had a ticket and he needed to be admitted.

Finally, the manager came and explained how people had been passing out from the film and he would let the kid in if I was willing to take responsibility if the kid fainted. I said that I would take that responsibility.On our way in, the ticket taker snarled at me " I hope both you AND the kid pass out and when you do...don't expect any help from me.

Throughout the texting Mary kept responding OMG and LOL.

At the finish she said "you did it."

And by God, I had thanks to a spark from Mary on Halloween.

Ava's Shower

When we moved to Tumbleweed, we had to enroll Mary in a brand new school. She was in third grade and had a broken leg. She arrived in time for school pictures. When the class pictures came out, I noticed this little girl with big glasses. Her name was Ava. I pointed her out to Mary and said "She looks like she'd be a good friend." Sure enough, they became besties and remain so to this day almost 30 years later.

This is the story of Ava's shower

I know this wasn't a dream because when I dream I always try to get the picture but the camera never works.

It was my first bridal shower. My gender had always rendered me ineligible but this shower was co-ed. We were enjoying our drinks and conversation downstairs when I noticed that the main female stars were missing.
Ava was trying on her wedding gown upstairs. I'm not sure who invited me but somehow through the grapevine I came too know that I would be welcome in this room and so would my camera.

This happens often in my dreams but in my dreams, the camera she don't work.

I walked up the stairs and entered the room. I was the only male but everyone seemed to welcome me. Everyone was admiring Ava in her dress. Ava was radiating joy and reflecting the admiring glances that were coming her way. The dress was perfect. Everybody knew it.

I've been taking Ava's picture ever since she was a little girl. She is the best friend of my youngest daughter. I wanted to get a great picture of Ava at this moment. All of my years of photography had led to this moment. It wasn't gonna come again.

Ava noticed me. She looked into the camera. I snapped. The camera worked.

This was no dream.
Mine wasn't the only camera in the room. Ava seemingly picked up on all of the lenses by not concentrating on any of them but rather enjoying her moment of celebration.

A model of decorum.

I got my pictures. Everybody got their pictures. The cameras disappeared. I lingered with my lens.

At that moment, at that second, in about the time it takes a car to swerve a deadly swerve, Ava's expression changed. For an instant memory, vulnerability and pain flashed through her entire being in a collision of joy and pain.

I imagine she was thinking of the older sister who was not in the room. The older sister who ended up on the deadly end of an unsignaled swerve on a dark Halloween night almost 10 years ago. A tragedy that changed everyone.

Suddenly Abby was in the room.

I didn't see Abby but I did see Ava seeing Abby as did my camera.

For one split second grief and recognition flashed across Ava's glowing face. In that split second I had to make the decision whether or not to snap the picture and "capture" this exceedingly private, candid, personal and vulnerable moment.

I was almost certain that the camera was going to malfunction revealing the entire scene as one more dream forever undocumented.

I snapped.

The camera worked.

Ava's expression returned to joy.

A few weeks later, I told Ava about the picture. I told her this story. I told her I wanted to write about it but couldn't do that unless she approved.

She said it would be an honor.

The wedding is this weekend.

This writing and this image is in honor of Ava

and of Abby.

Class of 1917 reunion

1967 was a very good year for Sinatra. I was a junior in college and at the top of my undergrad game. I was still young enough to rock and roll. I was a drummer in a band that had gone from garbage to garage to bar to cover to dance. Everybody on campus knew me. I had a beautiful, blonde girlfriend. We were in love... "Oh How Happy" she had made me.

Viet Nam and LBJ were concerns but the shit storm that was 1968 was still obscured by clouds over the horizon. I attended summer school, mostly to play in the band. The beginning of the summer sessions were fun because that's when reunions happened.. I remember one reunion in particular; a 50 year reunion. I couldn't believe what a bunch of old, out of it fogies were in attendance. Right then and there, I hoped I'd die before I got old.

They had no idea how to party so aside from freaking out, I avoided involvement with them. I never bothered to subtract the 50 years so I didn't realize that these were folks who graduated in 19freakin17. When these folks were my age, they were raggin' out to "Darktown Strutter's Ball", "Tiger Rag" and the most popular recording artists of the year The American Quartet who had made the charts consistently with numbers like "Oh Johnny, Oh Johnny, Oh"...."Goodbye Broadway Hello France"...."Sailin' Away on the Henry Clay" and the number one song of the year.... "Over There".

If they were 21 when they graduated, that meant that these old farts were born in the nineteenth century...right at the turn of the century when, according to BeeGee rumor everything was happening. I failed to realize that these folks had lived through the first selective service draft and had lost friends and relatives in WWI. I further failed to understand that in the year they graduated life expectancy around the world was 52 years and in 1918 because of war and the unimaginable devastation of flu it removed 13 years from that expectancy. Obviously, everybody at he reunion had survived.. They had lived through, among other things, Spanish flu, Prohibition, Depression, Two World Wars, the Korean War and were now living through the Viet Nam "conflict" They didn't show a lot of empathy towards the long hairs and filthy hippies who were as usual trying to do the impossible and "shocked" when the impossible failed to be realized. All we were sayin' was "give peace a chance" like a bunch of pansies.

Unlike the oldies, most of us had no real concept of war but we knew it wasn't righteous, brother. To me, the 50 year reunion folks seemed to be more about remembering the dead than celebrating life.

I attended a keg party. The highlight of the party was a piano player who hammered out the traditional, fraternity drinking songs like *Show Me the Way to Go Home*, The *Sheik of Araby*, *Give My Regards to Broadway* , *Rock a Bye Your Baby With a Dixie Melody*.etc. To me these songs were the height of camp....it's taken me all these years to realize that to the fifty year old fogies, these were the anthems of their lives. I might have connected but chose to dis, aloof as I was. I didn't want to imagine my fiftieth reunion. First of all, as a rock and roller, I didn't want to live that long and as a fool, I never wanted to be uncool.

A few months later, 1968 arrived. I sold my drums. I started my career. I got blindsided and blue shaded by a "buddy" who stole my girl by pretending that he was dying. I earned the blues the hard way, I suffered for them. I was starting to grow up. The draft was devouring boys/men of my age. We learned about war. I didn't want to die for something I didn't believe or understand. Most of my cool disappeared replaced by anxiety, beer, cynicism, incapability and the ferocious shadow of going over there.

I attended my 50th reunion last year. We were still rockin'. I got a chance to play the drums for the first time in forty years. I chose *Gloria* for my number. Before I got my chance on the skins, the dance floor was pretty quiet even though Mike Woods and his band Easy Money were killing it. Then, while Easy Money was playing *Memphis* some of my brothers and buddies showed up. Linda Miller and I started air guitaring in the aisle and singing all about "long distance information" as if we were twenty again. The music stopped for a second and I spotted Wild Bill coming in the door. The dance floor was still pretty empty.

I said, "c'mon Bill" and we went down to the floor and started our crazy dancing. Before long, the floor was full and we old farts were dancing furiously and foolishly. I noticed two young girls, maybe even students, gather around Bill trying to imitate his moves as he nodded and grinned, feeling every note and beat. Beautiful. Nobody feels music like Wild Bill.

Soon I got my chance on the drums.Mike said, "we'll set the rhythm" which means the drums come in after the opening guitar riffs. I had forgotten a couple of things about high hat use but eventually got into the groove.

G L O R I A. It was the first time and probably the last time that Lynn watched me play the drums. She liked it. She was dancing with Wild Bill both of them responding to my beat.

When we finished the song, I thanked Mike for convincing his drummer to let me sit in. It was the Friday of the weekend celebration. I realized that the weekend had peaked plus we were homeless, Lynn and I. We had closed on our Rochester home that morning and we were on our way to close on our new home in Carolina. My only regret was not having Wild Bill on stage with me. Bill sings the best Gloria this side of Van. I closed the book on Geneseo and went out kickin' ass. That night we headed South and I felt like a rock and roll star. Redeemed. No More Shades of Blue.

Shades of Blue

I thought every kiss was precious
I used to count them
Until I lost count
at over a thousand times
each of them meaningful
if meaning is love
and love is making happy
and oh how happy
you had made me
all of this before
we made love
which reduced the meaning
of remaining kisses
until they became meaningless
and we became he and she
and you and him became them
and kisses became strategy.

Bonds of Steel

Fraternities are getting a bad name in the twenty-first century and deserve some of it. We are outraged when we hear about hazing stupidities and we should be. The collegiate atmosphere was very different in the 1960's when Greek organizations were at the center of collegiate life. I joined Delta Kappa Tau at this time. We had a fraternity house that resembled the Delta House in Animal House. We drank a lot of beer, played a lot of music sang a lot of songs. We had a good

time in spite of Hell Nights and paddles and assuming positions. We stayed in bounds and were proud to wear the maroon and white.

I've had second and third thoughts about all of this. Sometimes, I've wondered why I joined at all. I've taken up this question with various brothers over the years. Phil Thrall is one of the most legendary of all DKs. Last summer, I asked the question of Phil. Why did he join? Phil gave me the answer that I've been searching for. Phil said that he joined for the possibility of making life long friends.

That's a good answer and a true answer.

Sixty years distant from Geneseo, I still have tremendous relationships with my fraternity brothers. We turned out alright; more than alright. We produced dozens of teachers who influenced thousands of lives. We became doctors, lawyers,   builders, sportscasters, scholars, soldiers, officers, coaches, musicians, therapists, artists, authors, administrators, businessmen, photographers, engineers, fathers, husbands, and grandfathers. Through all of those changes, we remain close.

Our fraternity song is entitled Our Bonds of Steel. Those bonds still exist.

This summer, Delta Kappa Tau will celebrate its 150th year of existence at the 2022 Homecoming. Fraternally, our Delta Kappa always leads the way.

Contact Snap

In the game of baseball, bat speed equals power. The most powerful hitters are in the Major Leagues and throughout history, the New York Yankees have always had some of the mightiest bashers from Babe Ruth to Lou Gehrig to Mickey Mantle to Roger Maris to Reggie Jackson to the current day sluggers Giancarlo Stanton and Aaron Judge.

The game has changed over the last decade as major league pitchers routinely throw the ball at a speed of 95 MPH. From the time that the ball leaves the pitchers hand until the player starts his swing is about the same time that it took you to read the above line that began with player.

Power requires quickness and decision making as well as bat speed.

Most of all power requires contact and contact depends upon where on the bat and where on the ball the collision occurred. If contact occurs too far down the bat handle maximum power can not be attained. If contact occurs on the top of the ball even if contact is made with the sweet spot of the bat, the result is likely to be a ground ball.

Furthermore, there is the amount of spin or spit on the ball and the launch angle of the swing to consider.

And whether the wind is blowing in or blowing out.

One of my goals as a baseball fan, photographer and writer has always been to capture the moment of contact when a slugger, preferably a Yankee makes perfect contact at top bat speed on a fastball coming in at ninety five plus miles per hour for homerun that I could write about.

Ten years ago, I captured such a moment.

The batter was Mark Teixera. Tex was the starting first baseman on the last Yankee team to win a World Series. Tex played 14 years in the majors. He won't make the Hall of Fame but he was a star in his day before hurting his back and leaving the game.

My seat was in left field. I had a real good angle on left handed batters. Obviously, you can't snap a picture of every swing of every batter. You've got to have a feeling. I had that feeling. I said to Deke " I think he's gonna hit one."

The count was three balls and one strike. A three and one count is an advantage for the batter .The pitcher had to come in with a good pitch or walk the batter. Mark guessed fastball. I guessed that Mark would guess fastball and uncork. The pitcher felt that he could throw his fastball past Mark. Power against power. Pitch placement against power. He went into his windup.

The ball left his hand. I had a feeling. Mark had a feeling. Maybe the pitcher had a feeling. I could see Mark begin his swing. I clicked. Mark connected. The batboy must have been thinking along the same lines that Mark and I were thinking because he's got a grin on his face. A few seconds later the ball landed in the right field seats....the same place where Babe hit 'em.

I was pretty sure that I caught the moment as I stood up and cheered. I high-fived my brother and said "Deke, I think I got that one." I looked at the image and dayum, there it was. I showed Deke and he said "You got it."

Every day in the major leagues somebody hits a homerun. Somebody gets all the guesswork right. I'm not a major leaguer. I'm a minor leaguer and a fan but at that instant,

I got it.

I treasure a moment that I will never forget....a moment of contact and connection. Tex connected with the pitch. I connected with Tex connecting with the pitch and my trusty camera had the speed to capture everything.

Home Run Baby!

Bone Dry or Boundary

I was playing the ninth hole at the Canandaigua Veteran's Hospital golf course, when my brother Deke approached. I got a bad feeling as Deke got closer and closer. When Deke got to the green, he told me that our great friend John McCormick had been killed in a car crash the night before.

We always kinda knew that something like this might happen because John always lived on the edge. He loved taking risks in whatever he was doing. John regularly terrified his wife Nancy on trips to Roseland where he and Bruce would change planes in mid-air while they twirled at high speed. The risk was not only mortal but also immortal. If either of their timing was slightly off, they would soar off to their death and land, broken, probably somewhere near the Skyliner or one the miniature golf course near a windmill. It would make headlines that would go something like this "two morons kill themselves trying to change planes at Roseland." Tales of stupidity based bravado would last forever.

They did this stunt three summers in a row. Each time, they were kicked out of the Park for life.

I witnessed the third switch. I was standing next to Nancy when Bruce and John boarded the planes. Before boarding both John and Bruce promised Nancy that they wouldn't attempt the switch. I think the promise was sincere but it changed when the two of em got into the air. They did it again. Not only was Nancy furious when they landed and when we were all kicked out but also she was pregnant. She informed John of that fact on the spot. John said he would never do anything as stupid as the switch again. He was gonna be a Dad and he wanted to be a good one.

John calmed down quite a bit after that. He remained a stalwart at the Bagman Ball. He loved him some beer and some Waylon Jennings. John was a guy you could count on when things got tricky. He'd always lend a hand or cover a back. John was known as a guy who could do anything. He could weld for God sake. More than anything else, John loved his son Matt.

So as Deke and I came to grips with the news of his death we were more saddened than stunned. What else could we do but shrug our shoulders and turn our palms to the sky. John had been Deke's great friend first. Deke introduced John to both me and Bruce. Deke was the hub of this wheel.

Funny thing is John had been sober the night he died. He had cut down on his drinking nearly to the point of zero. He was riding shotgun when his brother in law skidded into a telephone pole. The pole put an end to John.

What had God wrought?

Five years later, I was down at the lake visiting Deke. Deke told me to "get in the car we're going for a ride." He stopped at the corner store and picked up a 40 ounce Budweiser. The purchase surprised me because Deke rarely drank beer.

"Where we headed, Deke?"

"You'll see. I do this every year. It's amazing."

Deke has seen a lot of amazing things in his time so he isn't easily amazed. He's one of the few people I know who saw Ruby shoot Oswald.

After a twenty minute drive through the countryside. Deke pulled into a graveyard.

"Follow me"

I followed until we reached John's grave.

"There he is. Now watch this."

He took a deep swig from the bottle and handed it to me. I followed suit.

Deke poured the remainder of Budweiser on the dry dirt over John's grave. A few seconds later the dirt was Sahara dry again, the beer completely absorbed.

"That happens every time. I figure John's a little thirsty."

We walked back through the graveyard into the car. We drove back to the lake trading legendary stories about John. How much we missed him. How much we loved him.

We played some Waylon Jennings on the ride home.

Cricket?

I've never played cricket nor have I ever seen a game of cricket played but I'm very familiar with the phrase "that's not cricket" which figuratively describes a form of behavior that flaunts the accepted rules of conduct to the advantage of the flaunter.

Literally, "not cricket" refers to everything else on earth that isn't a cricket, even members of Buddy Holly's band who, let's face it were human.

Let me tell you a few things that are cricket.

Crickets are nocturnal creatures who chirp at night. They are dark in color, they have long antennae and four limbs. Only male crickets chirp. They make their chirp by rubbing forewings together. They use the sound of their forewings rubbing together as a courting song when a female cricket is near. The foreplay chirp has frequent pulses and romantic intervals between. The process of creating this song is called stridulation.

Before stridulating a courting song, males issue an aggressive chirp with less pulsation and shorter intervals between pulses. Imagine the aggressive song as a shout out for other males in the area that translates something like this: "hey dudes, I'm in this area and so is a beautiful female. I'm getting ready to make a move on her so stay the hell away from here."

If there is no response, the cricket goes into his courting song.

Imagine the female cricket during all of this hullaballoo. She's minding her own business when she hears the "shout out", she looks around and doesn't see any other females around so she goes "oh, oh" and a few minutes later she hears the courting song that her mother has been warning her against while simultaneously preparing her to accept. She reads between the chirps and prettys up for the seemingly inevitable.

Ah, sweet mysteries of life......etc

A few minutes later, the male chirps his celebratory song...thanking the female for her time and urging her to produce the eggs from their union.

Yeah, that's cricket.

Now let me tell ya something else that's not cricket.

Jiminy Cricket.

What the hell is Jiminy Cricket?

First of all he's green.

True some crickets are green but most of them are brown or black.

They all have long antennae. Not Jiminy.

They walk on four legs. Not Jiminy.

At first glance, Jiminy look more like a grasshopper than a cricket but a closer look reveals that Jiminy doesn't resemble anything on earth so ya might as well call him a cricket, why not. He's definitely not a fish nor a turtle nor snake nor aardvark.

Besides the obvious fact that Jiminy Cricket is a fictional, animated character drawn by a Disney artist for Pinnochio , nothing is Cricket about Jiminy from his hat to his gloves

There is one thing in his favor.

Jiminy sings

And he sings at night when Crickets sing.

He sings to the stars.

He wishes upon those stars that his dream will come true.

What is Jiminy's Wish upon those stars?

Jiminy wants to become a real cricket.

In the meantime, Jiminy is like all the rest of us....literally not cricket.

Big Surprise

Trauma is always a surprise. Nobody gets up in the morning dressed for the ambulance or the emergency room. Personally and culturally there have been so many traumatic surprises in my lifetime that they become too frequent to enumerate. In my writing, I tend to avoid the big surprises in my life, the moments of catastrophic non-linearity that have caused me to invent and re-invent myself. Too personal, too painful to relate.

I wish I had a "safe place" in my memory where I could put these painful memories and having placed them there, lose them forever in plain sight until their meaning reveals itself to me in a way that I am more equipped to understand.

I'm "happy" today. All's well that ends well.

I have learned that what we think never should have happened should have happened, we just didn't think that it would. We didn't want it to happen. We didn't expect it.

Let's take one cultural shock for example.

Watching football one Monday night, I heard Howard Cosell announce that John Lennon had been murdered in front of his Dakota apartment in New York City.

Remember that one?
Remember how long it took to believe that it really happened?
We didn't want it to happen.
It shouldn't have happened. Why did John pause to give Chapman his autograph?
It didn't make sense then.
We were surprised.
The reason he paused is because he had to pause and the reason Chapman was there in   the first place was because he had to be there.
Nobody knew why or what for except maybe Chapman.

John didn't know.

JD Salinger didn't know that Chapman would be carrying *Catcher in the Rye* and that his book would enable John's murder.

Howard Cosell didn't know.

We were all still enjoying *Double Fantasy*.

John was back and then he wasn't.

What a surprise. How unexpected.

It couldn't happen but it did.

We would get over it.

We got over it sorta.

Yet every day, cars pause in front of the Dakota hotel and somebody points to it and tells an out of towner...."There, right there is where John got shot."

I know. I've been in one of those cars. Wild Bill was my driver. He did the pointing. In the rearview mirror I saw another driver starting to point and behind him I'm sure there was another and right now today someone is pointing and shaking their head about an event that nobody expected, nobody wanted and nobody could believe except for Chapman. Strawberry Fields had to come to Central Park to serve as a reminder.

Live life while you may.

There's always somebody who believes the unbelievable and has the whole thing figured out.

A supernatural executive prepared to execute the eternal idea.

When my time comes, it won't be me doing the execution.

It'll be a big surprise.

Radar Readar Reader

Take out your radar guns and stop watches. We're about to discuss baseball, speed and reading.

If you wanna be a major league batter, you need to be able to hit a 92 MPH fastball. If you can't hit that, a fastball is all you'll see. No need to throw you a curve or a slider. They'll just blow the fastball by you, make ya feel like a fool.

If you wanna be a major league reader, you got to read at least 350 words a minute. If you're slower than that, your mind, which is traveling at about 1000 words per minute, will get bored and start looking for distraction which will lead to a loss of comprehension which will lead to re-reading which will slow your reading down even further which will lead to 'studying' which for most of us means reading the same few paragraphs over and over again until we fall asleep, decide to grab a beer or turn on the teevee and pray that the teacher asks a question that can be answered by the paragraphs that we've read over and over again even as we gave up on the majority of the reading. If we're reading at a speed less than that in a classroom, we're liable to start throwing paper wads at the nearest student who is also looking for a distraction and is relieved by it.

We slow down our reading when we subvocalize. Subvocalization means we are saying the words aloud to our selves in our mind which automatically takes us back to the earliest days of our reading when we were learning how to read by syllable which means we were decoding. It's easy to spot a subvocalizer because they move their lips when they read. Moving your lips is a tell.

Stop that inner voice. It's slowing down the speed of your swing. Bat speed equals power so if you're lucky enough to get around on a fastball, you won't hit it far which means that you can't hit the fastball which means you're not in the major leagues.

Let's face it, so much of what we used to call schooling is based on reading. If you are a slow reader, you've been punished for that lack of speed through most of your academic career and probably don't read much anymore as a consequence. We sorta give up on reading instruction somewhere around the third grade as by that time, we have already figured out who is "smart" and who isn't.

Next we move on to comprehension. By the time we get to high school, English class is all about comprehension which is a problem for those who didn't do the reading in the first place because they fell asleep or were bored or were distracting or distracted When teaching is done skillfully, teachers test what they teach and teach what they test. The tests are mostly about comprehension as we have stopped teaching reading at about fifth grade. For many pupils, reading speed has kicked in at around eleven years of age and stays that way until an effort is consciously made to increase that speed.

According to rumor JFK could read at a thousand words a minute. JFK was known for his speed. According to Angie Dickinson, having sex with JFK was the best 20 seconds of her life.

Not to be outdone, Donald Tump can read at 2000 words a minute. After reading the Tolkien trilogy in record time, Trump said "It's about wizards and shit."

Kennedy was even faster at writing. His best seller Profiles in Courage was written in no time at all. Same with Trump's Art of the Deal.

Many decoders (both North and South) are baffled by multisyllabic vocabulary words because of an inability to read in context. Good readers don't need a dictionary to look up the words because they can grasp their meaning due to the context of what they're reading. Take the word "lugubrious' for

example. Victor Hugo uses that word a record 46 times in Les Miserables in describing sad or mournful situations. If you read in context, you already know the meaning of the word. If you've read this far, you probably knew the meaning at the start.

I could go on but I'm running out of my allotted writing time so let me 'splain. I've emboldened every hundredth word (approximately) I'll give you a word count at the end so you can use your readar guns to determine your reading speed. If you got to the *probably* in the first minute, you're at around 300 wpm. If you got to *situations*, you're about 600 words a **minute.**

Now just for shitz and giggles read from the beginning of this piece down to here in 30 seconds and you can see what it looks and sounds like to read well over over a thousand words a minute. You're gonna have to force yourself. You're gonna need your timer or better yet someone to time you.

Might as well throw in a couple of comprehension questions just to make sure you aren't reading like Trump.
1) What did Angie Dickinson say?
2) what is subvocalization?
3) How might Trump describe the trilogy?
4) what's the name of JFK's best seller?
5) what does lugubrious mean?
6) How often is it used in Les Miserables?
7) What's your speed?

There is much more to say on the subject but my time is up as Lynn just returned from shopping, I'm still dicking around on the computer and she's timing me.

If this whole thing took you a minute to read....you're at about 850 WPM. Two minutes, means you're at 425. Five seconds and you're Donald Trump

A Tale Of Turley Lura

Nobody remembers Gambar anymore. If anybody recalls Gambar at all, they get him mixed up with the Orangatang who picked his scabs for twenty years at the Seneca Park Zoo.

I'm not talking about that Gambar. I'm talking about the Gambar that Gambar at the zoo was named after. The Gambar, I'm talking about lived hundreds if not thousands of years ago in a land unknown that exists but no longer exists under the name that Gambar and his pals called it when they lived in it. They called it Turley Lura At that time, "living" on Turley Lura was shorthand for hunting and gathering. Gambar wasn't much of a hunter and an even worse gatherer. Gambar was good with the women though.

Not.

About the only thing Gambar was good at was holding his breath. He could go for nine minutes (or what we today call minutes as the concept of "time" in Turley Lura was also up for grabs).

Nowadays only a few of us can go for one minute. Only a few of us would even be tempted to try unless our life was passing in front of us and planet waves were crashing above us or we were trying for a part in *Avatar 2*.

Just in case YOU are one of the FEW...... Then go ahead and try right now.

I'll count:one, two, three, four, five, six, seven, eight, nine, ten, eleven, twelve, thirteen, fourteen, fifteen, sixteen, seventeen, eighteen, nineteen, twenty, twenty one, twenty two, twenty three, twenty four, twenty five, twenty six, twenty seven, twenty eight, twenty nine, thirty.

Okay that's good enough.

Don't kill yourself. It's only an exercise in appreciation of the seemingly hapless Gambar.

If I was counting for Gambar while he was holding his breath, I'd still have another five hundred and ten numbers to type.

Forget that concept.

My life ain't passing before my eyes although a segment of Gambar's life will be passing before yours if you keep reading. So keep inhaling and exhaling. Including and excluding. You'll find it hard to read if you're not breathing.

Back in Gambar's day, there wasn't a lot to do besides standing around and staying alive. Staying alive depended on hunting and gathering. Since Gambar was a tribal liability to both of those life sustaining and time consuming activities, he spent most of his hours standing around. When even that minimum exertion proved too strenuous, he devolved to sitting around and then lying around.

While sitting around one day Gambar and his companion, another total tribal incompetent named Glork, decided to pass the time by seeing how long they could hold their breath. Gambar's competitor had a much stronger will than Gambar. Glork held his breath until he thought he had killed himself.

In that one moment of stupendous obstinacy, Glork reached his full potential with his discovery that death was nothing to fear. Unfortunately for Glork (but fortunately for his descendants who went on to become eagle killers) his involuntary respiration system kicked in and forced him to breathe after he had blacked out.

Thus, literature arrived at its first anti-climax which arrived even before literature

Even the apparent death of his competitor didn't stop Gambar from holding his breath. When Glork returned to his senses, the first sensation he experienced along with his surprised inhale was Gambar's massive exhale. Glork mistook Gambar's exhale as a sigh of relief and thought he had made a friend. Gambar was amazed that he had won at something.The two outcasts shared a moment of illusional ecstasy.

Then they got up and started standing around again. Glork thinking he had a friend. Gambar thinking he had a future. Whatever that was.

In Gambar's culture, the only sport less popular than breath holding was starvation. Outsiders, alienated from their tribes through their own helplessness, incompetence and sullen personalities, competed in the fundamental arena of who could live the longest with zero food.

Starvation was not technically a spectator sport aside from the starving stick figures themselves who had nothing else to do but sit there and watch each other shrivel up and die.

The most popular competitions were running, throwing rocks and staring. The starvers did a lot of staring too but since starving was considered an advantage in staring contests, the starving outcasts were not allowed to compete in organized staring contests.

Breath holding contests held a place between staring and starving contests in the pecking order of primitive sport.

Glork was a formidable starer, who was moving down the competitive ladder in status when he engaged Gambar in their one sided breath holding competition.

After recovering from his blackout and mistaking Gambar for a sympathetic soul, Glork decided that Gambar might have a talent for staring.

It would seem that the ability to hold one's breath would be very advantageous in a staring contest. However, it is even more important to be able to look your competitor in the eye when in the contest. Gambar, due to his profound alienation, found it impossible to look Glork in the eye as they stare sparred.

Still Glork believed in Gambar.

And he had a secret to pass on when Gambar confessed that the problem was looking into another human's eyes.

Glork passed on his secret to Gambar.

If you can't look 'em in the eye, look 'em in the eyebrow.

And hold your breath.

Glory suspected that he might gain an advantage on the "talent" of Gambar but for God sake they had to get the hell out of Turley Lura if it was the last thing that they ever did. They didn't know which way to go, Glork said "let's follow the big orange ball because tomorrow may rain". When they left, nobody looked up to see that they were gone.

If you're the type of person who pronounces nuclear as nukeyeller or ginseng as jingjang or orangutan as rangatang, then you're probably a lot like Gambar who would have been one of those persons if he had any idea of the concepts of nuclear, ginseng or orangutan or even the future. You're also a lot like Gambar if hundreds of years from now, they unknowingly name an orangutan after you in a zoo in a declining city. You're also a lot like Gambar and an orangutan if you're immature. If you're male and immature then the similarity between you and Gambar and an orangutan intensifies.

A fully adult orangutan male is flanged. When fully flanged, the orangutan has the large cheek flaps and throat sac which enables him to emit a deep booming sound which surpasses a lions roar in volume and intensity.   Male orangutans are not fully flanged until about thirty five years or older. No other animal takes that long to reach full maturity, with the exception of the human male, who in most cases is only fully mature just before death, and even not then in all cases. Gambar, in our story, was a typical male which means exasperatingly immature. Yet, in spite of his immaturity or perhaps because of it, Gambar was closer to death than he suspected from the moment he locked eyeballs with Glork.

Then, of course, all of us are closer to death than we think.
That's why God invented Doctors.
And witch doctors
And politicians
And security alerts

And executioners

And staring contests.

And that's why the most common last words we speak, when maturity and mortality are knocking down the door are these two words.

"Oh! Shit."

The people who lived near the beach called themselves islanders. They were familiar with stragglers like Gambar and Glork and referred to them as inlanders.

The islanders had never encountered two men as inland as Glork and Gambar.

When Gambar first saw the surrounding water, he thought it was blue land with ripples.

That's about as inland as ya can get.

The islanders were sophisticated in their staring. They were very aware of the "look em in the eyebrow rather than the eye" technique which Glork in his ignorance thought he had invented and which Gambar in his innocence obeyed. The islanders had outlawed this technique. Anyone using the technique was referred to as a "brow beater".

After Gambar had won a few staring contests near the shore, the word started to spread that Gambar was a brow beater. Eleeza would put Gambar to the test.

Eleeza had been born a unibrower. Her parents decided that rather than have their daughter go through her life as a unibrow, they would shave off her brow entirely. Without her brow, Eleeza became a litmus test for inlanders suspected of browbeating. Those inlanders would be in for a surprise.

The Islanders had never seen inlanders as inland as Glork and Gambar.

Three years before Gambar and Glork followed the orange ball to the edge of the island, a restless crab irritated a relaxed oyster.

We'll call the crab Buster and the oyster we'll call Paul. Why not?

Paul hadn't moved in years. A strong set of organic threads attached Paul to a reef named...

Okay, we're not gonna name reefs.
That would be as silly as naming organic threads. We're not gonna do that either.
Although I am tempted to call the organic thread Fred.
Let's resist that temptation and get back to the oyster named Paul.

Anyway, Paul was serene and content, filtering plankton through his gills when Buster, always looking for an advantage and passing for plankton, managed to find a place within Paul.

Of course, Paul was insulted.
When irritated by Buster, Paul did what pearls always do. They cover it up.
Paul secreted epithelial cells from the inside of his shell.
Scientists know these cells as nacre.
We know the cells, if we know them at all, as mother of pearl.
Paul had another name for Buster, the filter, the mother of pearl and for the hollow in his soft tissue, near his gonad.
Paul called them fookin nuisances.
He clung to his reef even as the nuisances grew more perfect.
As if a nuisance could ever be perfect.

Meanwhile back on the shore...Eleeza entered the staring contest with a blue veil over her face. The staring starter counted down to the start of the stare.
At the command to "stare", Eleeza removed the veil from her face.
Gambar held his breath and honed in on her eyebrow.
There was no eyebrow upon which to focus.
Gambar exhaled and looked into Eleeza's eyes.
He fell in love.
He blinked.
He lost.

Two seconds into the match, it was all over.

Gambar's gimmick was revealed to all.

He was a brow beater.

Eleeza replaced her veil and departed. She was shaken and all awhirl as nobody had ever looked her in the eye before. She was in love.

The Islanders seized the inlanders.

They loaded the inlanders onto a boat made of the skins of previous brow beaters.

They tied a rope around Gambar's leg. They attached a seventy five pound stone to the rope around Gambar's leg.

They paddled the boat away from the shore for "fifteen" minutes which they called tatatatas.

They explained to Gambar and Glork that after ten tatatatas underwater, they would pull Gambar to the surface. If he was still alive, his brow beating would be forgiven. He and Glork would be allowed to become slaves.

If not, the skin boat would get a little more fortified.

They threw Gambar, the rope and the stone into the blue earth with ripples.

Glork watched Gambar disappear into the blue earth.

Gambar thought only of Eleeza and her eyes.

He held his breath.

Gambar instinctively held his breath when thrown from the boat of many bodies.

He expected to land on the rippling blue land, he didn't expect to land in the land.

He also didn't expect to be flying within that land.

it took him a moment to realize that he wasn't flying, he was falling

The rock hit bottom before Gambar did.

When Gambar hit bottom, he began to look around.

This land had all kinds of activity that Gambar had never seen on the land he had lived upon until the moment he was thrown into this new shimmering land.

Still holding his breath and dragging the rock behind him, Gambar began to explore his new domain.

Beautiful.

He noticed what we would call a reef.

He noticed something attached to what we would call a reef.

He went over and like you and I might pluck a rose from a garden, he plucked the something that was attached to that which we would call a reef.

That something that was attached to the reef was something that today we would call an oyster.

While he was looking at what today we would call an oyster, he felt himself flying again; a lot like some people today would imagine something called the ascension. He took the oyster up with him.

An oyster that we would call Paul.

And within Paul, the imperfect nuisance of a memory named Buster.

When Gambar's ascension broke the surface, he opened his eyes and exhaled.

When Gambar opened his eyes and exhaled, the Islanders on the skin boat exhaled as well.

I guess we can call a scream an exhale.

The Islanders had never before seen a dead guy open his eyes and exhale.

They pulled Gambar upon the boat.

They knew that he had died.

Now they knew that he had come back to life.

He had visited the land unknown.

He brought something back from that land.

That something knew itself as Paul.

This was the first time that anyone, Islander or inlander had ever seen an oyster.

We call it an oyster. It called itself Paul. They thought it was a souvenir from heaven. They called it knowledge. Gambar was the bearer of knowledge. Glork was his friend.

Glork realized what he wanted to do. He immediately dropped the "K" sound from his name from his name and added a y sound. Upon this realization his future as a slave disappeared and his life as a prophet known as Glory began

Glory would tell the world about Gambar, the bearer of knowledge. Gambar who had returned gloriously from the dead. Glory days began. Gambar became Glam the Gambler

Hundreds if not thousands of years later, this site became the resting place for dozens of sunken galleons.

Imagine a fleet of sunken galleons stretching along the bottom of the ocean as far as the eye can see. Each galleon is loaded with diamonds. You've heard about this sunken fleet for seventy years and one day, you locate it and it's accessible. You alone know of its location, existence and accessibility. You have only a certain amount of air to roam through the precious shipyard and gather the infinite jewels that you find. You recover as many as you can bring to the surface on each dive. This image describes the delirious joy of discovering an unlimited imagination and the tools to articulate that imagination. It becomes our duty as well as our pleasure and obsession to explore that imagination and do all that we can to bring it to the surface. We are writers and this is our job. Particularly in times of quarantine when we are in our homes, in our dens, on our keyboards diving, retrieving and sharing before we run out of air. We know that we will run out of air before the galleons run out of riches so we do what we can do while we can do it and we rejoice with every breath, thankful for the time as well as the opportunity to realize the purpose of our good fortune.

Glory and Glam the Gambler will return in Ethereal Serial, if this isn't the last time.

Start imagining it now and maybe it's already happened.

Imagicnation works that way.

Jazz Oh Yeah

I've been digging some jazz lately on record, on tube, on Spotify and in person.

I got my first taste of jazz in Greenwich Village in the sixties where I saw Dizzy Gillespie, Charlie Mingus, Gerry Mulligan, Dave Brubeck, Wes Montgomery and Jimmy Smith perform at different times. Plus, I was good pals with Dr. Roger Eckers, Sunny Jain, Rich Thompson, Dan MacMurray and Mike Cottone.

My buddy Al and I used to say that it was good jazz when we could say "oh yeah" at any time during the rendition of whatever that whoever was jammin' and those two words would fit in perfectly.

Oh yeah.

The best "oh yeahs" came when our eyes were closed and when we opened them, we noticed that the musicians eyes were also closed as they escaped into the groove. I knew that they were getting even higher from the music than I was and I envied that elevation.

For many years, I've wanted to write like that, so goddamned high that I don't even know where I am because I am nowhere and everywhere at the same time but undeniably HERE from what I HEAR in the music that surrounds, comforts and challenges me and the words/notes that somehow emerge and the moods they reveal and the lessons they teach without trying to teach.

I can't quite get there and part of the reason is that after all these years, I still don't know how to type. I went to college in the sixties when college was more or less a typing contest. I was a shitty typer than and I'm not much better now except now we don't have to fiddle with whiteout and typeovers and tearing typing paper out the typewriter and throwing it into the trash can and lighting another cigarette and starting all over again on a new piece of typing paper that might live for ten minutes before being balled up and thrown into the same garbage pail as all the others while the clock on the wall ticked away the hours and minutes until deadline and the goddamned thing was through and you're still kinda drunk etc oh yeah.

We produced a lot of typists in the sixties before God invented word processing.

See, if you're as good with a keyboard as Gerry Mulligan was good with his sax, you don't have to look at the keys at all. You can forget about them, yeah. You know where everything is and that includes the vibe that you're laying

down and you don't even have to see it until you're done with it and then it stands as proof that you were away for a little while. Technique, imagination and resilience delivered via inspiration right now

The Force is with you yeah. You're feelin' it, ya feel me?
No need for garbage pails or white-out. The proof is on the screen. Hit save. Print it out or publish it. You were there baby, you were there but you did the whole thing looking at the keys and looking at your fingers and God knows there's another realm above and beyond, the order of pecking. Yeah, you're finger lookin' good but that ain't good enough....not free enough....not invisible enough. Too much gravy not enough train.

I want to get that high place someday. And take y'all with me. Today was close.

Yeah.

But no Charley Parker..

Charley Parker played the sax like he was trying to forget something sad and in the process of forgetting, Bird remembered something beautiful. something alluring, something breathtaking, irresistible,tantalizing, tempting

Charley Parker played the sax like he was trying to cram sixty years into thirty, trying to live three lives at once, trying to forget the future death of daughters unborn, to be born with holes in their hearts, hearts filled with innocence, fatherly neglect, exclusion, marginalization and omission that would in the beginning of their eternity fuel them to jam, to jive, to harmonize with those angels who bring Autumn to New York.

Simple, really, so simple that Bird could fly without effort; soar free past narrowing clouds of bald scentless vultures closing in on their next fresh, lifeless meal signalled by eyes, microscopic, telescopic and eight times brighter than the windows of the world's most famous junkie spending each night on a subway, pawning saxophones to feed the beast,asking Dizzy for help, for brief respite that neither Chan nor Mr. G had any idea how to supply much less provide a stoplight nor shelter for because he, she, they, themselves perceived infinite numbers of snow headed cool guys huddled neck deep in Big Muddy, hoping to thaw, watching the Mississippi recede at every futile sip.

Charley Parker played the sax like there was no space, no time between where he placed his fingers on the keys and where his heart lived even though his body barely moved. Charley Parker played the sax with extended intensity that eventually surrendered to splay fingered melody that made silent Thelonius Monk get up off his stool and dance.

Charley Parker played the sax. Simple paragraphs, full of complex sentences, conflicting synonyms of symmetry, celebration and sadness. Stream of consciousness for sure.

Repetition, repetition of course yet never the same way twice, not even love two times. Right up until the end, after the telegrams, the Baroness and the juggler. Charley Parker played the sax.

yeah, that's closer

Two Minute Ice Bowl

Yesterday Lynn asked me a very tantalizing question. "Do you feel like going bowling today?"

After twenty plus years without it, I had pretty much lost all contact with the "feeling" of going bowling. I was much more familiar with the feeling that I was having when she posed the question, namely the feeling of reclining on the couch and reading the suddenly appropriate "Love in the Time of Cholera."

I resisted the urge to just say no. Other than the total absence of feeling and presence of physical atrophy, I had no reason to reject the idea. So to my surprise, I said, "why not" and twenty minutes later, we were off to the bowling alley.

Back in the day, bowling alleys were everywhere. In the twenty first century there are fewer alley but the ones that survive are rigged up with all kinds of video, electronics, colors and sounds. When I first started bowling, it cost $0.35 a game and shoe rental was an extra quarter. Yesterday, the charge was $25 an hour and the shoes were $4.50 a pair.

$34 bucks would have bought me 100 draft beers back in the day and my couch was still calling so I looked at Lynn and in my best 'I'm not a cheapskate and I wouldn't rather be home on my ass reading a book' tone of voice I said to Lynn, "I don't know Honey, we just spent $50 on lunch a couple of days ago."

Lynn did the math in her head and came to the conclusion that the cost was "kinda high for just two bowlers and if we had four bowlers it would be a better deal."

I looked over my shoulder and shrugged, indicating that I didn't see the two other bowlers who would turn this outing into a better deal. Lynn caught my shrug but surprised me by saying, "Well, we're here. Let's go ahead and do this thing."

Of course, I agreed.

The attendant asked us our shoe size. My shoes turned out to be too big and Lynn's turned out to be too small. We had to find the balls that we were going to use. I asked the attendant when would the clock start running. She said that. "from the time you rent your shoes, we wait eight minutes before we start the clock."

I figured that was a fair amount of time to find the right ball, go to the designated alley, put on our shoes and start bowling.

I wondered how much research had been done to determine how much time was needed for those tasks. If a person brought his own bowling ball and shoes, did he get less than eight minutes to go on the clock ? What if the person only had one leg....did they give him more time.....did they only charge him for one shoe....is it possible for a one legged person to even bowl a game? Call Larry David.

So now I'm on the lookout for the ball that I'm going to use and there are literally a couple hundred from which to choose. Back in the day, there were maybe dozens to choose from and they were all black. Nowadays, they come in all different colors and are arranged according to weight and finger size.

Back many years ago when I bowled regularly, I owned my own ball and shoes. My ball weighed 14 pounds. Pro bowlers use a sixteen pound ball. I had reached a point in my bowling career that I either went to a 16 pound ball of quit bowling. Ya know that point where you're pretty good at something and if you spend some more money, spend some more time you could become GOOD at whatever that thing is but you also realize that you don't have the same aptitude for that thing that those who are BETTER than you have and the time you spend at that thing that you have less aptitude for might be time you're wasting from something for which you have a higher aptitude.

I kept bowling 165 over and over.

I didn't get the sixteen pounder. I quit bowling until yesterday.

So I started looking through the selection of 13 pound balls. I found a yellow ball. The ball was designated XL for finger size. The ball was too large. I checked out another 13 pound yellow ball this one designated as L. This ball was too small. I have the same problem when I'm buying pants. Meanwhile the clock was running.

I tried a couple more balls, again too small and too large. I have the same problem buying pants. I decided that too large is better than too small so with about a minute to spare, I had my ball.

We headed to our alley. Thank God, our shoes were Velcro. I knew right away that mine were too large. So there I was with a ball and shoes that were too big and only a few seconds before we were on the clock.

I picked up my loose yellow ball and was ready to roll.

I almost tripped when I stepped on the bowling lane. Back in the day, we had to step up from the scoring area to reach the lane. Here the lane was on the same level as the scoring area so as I attempted to step up, I almost fell down.

Now that I'm older and my balance is shot, I fall more frequently. Memories of recent falls tend to gather with each stumble and accrue a momentum of their own. My mind began to fill with images of "I've fallen and I can't reach my bowling ball" scenarios.

With my confidence already shaken by the immediate misstep, I walked onto the lane. I went to the spot on the lane that I used to take when I was a pretty good bowler. I took my stance and prepared for the five steps and slide to the foul line accompanied by backswing and finally release. I counted on muscle memory to take over but unfortunately the memory that had taken over was the last fall that I had taken when my shoe stuck to the floor in a grocery store and I lost my balance and flew ten feet towards the shopping carts in a vain attempt to get my balance which I never got until I smashed nose first into the floor, cut the shit out of my face. lost consciousness for a few seconds and awoke being assisted by a Hell's Angel's guy who happened to be passing by and saying, "are you all right, brudda?"

Yeah

Many years before, I had coached my sister Terri how to make an approach and slide on her left foot then follow through with her right hand as if she were trying to shake hands with the pin. I ran my own advice through my head.

Fuggedaboudid

So my first steps were, let's say tentative and the pendular weight and momentum of the back swinging yellow ball wasn't helping any. The next four slow motion, fearful wobbling steps brought me about three feet from the foul line. Back in the old days, I would be two and a half feet closer and my slide would take me to the line where I would smoothly release the ball and the ball would quietly begin its roll to the headpin.

When my steps ended so far away from the line, they ended abruptly. There was no slide so there I was standing still, a mile from the foul line and still in my backswing which I had started late due to the catastrophization that was clouding my mind and obliterating all muscle memory other than the fear of falling.

The momentum from my release forced me to throw the ball underhanded in the air rather than roll the ball on the alley. The ball landed with a furious THUD and slid its way directly into the gutter seemingly embarrassed to have made such an overly percussive sound as it collided with the lane, anxious to get out of sight before any of the hundreds of other balls on the racks had a chance to wake up and take a gander.

I turned around and looked at Lynn. Her expression was more of concern than pity but it was somewhere between the two.

The ball, seemingly recovered from its last THUD had been forced to return through the darkness of the underground system of automatic ball return and was more ready than I for the second shot of the first frame.

We're about two minutes into our hour of bowling.

Nobody was hurt yet, though the alley might have been slightly bruised.

Immediately After reading Camus & Marquez

Not only do we have an opportunity to explore the treasures of our own submerged galleons but we have time to appreciate and collect the diamonds of others that have been present but undiscovered, some for decades and some for centuries.

In other words, we have time to write and time to read and time to write about our reading and read about our writing. In the midst of our current international voluntary mitigation, ABC tales in London serves as a lighthouse and a gathering place.

So today I read and write about my reading.

Last December when we still had all the usual distractions of non-quarantined life, I became obsessed with reading Camus. Weirdly enough, I began my study with *The Plague*. Little did I know that I was getting a preview of the oncoming pandemic. After concluding *The Plague*, I moved to another galleon that had somehow avoided my reconnoiter....*Love in the Time of Cholera* by Gabriel Garcia Marquez.

While being overwhelmed by the ferocious romance and magical realism of Marquez, I heard for the first time rumblings coming from China and began to imagine the claustrophobic quarantine of *The Plague*. The horror was nearly impossible to process. Little did I know

At the end of February before the virus had spread to the United States. I came down with a suffocating something. I struggled with that something for a couple of weeks before writing about it in my blog on March 12th. What follows is my blog entry for that day...

"If I didn't/don't have the virus than I came/come real close. I'd been sniffling, coughing, malaising and sleeping for almost two weeks now. Maybe I got lucky and it was/is only pneumonia cuz only pneumonia knows the way I feel tonight. I got flu shots and pneumonia shots at the beginning of the season so whatever I had/have could have been worse without those shots which is a frightening thought.

I don't think it's the Corona because I got it before it arrived in the US and I don't get out much around here as a recluse, I'm pretty much on a self-imposed quarantine other than an occasional trip to the movies. The last movie we saw was *The Invisible Man*. It was out of focus and I didn't even have the energy to demand my money back." Whatever it was, I don't want the other thing. Just tell me what I got to do to not get it.

Krell On Covid

Way back in 2015, it didn't take a genius to predict that a pandemic was on its way.

Thornton Krell was no genius but he did have the ability to think both horizontally and vertically at the same time. This combination enabled him to think logically while understanding that his logical thinking was incapable of grasping anomalies. Thus Krell became a devotee of misunderstanding which he saw everywhere as an indication of the possibility of progress.

This kind of thinking established Krell as a nut.

A Charismatic lunatic.

Krell became increasingly nutty when he tried to explain things to the horizontally entrenched folks who depended upon logic and the senses to dictate "reality" which Krell automatically resisted.
Krell was never perceived as "normal" which he took as a compliment.
Krell was didactic. He was self-taught. He had his own curriculum.

Krell also knew something that only a few folks outside the ever changing world of medicine, specifically bacteriology and immunology understood only too well, namely that epidemics..even pandemics have long been a staple of "civilized" life and that we were due for another one at any moment.

As was his wont, Krell tried to oversimplify the danger and the process which infuriated so many who preferred logic to reality...the don't worry be happy folks who constituted the vast battalions of the normal.

Krell subscribed to enigma.
He knew some things about viruses.
Viruses are an enigma that exist on the edge of life.

Most of what people considered to be "alive" were involved in metabolism which included inclusion, exclusion and toleration which means including food, burning oxygen, producing waste and reproducing by division.

Those processes define life even in the realm of bacteria. Those processes are normal.

A virus does not eat or burn oxygen for energy. They avoid any engagement that might be considered metabolic. They do not produce waste. They do not have sex. They make no side products. They do not even reproduce independently. They are at once, less than life and more than an inert collection of chemicals.

Ya wanna talk about low life...talk about virus.

A virus has only one function; to replicate itself but is incapable of doing that on its own rather it invades cells and cells that have energy and like a Gepetto from Mars takes them over and forces them to make hundreds of thousands of new viruses.

This didn't start yesterday.
Any didactic will tell ya that.
This has been going on ever since Eden or whatever.

It's all about genes and genomes. Genomes are combinations of genes just as chords are combinations of musical notes. All about DNA and even more about RNA. Genes tell cells what to do. Genomes respond like a player piano, making a music of its own without the assistance of Liberace or Elton John.

When a virus invades a cell it inserts its own notes into the chords. The player piano then begins to produce the music of the virus instead of what the cell needs for itself.

The cells starts playing a different tune turning out hundreds of thousands of viral proteins which which bind together to form new viruses....new music...strange, deadly music until the keys on the piano lock permanently making the piano useless as a piano.

The new music, out of control, bursts through the cell wall to invade other cells, other pianos.

Covid is the latest virus to invade our pianos and change the music of our species.

By now, we've all seen the imagery of the Covid; The crown like protuberances on the top, the corona. It is these protuberances that allow the virus to unlock cells within our bodies that fool our immune systems into thinking everything is awright. They become a skeleton key fitting with exquisite precision into our cells bypassing our immune systems.

No previous virus had ever had this key before.

Viruses combine to cause 90 percent of all respiratory infections. We tend to underestimate this ongoing invasion as the "flu". No biggie

We get a shot.

We get a cold. It's an endemic disease. It's always around.

Krell knew that throughout history endemics have become pandemics. Antigenic anomalies occur just as certainly as night follows day.

Krell knew all this but when he tried to tell people about these processes, he was regarded as an abnormal nut.

Krell didn't mind.

He got his flu shots every year. He told everybody to get theirs but he knew this was not gonna be enough when a new variety of fit would eventually hit the shan.

Just a matter of time.

Krell like everybody else had no idea that his time was running out.

Stay tuned
And get the goddamned vaccine
Then I'll tell you more.

Ovid During Covid

by Ovid Warren Peets

I've always been an advanced student when the subject is projection, metaphysician or learned helplessness. I catch on quick. I'm good at letting somebody else do it.

Since Julia has taken over most of the decisions in my lifetime, my helplessness was already very advanced and prospering before Covid came along to validate.

She cooks, I eat what she cooks. She's a great cook.
She shops and brings home the food that she's gonna cook that I'm gonna eat.
She takes care of the yard.
She drives. I sit shotgun.
She pays the bills and balances the checkbook every month.
I have a schedule and I stick to my routine.
I have an allowance and I stay within it.
I have a man cave for sports watching and privacy.
I was so happy, so idle, so increasingly helpless that I began to feel guilt.

Then Covid showed up.
Fear began to replace guilt.
I could justify my ongoing lessons in learned helplessness and projection.
I increased my couch time. Much easier to fall asleep in the afternoon than at night.
I increased my snacking time.
I reduced my exercise.

And I felt justified in doing so goddamned it, I'm fighting the Covid. I'm doing my best to save the life of everyone I know by becoming a recluse in my bunker and not letting the wreck loose in my community to infect and/or to be infected.

Helplessness found fertile soil to grow.

And grow I did...thirty pounds worth.

Julia cut my hair. She's a better cook than a barber so I looked in the mirror recently and discovered a pale fat, helpless slob with a lunatic haircut who just wanted to go up stairs, watch teevee, take naps and read, read, read until time to come down for dinner. Lots of reading about various Kennedys and novels by James Patterson topped off by a book by Patterson about the Kennedys We turned on the teevee after dinner, were astonished and horrified nightly by the absurd fandango known as the Trump presidency. We watched one murder show after another.

Aside from the horror show in the mirror and the carnage surrounding me, I loved my Covid life.

Even enjoyed the masks as I always wanted to be a masked man when I grew up based upon my love of the Lone Ranger. I always wore masks to concerts, the difference being that my masks didn't cover my mouth bandit style but rather my eyebrows and cheeks Lone Ranger style.

I'm glad I don't have to get too close to people. Six feet is fine. I still remember the time I got too close to a fake Robert E Lee moments before Julia changed my life.

I love giving and getting the right of way when we walk. I'm quick to step aside. I enjoy waving at people.

Now it's all coming to an end. They say they have a vaccine

I'm as helpless and happy as a turtle in his shell.

Maybe I won't get the vaccine.

Merle on Covid

Attention you bat biting, snake chewing, hedgehog gobbling, turtle dove devouring Orientals in the wet markets of Huanan, thanks a lot. Same to you, wet market butchers who render both the produce and the wildlife on the spot before the blood, gut and shit stained pavements are hosed down to keep them "clean". In case you haven't seen Dracula, scientists have long insisted that bat-human interactions including the presence and consumption of live bats in wildlife markets in Southern China "ain't gonna end well for anybody and might just fuck up everything."

But wait a minute, before we start kissing the ass of Asian scientists let's remember that low paid research assistants had collected samples of the virus directly from wild bats not the bats in the market. They analyzed this bat poison without appropriate protective procedures. All of this batshit crazy research was done right smack dab in Huanan, in a laboratory just a few minutes from the wet market as the turtledove flies.

Whether it was researchers or shoppers, traders or visitors the China virus started and today it has become uncontrollable through out the world as it spreads exponentially. I get the flu...I give it to three people...those three people give it nine people...those nine people give it to twenty seven.
You get the drift?

So whaddya we do now. I got it. Let's elect Biden and go to communion every day . What? No communion? Social distance? and what? The latest Premature Saint knew all about sex crimes and din't say anything about them while getting his face lifted and porcelain grin refashioned, actually covered them up?

Thank God, Trump won the election.

(Merle Seton is known nationwide for intentionally disseminating marketable misinformation to both side of the divide based on plagiarism, rumor, fake polls and xenophobic hate mongering. Currently Merle is waiting for the return of JFK Jr while advising Robert Kennedy Jr in his sensational expository regarding Fauci)

Recognizing Rivers

by Thornton Krell

Julia didn't want to be recognized so she removed her leopard skin pill box hat and put in on the table next to her Stella Artois draft. Ovid wanted to be recognized so he left his mask on his face while he sipped his Long Island Ice Tea.

Julia and Ovid were comfortable on the deck outside Big Daddy's Burger joint. Yeah, it was kinda hot but kinda low humidity so a great day for drinking a couple of beers and doing some people watching. Some restrictions had been lifted just the day before.

"Hey, look at that dude over there."

"Which dude? I see several."

"The guy with the beard. See that guy? The guy who looks like Hemingway mixed with Sean Connery except with better hair than both of them?

Ovid immediately knew which dude Julia was referring to.

"Oh yeah that guy, the guy with the SLR hanging around his neck?"

"Yeah, that guy. I'd call him the definition of a brown eyed handsome man." Julia was surprised by her own observation.

"I don't know", said Ovid, the gray hair is more prominent than the eyes. I can't even tell what color his eyes are but the hair, Jeezuz Christ the hair."

"I love that whitish gray with the streaks of pure white which makes the gray look almost black in some places."

"I bet he was a teacher."

"He looks like the kinda guy who was handsome as a young man and grew even more handsome as he aged and wisdom started to replace impetuosity."

Julia asked, "Whaddya think he is now....a writer or a photographer?"

"Judging by the camera, I'd say he's a photographer who writes. You don't see a lot of SLRs around anymore. Maybe he's a writer who takes photographs. Maybe he's a teacher who writes. Maybe he's a writer who taught."

"Do you think he's famous?"

Ovid thought he was probably as famous as he wanted to be, probably delighted with his obscurity although a little disappointed at how meager were the sales of his books.

Julia thought she might try to get his attention. She coughed and dangled a sandal. She ran her fingers through her hair which suddenly took on a new lustre.

She had no idea that she was a factoid and the dude she was dangling for knew exactly what she was doing, what she was saying, what she was thinking.

He was Ice Rivers after all.

What else could she think?

What else could she do?

Rivers had a few ideas about that as well. He made her even prettier, smarter and happier.

He took 10 pounds away from Julia and stopped her from snoring.

Ovid was indeed a lucky masked man.

Ovid took a closer look at Julia. Once again, she looked different from how she had looked a few minutes earlier. Ovid notched that up to the nature of all beautiful women. Once again, he considered himself a very lucky, lucky man.

He looked adoringly into her magnetic eyes and said, "We've got a lot to live for; let's get the shot."

Covid Baseball

I've loved baseball for 65 years. Strangely, I didn't miss it when Covid eliminated the first three and a half months of play. The game returned a couple of days ago and my love returned. I've heard it said that we will always love whatever we've ever loved although sometimes we lose that love. If we are going to find that love again, the best place to look for it is the place that we had it last. The return of baseball immediately sustained that theory.

Here's another theory; love is strange.

Here's one of my favorite books: *Stranger in a Strange Land.*

Watching baseball in this covid season made me feel like a stranger in a strange land who had rediscovered his love and God Awmighty was it strange.

The stadiums are empty or sparsely crowded with cardboard cut outs. The sounds of the ballpark are recorded and played back at appropriate moments. The players are wearing masks. Ballplayers who are not expected to play on a given day are seated at a social distance in the empty stands.

No spitting is allowed on the field.

Let's talk about spitting for a moment. The kid who taught me how to play baseball was a kid who spit all the time. When I asked him why he spat, he said because it was part of the game. I started to spit. We all spit like maniacs when we were on the Little League field emulating the major leaguers who spit when they were on the field. Those major leaguers no doubt learned how to spit when they were kids and somebody taught them that spitting was part of the game. Therefore, if you were a major league player, you were a major league spitter. All of a sudden, spitting had become illegal and God bless 'em the ballplayers are breaking an age old habit with admirable Covid discipline.

For those folks who don't like baseball, it's usually because the game is too long and so is the season. The length of the season reduces the importance of individual games which only increases the tedium of the non-fan. This Covid season is only 60 instead of 162 games which makes each game more significant. Further, almost every game is now available on teevee. For the past couple of years, I've learned the skill of "watching a three hour game in about 35 minutes. I tape the game before I sit and watch it and then I play the game back at double speed until I get used to that speed and then speed it up to four X speed once I become accustomed. I slow the speed down to real time if there is a critical at bat or if I am interested in a particular batter or pitcher. Of course, I go at four time speed during commercials. Watching baseball on teevee has become an art form. You gotta be good with the remote.

So there I was yesterday, watching a game between the Pirates of Pittsburgh and the Cardinals of St. Louis. I chose that game because the pitcher for the Cardinals was a guy on my fantasy league team that I had never seen pitch. The game was traveling along at double speed when I noticed the umpire making a gesture. I slowed the game down to real time.

Yup, the umpire was throwing somebody out of the game, presumably the manager of the Pirates. The manager leaped out of the dugout, wearing his mask and made his way to the ump. The ump whipped off his iron mask, threw on his Covid mask and there they were, two masked men arguing with each other while keeping a safe social distance.

The umpire returned to his position behind the plate. The Pirate manager made his way to the dugout, on his way to an early shower in the clubhouse. The manager stopped on the way to the clubhouse and took his usual spot in the dugout. The announcers (who no longer are in the stadium but rather in a studio watching the game on teevee while hilariously trying to decide whether the last pitch was a slider or a change of pace etc and calling almost everything a slider) were confused until one of them came to the conclusion that it was not the manager who was being thrown from the game. They took a look at the replay to try to catch anybody doing anything suspicious. One of the announcers noticed a ballplayer in the empty stands start to run away as the umpire was kicking someone out of the game. The announcer said "I think that was Holland running away".

Sure enough it was Holland. Holland is my wife's maiden name so that's weird. Apparently Holland had been chirping away at the ump from the

STANDS around the third base line. Normally, chirping from the third baseline would never be heard by an umpire drowned out as it would be by the sounds of the crowd. Because the stands were empty except for a few ball players who were forced to sit in them for Covid reasons, Holland's chirping was heard by the umpire who didn't care for it and "threw the bum out".

Now let's slow this down for a minute. The umpire ejected a guy from the game who was sitting in the stands which meant that he wasn't expected to play anyway, so Holland was forced to leave a game that he would have never entered in the first place for commenting on the umpire whom Holland thought would never hear him in the second place.

If a tree fell down in an empty stadium would it make any noise? Apparently, it would.

A few minutes later, my fantasy player got lit up for a few runs and was out of the game. I watched the rest of the game at 7 times normal speed and was done with it in 25 minutes.

Writing this story took me more time to write than I needed to watch the ballgame that I am writing this story about.

Baseball 2020.

I had witnessed something that I could never have imagined happening and so had fifty or so cardboard cutouts.

Love is strange.

Quiet Village

Birkdale is described as a village. I went to college in a village so I've always enjoyed the village vibe particularly the Main Street. If It wasn't for Main Street in Birkdale, I might have put up more resistance to moving down South. My first impression of North Carolina was that it didn't appear much different from Rochester. I was expecting much more drama in the landscape.

The best thing about our first visit was the hospitality of our kin who had relocated before us. On the last day of our visit, they took us for a visit to Birkdale and I kinda fell in love.

Birkdale has a Main Street straight out of my dreams. All kinds of shops and even the famous Birkdale Regal. Always music and LIFE going on in Birkdale. Until yesterday that is and even more absolutely today.

I've been through a number of ghost towns in my life but this was the first town I had visited that was an hour away from the invisible spirit.

Birkdale was shut down except for my favorite spot in Birkdale, Kilwin's Ice Cream Shop and Kilwin's was in its last hour of operation until ?.

Have you ever noticed how everyone in an ice cream shop seems so healthy and clean and clear eyed and friendly. Kilwin's is that to the max and even though they were closing down and about to lose one of their most prosperous holidays...Easter.....the whole staff including the owner greeted us with the usual enthusiasm and bon homme.

We got our cones. I got my mint chocolate chip in a medium waffle cone. Lynn got a small toasted chocolate coconut. Needless to say they were delicious.

I noticed a sign that said, "Buy one slice of fudge. get one free."

Naturally we bought one...double chocolate and got a free dark chocolate.

I noticed some fudge caramel apples behind the counter also BOGO. I enquired about them and the server said that since we were the lasrt customers we could have two for free.

We grabbed our free caramels and wished everybody good luck. They thanked us for our support. We assured them that we would be back ASAP.
Lynn paid for the sweet delights and we headed for our car.

Once we got to the car, we discovered that the owner had inadvertently charged us for both fudges, surely out of habit.

Old habits die hard.

We decided that they could have charged us twice as much and everything would have still been good.

We went home where we're gonna be for awhile until we return to Birkdale.

Covid Ambiance

Tuesday afternoons have been special times for Lynn and me since we moved down South. We visit the mall village of Birkdale and go to a matinee then we stop over at Bonefish grill where I always get an order of bang bang shrimp while we discuss the movie and our plans for the week. The pandemic has altered all of that and I chalked it up to societal sacrifice until Lynn came up with this idea.....let's rent a recent movie and have Bonefish deliver our lunch. Such a simple and clear idea/remedy.

In the meantime, Lynn went outside and worked on her garden while I went up to the cave and began yet another round of digital solitaire.

Lynn finished her gardening and took a shower. I woke up from my nap. We called Bonefish. They were on a limited menu so no lobster bisque. I ordered my bang bang and Lynn ordered lily chicken with a side of mac and bacon.

While we waited for the food, we tried to decide what would be an appropriate movie for our first Tuesday stayvake. The hottest movies like *Quiet Place 2* are being held back by the studios although I think they're missing an opportunity. Studios should release all of those movies for tee vee rental now when people are searching for ways to pass the time in social separation yet still are willing contribute to the economy. The latest movie available was *The Invisible Man* which we had already seen and in lieu of the invisible enemy that we all are fighting, didn't seem like an appropriate choice plus we already saw it although it wasn't in focus which Lynn and I had fought about when we saw it at the Birkdale Regal. Just to start a little trouble, I told her that "yeah, it's inappropriate and we didn't like it the first time but maybe if we saw it IN FOCUS, we might like it better"

Lynn said, "you were a jerk that day. Don't start being one again now."

It came down to *Bombshell* or *Birds of Prey* both of which star Margot Robbie. We like Margot. She's been on quite a hot streak including Tonya and Tarantino.

Bonefish arrived moments after we made our movie selection.

The food was good but not as good as we had grown to expect and the reason is simple. We ate the food out of the plastic containers in which it was delivered and the fact that the meal was showing up on OUR kitchen table put the meal in competition with the meals that Lynn prepares. To me, Lynn is the best of all possible cooks; so sorry Bonefish.

Yeah, the ambience was missing so if you decide to try this idea, I'd advise that you use your best dishes and silverware and maybe even light a candle because yeah, ambience counts for something.

Of course, not having to wash dishes counts for something as well.

After eating, we fired up *Bombshell* which proved to be a teevee movie that was released as a big screen movie the essence of which had already been covered by a tee vee movie that never made the screen with Russel Crowe starring as Roger Ailes. We preferred the Crowe version but enjoyed this one for what it was...a pandemic distraction.

Later we watched the final episode of *Curb Your Enthusiasm*.

Lynn played some Words With Friends. I returned to my current solitaire addiction. We kissed goodnight. We turned out the lights and went to sleep.

Aside from the delivery person, we hadn't come within 600 feet of anybody and we had contributed to the economy.

Also, we got a coupon for a complimentary bang bang shrimp.

Who knows when or where we'll use it?

Open Letter to Covid

Scientists measure the spread of an epidemic by a number called R0, or "R naught." That number is calculated this way: for every person who develops the illness, how many other people do they give it to before they are cured (or dead) and no longer infectious? The R0 for coronavirus appears to be a number close to 3 – an extremely frightening number for such a deadly disease.

Suppose you catch the virus. You will give it to 3 other people, and they will each give it to three others, and so forth. Here is how the math works, where you, the "index case," are the first line:

1
3
9
27
81
243
729
2,187
6,561
19,683
59,046
177,147
531,441
1,594,323
4,782,969
14,348,907

Here's the deal though.

In case you haven't realized it by now, life is castrophicaly non-linear. This means that we can get something good going and it looks like it's gonna keep getting better and better until damn something effed up happens and all of a sudden we're going in the opposite direction. Take most of our love lives for a quick example. We're going along fine until boom disillusion, disenchantment, disenfranchisement and finally dis sucks and I'm getting the hell out of dis (but it's not my fault or yours) etc or as Johnny Lennon once asked "how can I go forward when I don't know which way I'm facing."

Well guess what virus....you're alive right? everything's going your way right? Look at those numbers. You're kicking ass and taking names right? You're black swanning everybody and having the time of your shitty life. Bad news asshole. It's not gonna last. If you're alive, you can count on catastrophe and fuggedaboud linearity.

Ya finally had the balls to come over to America. Well guess what? After we stop bungling around and get past the misinformation, we're coming after you. We got the full court press on your ass right now. We're socially distancing and spiritually connecting. Yeah, we're staying indoors. Yeah the schools are closed. The kids are driving us crazy. We're bickering. We're washing our hands like maniacs. We're coming for ya asshole. Nobody wants to piss off the good old USA and our motto: we won't fuck with you but if you fuck with us we gonna fuck you up. We're taking your ass seriously now. We're starting to mobilize. Nobody spends more money on defense than us and we're about to declare all out war on you Corona.

You're gonna join the rest of those virus a holes like cholera and the plague and the Spanish flu and whatever else is rotting on the scrap heap of extinct chumps. Nobody's gonna miss ya. You're going down as a real asshole who overstayed your welcome and you were never welcome in the first place.

We're coming at you with money with society and with spirituality. Remember when Moses came down from the mountain he said "don't covid thy neighbor's wife" and "don't covid thy neighbor's goods". Well, we're taking it one step further. We won't covid our neighbors or they wives. We're gonna watch out for each other. We're gonna stay at home and man did you pick a bad time to make us "stay" at home.

We've got teevee. We've got internet. We've got facebook. We've got Twitter. We've got Kindle. We can get virtually any book we want and we can read our asses off. We can go on walks and it's gonna be Spring soon. We can spend quality time with our families. We don't need your ass around here.

Yeah, we're gonna lose some folks around here but you ain't seen nothing like the courage of our health providers nor the brilliance of our researchers nor the generosity of our government nor the flexibilty of our economy nor the spirit of humanity that is still rocking in the freeworld.

Have your putrid fun, scumbag. We're gonna getcha. Get used to it.

GTFO.

Food For Thought

When I sat down to type this morning, food was the last thing on my mind as I had already consumed my breakfast, the same breakfast that I have every Saturday when I allow myself two slices of heavily buttered and peanut buttered slices of toast.. Then I came to inspiration point and found food for my next group of thoughts which will follow immediately as I imagine and capture them.

Okay, here we go.

Raccoons and opossums became unexpected food sources when Burmese Pythons were introduced, intentionally or accidentally into the Everglades in the 1970's.. Since that time, 99% of opossums and raccoons have disappeared from the area.

Millions of years had passed since snakes of that size had last been seen in North America so their sudden re-appearance took the raccoon/oposum community by surprise. Rocky Raccoon, Ozzie Opossum and pals continued their previous habits and blundered their way into the python realm where they were met with the friendly, overwhelming persuasion of constriction followed by digestion and excretion. The pythons weren't hunting their raccoon food as much as the raccoon food was naively going where they had always gone, doing what they always had done. You can't blame the snakes for the naivety of the opossums. Most of us will eat what is served to us if it tastes good. Rocky and his opossum friends could be commended for their good taste if not their inability to cope with change.

More than 2,000 have pythons been captured which suggests that one of the world's largest snakes is now entrenched in the local food chain.

When a species becomes vulnerable due to a change in its environment, particularly a demotion in its place on the food chain, that species must adapt or face waves of death nearing extermination within the danger zone of that changing environment. The pythons are out there but they're not really hunting. Why bother hunting when food is delivering itself and pretending that nothing's changed and life will just go on the way it always does?

Until, suddenly, it doesn't. And an opossum begins its journey into python turdsdom.

The opossums and raccoons are gone from the Glades. Lots of people are wondering what they were doing there in the first place. The answer as always is very simple, they were looking for food.

Oh yeah

Alligators and full grown deer have replaced Rocky and Ozzie.

Alligators have never been accused of naivety. The pythons are gonna have to hunt for these meals and hunting is a whole different ballgame.

Most of the pythons will not be able to cope with the food chain disruption.

They don't belong in the neighborhood anyways. The pythons were better off in Burma with the leopards.

Eventually they will disappear. Currently they are on the wanted dead or alive list. Some intrepid capitalists are capturing pythons alive, mating them and raising generations of pythons only to turn them in for money when they reach a certain size and qualify for reward from the pro opossum group.

And that, my friends concludes an unexpected torrent of thought on food. Life is different whenever a new predator is introduced into the food chain. And wear your masks because things are different now. And get your shot

Wowsky the Pandemic Pomsky

When I imagine pandemics past, the sky is like granite with howling winds drizzling rain and catcreeping fog. Today, we are in the latest style of pandemic. The weather is gorgeous. The sky is a deep blue accentuated by the stainless white cumulus clouds. The temperature is 80 degrees. I'm sitting in a rocker on my front porch, socially isolated at least 20 feet from the walk in front of our house.

I love our porch. It has six pillars and is very Southern. Our house is located near the top of a hill on a street called Serenity. People on their isolation strolls pass by our house regularly. The people going up the hill are moving at a slower pace than the people going down the hill. When we say, "hi"neighbors tend to pause in their strolls for different reasons. The folks going up the hill pause to catch their breath and wish us well. The folks going down the hill pause to slow down and share the good fortune of coasting.

There are exceptions of course. A few minutes ago, a young mother passed our porch while jogging and pushing a stroller containing a set of twins. She was wearing a baseball hat with the inevitable pony tail. She was young and healthy enough to glisten as she passed. I called out, "I wish I could do that."while she made her way to the top of the Serenity Hill. She waved and grinned.

A few minutes later, going down the hill, a woman, her 10 year old daughter and a dog of remarkable appearance paused before the porch. I said hello and remarked about the appearance of the dog.

The woman stopped. It became immediately clear that she was used to such interruptions in her walk because she was always in the presence of such a remarkable animal.

"Thank you," the woman responded. "She's a cutie. We call her Wowsky."

Even from our porch I noticed the remarkable clarity of Wowsky's eyes and remarked upon them noting their similarity to the eyes of a husky.

The woman agreed. "Her mother is a Siberian husky. Her father is a Pomeranian. She is a new breed called a Pomsky."

I took a moment to visualize the mating process which seemed impossible at worst and improbable at best. Trying to imagine a Pomeranian mounting a Husky sort of boggled my mind.

The woman recognized the familiar boggle which occurred regularly in her strolls with Wowsky.

"It's all done with artificial insemination. The husky gets the needle and delivers the pups. The other way around would be quite a struggle if the Pom were the mother. Ouch"

Most people seeing a Pomsky for the first time would want to possess one so we embarked on the usual questions to construct obstacles towards pandemic panic buying.

How much does it shed? Is it good with kids? Does it bark all the time? How often do you have to groom it?

The woman was used to these questions.

Yes shedding is a concern.

Wowsky is good with our kids,

She does have a distinct personality that she conveys regularly especially when she needs to go on a walk. We take her out twice a day for 20 minutes and that's what she wants. If she needs a walk, believe me she'll let us know. Wowsy needs grooming 5 times a week so we all share the duties. Wowsy can be a pain sometimes but she is a member of our family so we deal with her moods, demands and territorialities the way we try to deal with each other's.

I asked if Wowsy would pose for a picture. Wowsy complied. I snapped the picture. The camera worked. As I have stated repeatedly, when I'm dreaming the camera never works. This whole scene, my porch, the Serenity Hill, the passersby and beautiful sky and the surrounding pandemic must be real.

We waved good bye and Wowsky started down the hill towards the next barrage of compliments and questions.

We Got The Shot

The virus needs to spread to "live" and it lives to spread. In order to live to spread, the virus needs to mutate. With its spreading and mutating, the virus has been having a ball battering defenseless humans around the clock and around the world.

And in Divided America, the home of the free.

Now we're fighting back.

Our masks and social distancing helped but were only passive resistance. Still we resisted as best we could while our scientists in spite of some politicians searched for a more aggressive response. They developed several vaccines that will slow down if not stop the spread which makes it difficult for the virus to survive. If we get enough vaccines into enough arms, we can stop the son of a bitch.

We've got more than a puncher's chance after rope- a dopin' for the past year while hundreds of thousands of us died.

Now, we're involved in another arms race.

The virus is mutating so time becomes a factor.

Yesterday, I'm proud to say, I saw America at its best. I saw the beginning of the pushback. Thousands of folks, most of us severely endangered, headed downtown...to the front of the line.

In Southern North Carolina, we gathered in Charlotte. In Charlotte we gathered at Panther Stadium. Yeah, the NFL was lending a hand.

We were pro-active.

We made reservations.

We arrived at the right place at the right time.

As we headed into the stadium, we passed hundreds of people heading out.

Rope lines had been secured.

Everyone was calm, the helpers securing the lines were helpful, kind, patient, friendly.

The lines moved swiftly.

This was America at its best. Absolutely no division. Red, blue, purple, black, white, yellow, rich, poor, fat, thin, co-operating against a common enemy.

This is the America I remember.

Twenty minutes later, past the black curtains, I met Jaclyn.

I asked her if she was gonna give me my shot.

She was.

She did.

Beautifully.

No pain.

I thanked her.

She congratulated me.

I met Lynn and we went to the area marked off to wait and see if we would suffer any immediate side effects.

On my way to the area, I passed an entrance to the field. I asked the guard if I might take a look at the field. He said, "Of course you can." I found Lynn.

She was doing fine.

We walked back to where I had met the security guy, he was gone but another person was in his place

Again another friendly person who said "of course you may."

We passed the guard.

I got a look at the field.

At the far end, the scoreboard was alight with these words....." I got the Shot."

I took out my camera. The camera worked. This wasn't a dream.

I had another opportunity to capture the moment. Lynn took her position. I waited for the sign to flash. It flashed. I clicked. Got the Shot once again.

After getting the covid shot, I got the shot of the scoreboard as it flashed "I Got The Shot."

Jimmy

We're getting numb over here.
Still we manage to smile
3300 Americans died of
Covid yesterday
More than Pearl Harbor
More than 9-11
Very sensitive subjects.
Supposedly there is no
comparative degree for "numb"

You're either numb or you're not.
Which leads us to number.
The numbers makes us even more numb than the original numbness
We see numbing numbers every time we turn on the news
They begin to lose all meaning
until we lose a friend or family member
Then the numbness wears off
The smile disappears
Another train crosses another bridge   Photo by Ron Stochl
Our friend wasn't a number
He was flesh and blood
Numbers are never real
They're simply symbols
Jimmy was real
He was a smiler
He became a number to the person
who counts up these figures
The person who keeps our numbness up to date
The ultra comparative
the unsmiling numbererer.

Wall Drug Ahead

Perhaps it's only fitting that the worst year in movies of my lifetime concluded with the worst Oscar show. From start to finish, this year's Oscar celebration managed to be both dull and finicky at the same time.

The best movie I saw this year was a garbled green screened mess called *The Invisible Man*. It was an easy choice every other "movie" that I saw this year was on teevee.

The teevee movie that resounded the most with me was *Nomadland*. I've spent time as a nomad and as I look back at my life, those times were amongst the best of times....broke as a joke....down to my last peso not afraid to say so but lovin life and campin' out every night under the stars as I criss crossed America. The life of a derelict is the life of a king etc.

A portion of *Nomadland* is set at Wall Drug. Let me tell ya about it.

When you start heading West from Atlantic to Pacific somewhere around central Ohio you pick up these unobtrusive distance markers revealing the distance to Wall Drug. 1200 Miles to Wall Drug....1000 miles to Wall Drug etc. Everything sorta looks like New York until you get into the vicinity of Wall Drug, South Dakota. South Dakota is where everything changes and it becomes apparent that you're not in Kansas anymore. Wall Drug had established itself as a watering hole for road bound Americans. Wall Drug, on first sight, resembles a stockade oasis with a cowboy motif. It's a collection of small shops and sure enough features the famous Wall Drug water...."reach out your hand if your cup be empty if your cup be full may it be again" with cold, clean, clear Black Hills water.

Nothing ever as intoxicating and refreshing as Wall Drug water. Preparation for the Badlands, the Black Hills, Mount Rushmore and Deadwood. America will never look quite the same to the thirst quenched traveler whose consciousness will be jostled even more with the subsequent discovery of Wyoming, Montana, Utah etc.

Wall Drug, dude.

Of course, not everybody nomads across America so up until *Nomadland*, Wall Drug was/is unknown to most Americans other than those who have tasted the waters or seen the Black Hill Gold. I would often tell folks about Wall Drug and the only thing they seemed to hear was the word "drug" especially when I talked about Wall in my high school classes.
For some this proved that "Mr. Rivers was on drugs etc,"

I always got a kick out of that.

However when somebody knew about Wall Drug because they had tasted the water, a gleam would appear in their eyes....a gleam of freedom and connection.

I stopped at Wall several times over the next decade. The last time I returned was as we were preparing for our wedding at the Field of Dreams in Iowa and wondering whether or not we had survived our collision with a semi-truck a few hundred miles East near South Bend Indiana, the home of touchdown Jesus.

I had been talking about Wall with Lynn for the past couple of years and of course, she also thought I was nuts. Until we got there. Wall had grown quite a bit but the spirit still remained. If were going to get married we needed wedding rings. A wedding ring is band of gold. Can there be a better place in America to find that band other than the Black Hills near Mt. Rushmore?

Black Hills gold.

We bought our wedding rings right there at Wall Drug. We're still wearing them today 32 years later. We've been through a lot over those 32 years. Lynn is a tough person. I've only seen her tear up a couple of times on our life journey. The first time was at Wall Drug when she tried on her ring while we wondered if we had survived the crash. I can still see that moment in my mind's eye.

I felt it again watching *Nomadland*. In a year with pandemic and without movies Wall Drug had somehow emerged and momentarily quenched my thirst with the water of hope and gratitude.

Awakening

Even though the contagion continues to increase throughout the South,
North Carolina rescinded our stay at home order.
We decided to take a short trip to Birkdale to observe the effect.
We were amongst the last folks to leave Birkdale before it shut down.
We brought our masks with us in case we decided to get out of the car.
Masks protect others from us.
Masks mean we care about the welfare of others.
Birkdale was bustling.
Very few bustlers wore masks.
Back to normal even in the contaminated air
Back to normal amidst the warnings.
Back to normal apparently
Still surrounded by the abnormal.
What we ignore, will go away.
Everybody friendly as can be
Back to normal hospitality.
We put on our masks and walked to the ice cream shop.
The ice cream shop had been our last stop before the shut down.
The shop was packed. We were the only two wearing masks.
Everybody was super friendly.
We maintained our distance.
We were encouraged to come closer.
We stayed back....we cared
When we got to the counter
A very friendly scooper asked us what we wanted
What I wanted to say was
"Don't you care about me".
The scooper was handsome
Barefaced and friendly.
We bought two chocolate dipped cones.
We said we were glad to be back
Our masks said we were concerned
He said "we ain't goin' nowhere...we're back"
Friendly, Hospitable

Old school Healthy
Not caring for us in the new way
We need to care for each other.
The Ghost had left the town.

Bangers and Mash at Galway Hooker

I was leaving my doctor's office and feeling pretty good. My blood test numbers were safely in bounds. The only concern was about my heart, some test had detected the beginnings of an aneurism near my aorta.

Then I heard a groan in the distance. I didn't check it out. If a person is gonna groan probably the best place for the groan to escape is in the doctor's office. I couldn't help wondering about my next groan and hoping that it would never come. Not today, anyways.

Lynn met me in the waiting room. We had plans for the afternoon. We didn't schedule any groaning. I decided to wait a little until I told her about the aorta bulletin.

We were going out for dinner, something that we have rarely done in the past seven months. We have dinner every night of course, it's the going out part that has disintegrated.

I'm a very lucky man. I enjoy my quarantine. I love my house. My wife is a fascinatrix who keeps me guessing and invigorates every discussion. A couple of nights ago we had a discussion about who knew more about John Agar which led to several hours of hilarious pillow talk before we fell asleep. We've never gotten along better. I have come to the understanding that all men make mistakes and that married men find out about their mistakes sooner than single men I learn new lessons every day.. We are no longer feeling like refugees from the North. We are becoming assimilated. We have established our own schedule and I love it.

Love, love, love.
It's the time of the season.
It's the time of our lives.

We got here somehow and we're enjoying it today and looking forward to tomorrow.

We even have a favorite bar. It's an Irish pub called Galway Hooker. It has the "coldest beer in Lake Normand". Not only is the beer cold, it's inexpensive. Pabst Blue Ribbon drafts are only two bucks a glass. We even have favorites on the menu. I order bangers and mash with a side of rice. Lynn gets Philly cheese steak. We sit outside on a rickety

table that needs to be propped up with coasters, which our masked server promptly props. The beer comes immediately. The food arrives while we still have unfinished PBR in our mugs. I take a picture of my plate.

It's a bright blue October day The temperature is 74 degrees. The humidity is low. The beer IS cold. We order seconds as we finish off our meals. I'm 73 years old. I'm in love with my wife. I'm convinced by her deeds that she loves me. We own our Cadillac. We live within our means. Tomorrow promises to be even better than today. We earned it, God bless us.

So there we were counting our blessings and aware that we were keeping track and grateful. Lynn left to use the rest room. I sat by myself just listening to the sounds of the street, the city, the state. That's when I heard it...a massive global groan in the distance. The groan lasted for only a moment but it served a sober reminder of the suffering that surrounded us, the contamination that was again rearing its head and striking even as we prepared to get in our car and escape once again into our cocoon, our fortress of solitude and turn on the teevee.

Two Different Targets

We drive a Cadillac and I'm getting cataracts. The decision about cataract surgery is when not if. I decided to get one more pair of glasses and put the surgery off for a year. Since the glasses are gonna be a short term fix, I decided to get a pair with the fewest bells and whistles (no transition, non-progressive, polycarbonate etc.)

Looking for a quick fix, we took my prescription to Target. We picked out a pair of dark glasses with oval Harry Potter type frames. Lynn did most of the negotiating as my hearing is almost as bad as my vision but my vision is catching down fast.

With all of the details sorted out, all that remained for me to do was to have the salesperson fit the glasses to my face.

Lynn decided to step outside of the shop to get a free flu shot which also included a $5 coupon.

Let's pause here for a brief discussion of contrasting accents. My accent is very similar to accents from other cities on the Great Lakes. I come from Rochester which I pronounce Rahchester. Down heyah, in the stayit of North Cayolinah the folks tend to draw out vowel sounds. I love their accent but we transplants from the North are beginning to endanger it.

The sales person wore a name tag that said Bernadette. She was a young thang of about 55, thin, blonde and spectacled with half her face concealed by a modest mask. Her axsayint was a little extreme but quite attractive if barely comprehensible to me, specially comin' thru that mask.

We sat down across from one another. She took out this measuring device that looked kinda like a pair of heavy metal glasses and got ready to put it on my face to measure the distance between my eyes. As she prepared to do so she said somethin' which I could barely hear/understand through her mask, my deafness and our colliding accents.

I non-verbally asked her to repeat herself by rising my eyebrows, turning my palms up, widening my eyes and shrugging my shoulders.

Bernadette got the message. She repeated herself.

"Do y'all have a problem with alkahall?"

I wondered why she was asking me such a profound and personal question.

I sat there speechless as she sprayed some sort of alcohol cleansing solution on the measuring device.

"I always have to ask that before we try these on after I spray 'em."

I replied " As a matter of fact, I quite enjoy alcohol."

Bernadette's eyes told me she was smiling under her mask so I went to the next gear.
"Although, a couple of years ago my wife was massaging my back with rubbing alcohol and I nearly broke my neck trying to lick it off."
Bernadette exploded in laughter.
Lynn walked back in.
Bernadette still laughing said to Lynn, "Oh, your husband is sooo funny. He's a regular Rodney Dangerfield."
"Oh yeah, said Lynn. He's quite the comedian."
Bernadette was still laughing when she checked us out at counter. Lynn was far less amused. I was once again caught in the middle.

The glasses would be ready in three weeks. We said so long to Bernadette.
Right outside the door was a girl in a lab coat with the job of encouraging folks to get flu shots and then giving them the shot herself. Her name tag said "Kitty". She looked like a nice kid so I decided to get my free flu shot. The Kitty kid did a great job. I hardly felt it.

Beautiful.

As we headed back to the Cadillac, Lynn told me what had occurred when she got her flu shot and I was alone with Bernadette. After getting the shot and before heading to straighten out whatever mess I was making, Lynn caught this transaction.

Kitty was doing her job. She asked a passerby if he wanted his flu shot. The passerby, was an older guy with a potbelly, baseball hat. Nuthin' wrong with any of that.

"Hell no. I wouldn't have you put that poison in my arm. It's guvment propaganda and you know it is. You know the facts. Look at 'em. Look at the facts. Ah'm sooprized y'aunt handing out those Covid shots. "

Kitty maintained her composure, " the facts I have come from doctors and medical science. I believe in medicine."

"Well you got the wrong facts and y'all should be ashamed." and the passerby passed by taking his storm clouds with him.

A few minutes later, I met the composed Kitty who gave me my shot.

Until Lynn told me the story, I didn't know how right Kitty was.

Genes and Covid

Lots of folks are concerned about getting their COVID shot. They are afraid that something worse than Covid will be the consequence of preventing Covid. This is known as the "cured from what we're suffering from but suffering from the cure" school of thought.

Yeah, this is bad but the future is worse.

Reminds me of a story.

Gene Phillips was suffering from a couple of things; public school and private parenting. The school had a couple of cures in mind. Gene was a spoiled child who had become an insufferable adolescent on his way to becoming a miserable adult.

Gene's father Gene Senior wasn't about to let that happen to his only son.

Matters came to a head one afternoon at the principal's office. Earlier that day, Gene had been caught urinating in the drinking fountain outside the girl's john.

I was asked to attend the meeting in case a witness was needed. Gene was known as "disruptive" and his father was known as a nutcase.

The principal, Dr. Fowler greeted the two Genes. He informed them that due to young Gene's erratic behavior and negligible scholastic performance, today would be his last day as a member of Ward Stokes high school. Formal expulsion procedures would occur directly after the meeting.

There was, however, one other possible alternative. Like many progressive schools, Stokes had come to the realization that traditional learning was not for everyone and had organized an alternative "school within a school" for students who had demonstrated an inability to cope with the factory styled learning still prevalent in the main school. Dr. Fowler informed the two Genes of the existence of A School which was the name given to the non traditional school within the school. For many of the Stokes staff the A had come to stand for Asshole but within the school and community the A was supposed to stand for Alternative.

Upon learning about A School, the elder Gene was irritated. His son didn't belong in something like that.

Fowler assured Father Gene that A school had been a life changer for many students who had got their act together at the finishing line and gone on to Community College.

Big Gene didn't want Community college for Little Gene. Big Gene who had gone to Madison and flunked out of Community College himself was of the opinion that Madison was for losers. Big Gene didn't want Little Gene to enter a high school program for druggers and soul brothers that would prepare him to qualify for a college program that would help him to become an even bigger loser than the losers he was hanging around with in high school while "studying" for a non-existent job in Forensic science

"No", said Gene the Father, there would be no A School for his boy.

Dr. Fowler tried one more time to help Gene Senior see the light when the father wanted to know "what the acceptance rate of Ivy League colleges was for the normal high school as compared to this so called alternative high school?" Gene Senior wanted to do everything in his power to get Gene into a top rated school straight out of high school, where Gene would grow up and settle down among the Bushes and the Clintons.

This insane conversation went on for a while until finally Fowler summed things up, "You have one decision to make...a turning point if you will. Gene can either choose the alternative school or this is his last five minutes in public education...we're tossing him outta here. There will be no college whatsoever as students who get expelled from school for public urination are not generally offered encouraging acceptance packages.

Finally...finally....the light seemed to go on.

Father Gene turned to son Gene who had been alternatively spacing out or nodding in agreement with his father's ideas. "Son, we're gonna sign you up for A school."

Gene said "Okkayy."

And that was that.

Gene got the vaccine.

The rest of his life was up to him but he wasn't gonna die that day or for the next few months.

Quarantine Cut

Right off the top of my head, I want to discuss a matter that is near and dear to me; my hair. Although bald is now in fashion, I consider myself blessed that a renewable follicular resource exists atop my dome.

However, escalation always proceeds revolution and my hair always begins to revolt moments after its peak performance, much like the cover curse of Sports Illustrated. Several days ago, I wrote an article about how happy my hair was making me. That happiness was not shared by my wife Lynn who viewed my elation with the raised eyebrow of spousal suspicion.

My hair was getting more and more complicated by the moment until it had finally escalated to a point of out and out insubordination which Lynn correctly identified as sloppy disrespect.

Lynn prefers a simple, clean approach to style so she made it clear to me that I needed her help. I suggested that perhaps an insane asylum haircut wouldn't help my staggering self-image. She assured me while unpacking her formidable electric shaver that we could proceed with finesse rather than with desperate, absurd hilarity.

Next thing I knew, I heard the familiar buzzing and felt the pull. I watched great clumps of my hair fall to the kitchen floor. Looking at the clumps, I wondered how much hair would be needed to fill a pillow, it seems like such a waste to see the severed follicles down for the count and submissively awaiting the sweep of the broom.

The buzzing continued, full of purpose, precision and pleasantry. I kept waiting for the "Oops" moment with the ensuing shrieks of laughter. The forlorn clumps on the floor continued to grow until Lynn backed away, rubbed the top of my head and said "finished".

It didn't take long. She helped me off the chair, making sure that I didn't step into my shorn gray and drag the stuff all over the goddamned house.

"You look so much better", she assured me with that wonderful happy wife, happy life lilt to her voice. Let's face it, we all like to admire our work when we're finished with it, especially if it turned out the way we imagined it would, which in my case is a rarity.

She sent me into the bathroom to grab a look in the mirror.

I followed her direction. When I glanced in the mirror, it was obvious that the rebellion was over. Although I've seen the effects of surrender many times before, I'm still surprised at the clarity of the outcome.

There I was again with a haircut very similar to the cut I had in my high school graduation picture, very similar to the one I got from Henry the Barber when I sat in his chair for the first time in the days before style

It took a startling moment in the glass but I had to admit that Lynn did a good job.

She suggested that we describe the new style as a "quarantine" rather than "insane asylum".

Good and accurate suggestion.

Later that day, we heard on the radio that Springsteen had also experienced a quarantine cut at the hands of his wife, so I figured I was in good company.

I jumped into the shower. When I emerged, my hair was ready to go without complicated combing, brushing, drying and or glooping. How simple life can be.

How clean.

How quarantine.

Approximate Fashion

Now that many Baby Boomers are retired, the younger folks are working out of their homes and so many others are in the hospital or in quarantine, there's not much need to dress up anymore. As a result many of us have experienced our bodies going through yet another pivotal passage. We're no longer off the rack and we ain't interested in tailors. Our clothes begin to fit approximately.

The zenith of approximate clothing is sweat pants. Stylistically we tend to top them off either with sweat shirts or unbuttoned flannel shirts with a tee shirt underneath and showing. Pajamas also serve a function as home office day time wear but not as formal as sweatpants.

I have five pair of sweat pants. I have two formal pair...they are both black and pretty much fit the height of my legs. I'll even throw on black socks on occasion if we're headed to Birkdale, especially when Birkdale isn't a ghost town.

I have two informal sweat pants...one is gray and the other is blue. They are not as form fitting as the formal. They work well with white socks and either my gray or black slip on shoes. They are great for walks around Vermillion.

When I want to relax but not go as far as pajamas, I have a gray pair sweats that is truly approximate. I have to wear suspenders to keep them up but that's a hassle so I only wear them indoors so when they begin to slip down the only one that can be irritated by the slippage is Lynn whose clothes fit much better.

In most cases I, like Dizzy Dean, resemble an unmade bed.

The last time I tried to wear a suit coat and slacks, I resembled the profile of the gill man in the *Creature Walks Among Us* and experienced similar alienation. Ten pounds of potatoes in a five pound sack trying to maintain enough equilibrium to avoid falling on the hard concrete.

With my current quarantine cut, the resemblance is even more striking/ pathetic.

When summer comes around I slip into the second best level of approximation, baggy shorts. I have five pair of those two of which are sane enough to wear into the pool when the heat and sun become too much.

Perhaps this momentum is part of a revolution or maybe it's just a development. We're all evolving while our styles are dissolving. William Bendix as Chester A. Riley might have described the whole thing to his neighbor Jim Gillis as a revolting development as they observed this trend while wearing their trousers held up with belts and their Cunningham aircraft work shirts. Ralph Kramden would be far more outraged than Ed Norton who was waay ahead of his time when it came to attire.

At this moment I am enjoying some creative informality with my blue, gray and black flannel shirt over a light blue tee shirt, white sox and no shoes. Let's face it, nobody is going to text me to ask me what I'm wearing.

I even have a formal sweatshirt...blue with Full Filler written in gold.

Mary made it for me and I love it when I need to get dressed up. It goes beautifully with my black sweats and socks. On such formal occasions, I seldom wear a hat even though most of them have a fitting buckle in the back.

Free Guy and Hogan Hat Marine

The movies are back and Birkdale is breathing again. Today we saw *Free Guy*.

It's nice to have fun at the movies. *Free Guy* is a lot of fun. It'll take your mind off the struggles of the day. Ryan Reynolds is a very likable actor playing a very likable character.

The movie is set within a video game.

I don't play enough video games to comment on the validity of the action but it sure is engaging, authentic and at times surprisingly rigorous.

I understood most of the cultural allusions and linguistic idioms within the film but I'm sure that my millennial daughter Mary will grok them significantly more than I. We thought of her throughout the film which only increased our enjoyment.

Definitely go see it.

It also helps to know what an NPC is. In case you don't know (which I didn't) an NPC is a Non Playable Character. The Reynolds character is an NPC who is involved in an ongoing Ground Hog Day experience until one day he realizes that there may be more to life than being a bystander watching the action like the rest of the NPCs who are part of his everyday existence and don't seem at all bothered by the endless repetition that has become their reason for being.

They don't really matter in the game. They are scenery. They love it. They know their role and keep their mouths shut.

Upon emerging from the theater, we encountered the real world of Birkdale. Birkdale is a village that is an array of upscale shops, bars and restaurants, an extended village green. People coming and going, shopping, eating, drinking, grooving, winking, nodding hello and getting on with their business. It looks a lot like the scene of a video game especially on a bright August day after departing from a dark theater.

I began to realize that all of the people that passed me or were passed by me were NPCs in my particular game of life. They are/were just part of the scenery. I realized as well that I was an NPC in their worlds. Nobody was gonna remember me just as I would not remember them. Most of them probably didn't even see me much less gather the fact that I was forgetting them as soon as I saw them, rebooting the scene with every glance.

Lynn decided to shop at one of the stores. I sat on a bench, enjoying the tranquility of NPC passivity amidst sedated quarantine. Then I noticed an older gentleman walking more slowly as he approached me and I got the feeling this man thought that I was in his game. Sure enough, he stopped right in front of me and said, "hello." I realized that the two of us were now in the same game at least for a minute and this gentlemen might make it into my memory thus becoming a character in a subsequent story which of course, this is.

He was nattily dressed. Trendy Skechers, blue ankle length Underarmour sweat pants and designer long sleeve shirt topped of by a Hogan style golf hat. The gentleman was short and straight with vivid blue eyes.

I nodded hello.

He sat down next to me on the bench.

"The women are in the pie shop, all they want to do is eat."

I assumed that he was talking about his wife and maybe his grand daughters. Birkdale has a custom pie shop not far from where I was sitting.

Once again I nodded.

Then the guy started on Biden. What a chicken shit.   How all these Afghanistan refugees were gonna invade our country, none of them vaccinated, spreading Covid while China was going to take over Afghanistan through Formosa and that we would be at war in a couple of weeks with our enemies killing us with our own weapons. And Putin's ready to invade the Ukraine. He said he was a veteran of the Korean War. He was an ex-Marine and we didn't need to stand for this Taliban horse shit. If our President had "any balls" it would be whole different story.

I just nodded to indicate that I heard him.

At that point, he was collected by a gray haired woman who I assume was his wife and two dark haired women who were related to him somehow. They were carrying a couple boxes of pie.

I don't think the three women even noticed me I was more NPC to them than they were to me as they were entering an odd game that I was barely playing with the Marine.

They went off down the street, heading toward the theater where we had just watched *Free Guy*.

Free Guy was a lot more fun.

Between Covid and Putin

Well, with all the troubles in our world and the various snakes devouring each other in their exercises of mutually assured destruction at least the boys of summer will be with us again soon as the sounds of spring training lighten our hearts, It's BASEBALL, Ray. Baseball marks the passage of time. Listen for the sound of gloves and bats...oh wait a minute....no spring training....season openers already delayed.....impasse between players and bosses. Why don't the players just give in and play ball? I'll tell ya why. The owners are pulling a Putin and trying to overwhelm a weaker opponent. The snakes are devouring each other but one snake is bigger than the other and swallows quicker. The surviving snake won't have much of a body but one hell of a head.

I know...what do we care? It's a battle between millionaires and billionaires right? Sorta, accept the billionaires (the owners) are trying to squeeze the life out of the players union and that needs to be addressed as all bullies need to be stood up to always and forever. Where's Marvin Miller when we need him? Miller started the player's union and led the ballplayers out of the pre-free agent days when the owners had total control of the game until the Supreme Court and Curt Flood stepped in and said "wait a minute". Since the departure of Miller, the union has been appeasing the owners for too long now just as we looked the other way while Putin was building up his strength and using our money to threaten us while we all pretended to be buddy-buddy. Most of us common folk don't talk in terms of millions, we worry about hundreds and thousands when it comes to money. The battle between millionaires and billionaires is like the battle between thousandaires and milionaires. It's a mismatch. We hear about the huge salaries going to the stars which in reality are not that much in comparison to the profits of the owners. Alex Rodriguez is the poster boy for salary bashing yet A ROD is no more representative of the overall situation than all cover boys and girls are representative of their own constituency. We all kinda hate A Rod for earning a pro-rated 550 million in the length of his entire 22 year career whereas the Dodger organization made 850 million in profit just last year. Of the thousands of men who played or are playing baseball, none have come close to AROD in their earnings. AROD is the only AROD and he didn't earn his money waiting for the bus, although he like his peers have waited for many a bus, many a train and many an airplane.

Support labor. The Putins of MLB need a setback in their momentum before they destroy the game forever and the money goes elsewhere along with the loyalty of the fans.

75, 000 fans showed up for a soccer game in Charlotte

We don't need another cold war. We need a cold conflict. We need resistance.

Here's the deal.....

For whatever psychological or technological reasons, professional baseball at the major league level is a highly profitable business. The players and their high level of rarified competition create the product and in some ways are the product. The owners get a much greater percentage of the ever growing profit than do the ball players. I know it's hard to sympathize with the players who must now worry about the lifelong financial prosperity of their great, great grandchildren while trying to put a round bat on a round ball that's curving and dropping while approaching at an average speed of 94mph over the course of 160 games at least half which are played away from home

It's no walk in the park to get to the majors. It takes a rare combination of skills and luck. Very rare. Some folks say that the ballplayers don't love the game...they just love the money that they make while playing the game. I find it impossible to believe that anyone who didn't love the game could make it to the highest level of that game and survive the grind that is the major league schedule with fans measuring your every move with continually evolving statistics, streaming television of virtually every game and social media scrutiny. The players are playing the game they love **for** money not **because** of it. They are professionals. They're no longer little boys with dreams. They are competitive human beings comparing the reality of their dream to the dreams of other equally skilled humans through continual conflict and resolution while the Putincrats get most of the dough and use elaborate tax evasion schemes to insure that the money doesn't trickle down to the low folks on the totem pole, we fans. Here's a perfect example among hundreds of available examples. When the Red Sox salary dumped Mookie Betts and David Price, they saved millions of dollars and they dropped the price of admission to Fenway. I don't think so. They saved a lot of money for sure but raised the price of admission and the cost of beer, although I must admit that beer tends to taste a little better at a ballpark.

Those players whose dreams are most accurate and whose skills are most fully exercised get paid the most money. I have no problem with that. Yet even they aren't getting their rightful share of the preposterous profits.

So what about the guys whose dreams have been far less accurate. The major league minimum is $550 grr a year. To we thousandaires, that's a lot of scratch but in the world of billionaires that's hardly an itch. The guys at the lower end are barely making subsistence pay while taking endless train and bus rides from one minor league town to another. The new union proposals are trying to improve their lot which the owners are resisting.

Finally, in the game itself, it's more likely that a player who had a bad year will have a better year the next year than that a player who had a great year will have an even greater year his following year. Why is that? It's because the guy who had the bad year has spent more time trying to address and change the problems that led to the bad year in the first place. The guy who had the good year is less likely to make any changes to his game which results in a certain degree of atrophy until he notices that atrophy and begins to make the changes he needs to regain his grip on his own dream.

If we want our individual dreams to be full filled we've got to continually fill fuller.

We've got to stand up for what we believe. We've got to fight bullies wherever they appear. The work never ends. Learn to love it.

Moa Less

If you go deep into the Hobbitland now known as New Zealand and listen carefully, you might hear the haunted/hunted echo of a deep resonant howl from the wildly elongated trachea of a spirit Big Bird being torn to pieces by a ghostly gigantic eagle. The eagle, top predator of his pre-historic realm, has once again slammed into a retreating Big Bird with the force of a block of concrete falling from an eight story building if they had either concrete blocks or eight story buildings back then which of course they didn't which was good for everybody.

This was going on for 60 million years and everybody loved it except for on occasion the gigantic big bird who had about as much fun as a turkey on Thanksgiving but hey, in the natural order, that's the way things go.

So everything was going fine until Gambar and eventually his Turleylurian pals showed up in 1300 BC (giveor take a few hundred or thousand years) and decided that Big Birds were good to eat. Over the course of the next 400 years, Gambar and the gang along with the giant eagles drove the Big Birds, known as the moa, into extinction.

Turned out that this was a bad idea for the giant eagles as well. Every once in awhile they would attack a Lurian for shits and giggles. That giant eagle would become part of Lurian legend until it too became prey of the pissed off Glams (the most fervent followers of Gambar), as some of the Lurians categorized themselves. It wasn't the Glams that drove the giant eagles into extinction. The absence of Big Bird for dinner led directly to the starvation and extinction of the giant Eagle.

Of course this ongoing extinction of birds is continuing today and is a forever endeavor which is apparently fine with everybody until it isn't when it might be too late.

But that's not gonna happen tomorrow, so let's love the one we're with while we can because we too are aware of the catastrophic non-linearity of potential. Some of us will realize our potential and thrive until catastrophe sets us back a spell. Others of us, will never come close to reaching our potential which will disappear into the heavens and be gathered by angels for re-distribution/de-extinction.

The moa were truly wingless birds and were fifteen times the size of the eagles that ripped them apart and twice the size of the Polynesians who feasted upon them. Size isn't everything but it worked well for Wilt Chamberlain.

So as the moa attempted to achieve the record for quickest extinction it faced a stiff challenge from another, much smaller bird....the beloved DoDo bird.

The race between moa and dodo to extinction is too close to call so scientists have come up with a remedy. Fossil remains have provided geneticists with enough DNA to begin the formalization of the process that might enable de-extinction of both birds and the one who comes back first will be declared the loser in the race to extinction derby.

The way we are proceeding currently, investigations into the probability of de-extinction are liable to increase in the next thirty years when currently unborn children will be watching re-runs of Sesame Street. They will see Big Bird and his DoDo friends in teevee time and then go to the zoo and see them in real time along with the giant eagles three cages over and passenger pigeons on a pond located on a fake tundra.

Patterns Exist For Close Readers

Patterns exist within our written language which benefit those who are aware of those benefits. This benefit is enjoyed by skillful readers who know where to locate what is needed quickly. Unskilled "readers" can spend hours looking at a selection of written material and not absorb as much as a skilled reader can absorb in a few minutes. That's why a guy like Karl Benedict can "study" all night long and still fail the same test on the same material that a guy like Crazy Joe can study for fifteen minutes and get a C on the test after a full night of drinking uptown rather than pounding his head against the desk in the dorm which is a great place to sleep but a horrible place to study. Joe understood a bit more about composition than did Karl.

Every effective composition is a collection of ideas called paragraphs which are composed of an arrangement of complete thoughts known as sentences. Collection and arrangement are concepts of equal importance. A composition is more than an idea, therefore, several ideas have to be collected and the thoughts within those ideas have to be put in some kind of order with the most important sentence usually the first sentence. Order is important. Joe for example did not call Karl "an ugly, fat, balding moron who has no idea how to read" until after he had returned from his carousing which he felt he could afford because he understood differentiation better than Karl.

Differentiations exist not only within the arrangement of thoughts but also within the the collection of ideas. Some ideas are more significant than others. A guy like Karl looked at every thought, idea and word as of equal significance which leads him to a kind of "reading" that is characterized not only by insidious sub-vocalization but also an attempt to memorize rather than to visualize. Karl would read a few words, test his memory, find it lacking, go back and re-read, test his memory again find it lacking again, re-read etc. Unable to visualize anything other than Joe being uptown having a ball while he was stuck alone in this hellhole on an over the hump Wednesday. Karl could not grasp the essential and as a consequence overdosed on incomprehensible triviality which he mistakenly confused as essential.

Ideas as well as thoughts can be categorized as essential, important, or nice to know. All students are expected to establish a grasp of the essentials. The essentials are the main ideas of any composition which means they are delineated by the most evident thoughts. If a student can exhibit a mastery of the essentials, that student will pass most evaluations. Karl, unable to differentiate, was on his way to another E while Joe, having discerned the essentials with a quick, cursory glance had a good shot at a bonus B because Joe knew how to use compositional patterns while time saving on his quest for another cold draft or ten; a C with an outside shot at a B was good enough for Joe. He wasn't going to bother with the nice to know, trivial crap that A students learn to accompany the essential AND the important. A students also learn to emphasize the essential while using the important and the trivial merely to accentuate their emphasis upon the essential.

Built in emphasis exists at the beginning of every idea so that's the best place to look for essential thought placement. Joe knew that the first ideas were the ideas that represented "takeoff ". Usually in takeoff mode, the "pilot" or "writer" announces the destination of the flight. After the takeoff, subsequent ideas represent the flight and the landing which are composed of complete thoughts. Takeoffs and landings take less time than the "flight" itself but are equally critical, therefore, thoughts at the beginning of each idea are usually categorized as essential whereas anecdotes, and illustrations no matter how cleverly embroidered, are merely nice to know.

Anecdotes are minor forms of emphasis and need to be regarded as such. Karl's comprehension, driven by compulsion to grasp trivial illustration resembles the reaction of an actor who after being booed for his rendering of Hamlet's soliloquy responds to an outraged audience by screaming back, " Hey, I didn't write this crap, I'm only reading it." Karl in reading this very composition might be afraid of a "trick" question and therefore attempt to memorize the entire soliloquy and then be amazed when that is not on the test, failing to grasp the purpose of the test itself to say nothing of the source material from which the test is derived.

All the ideas and thoughts, properly ordered should achieve a clear purpose which should be underscored in the conclusion which is the proverbial "telling your audience what you told them" even at the risk of redundancy. The last paragraph should some up all of the essentials which are seemingly an accumulation of the essential and enable the "student" simply by grasping the conclusion, to pass the test and maybe avoid being tossed out of college even though they are the oldest, fattest and baldest person in the entire class. Karl preoccupied by distraction never gets to the end of the composition so he misses the point of the entire effort yet feels justified in having spent six hours "studying".

Karl would never reach this last paragraph.

Patterns exist within our written language which benefit those who are aware of the patterns. Every effective composition is a collection of ideas called paragraphs which are composed of an arrangement of complete thought known as sentences. Differentiations exist not only within the arrangement of thoughts but also within the collection of ideas. Ideas as well as thoughts can be categorizes as essential, important or nice to know. Built in emphasis exists at the beginning of every idea so that's the best place to look for essential thought placement. Anecdotes are forms of emphasis and need to be regarded as such. All the ideas and thoughts, properly ordered should achieve a clear purpose which should be underscored in the conclusion which is the proverbial "telling your audience what you told them" even at the risk of redundancy.

Brother Tony reading closely

LUUUUUKE

For thousands of Baby Boomers in upstate New York, our favorite ball player of all time is Luke Easter. Luke came along at the end of the Negro Leagues and didn't get started in the majors until he was a 34 year old rookie with the Cleveland Indians. Luke played three seasons with the Indians and hit some of the most propelled home runs in the history of the game.

According to wikipedia, during his rookie season, he hit the longest home run in the history of Cleveland's Municipal Stadium, a 477-foot blast over the auxiliary scoreboard in right field. The only other player to match that feat was Mickey Mantle, who did it in 1960. Finally, during his twilight days with the Bisons, he became the first player to hit a home run over the center field scoreboard at Buffalo's home park, Offermann Stadium, doing so twice in 1957. On June 14 he cleared the board, and newspapers reported the blow at an estimated 500 feet. On August 15, he hit the board near the top, and it went through a space between the board and a sign just above it.

When told by a fan one time that the fan had seen Easter's longest home run in person, Easter is reported to have replied, "If it came down, it wasn't my longest."

Even though he was still a fearsome slugger, Luke was sent to the Buffalo Bisons in the International League where he began his legendary career in upstate New York. He tore the league apart, especially our home team the Rochester Red Wings. His number was retired in Buffalo when he was acquired by the Red Wings.

Luke stood six foot four and weighed 240 plus pounds. When he arrived in Rochester, he immediately became a fan favorite. Red Wing stadium would fill with cries of LUUUUUKKE whenever Luke came to bat.

This was a particularly fertile time for baseball in my family. My aunt Helen became a huge fan and started to regularly attend Red Wing games. She would transport her son, my cousin Davey and my brother Deke to Norton St to watch the Red Wings. Davey and Deke were the perfect ages to begin their fandom. Deke was 9 and Davey was 7. LUUUKE quickly became their idol. Nobody knew how old Luke was at the time but he was in his mid-40's at least.

Whenever they would come home from a ball game they would begin narrating the latest exploits of LUUUUKE.

"LUUUKE hit a foul ball that went out of the parking lot."
"LUUUUKE made a great play at first base."
"A fight started on the field but when LUUUUKE arrived, everybody ran for cover."
"LUUUUKE hit two home runs today."

LUUUUUKE......LUUUKE......LUUUKE.

My aunt Helen was also caught up in Lukemania. She was the first adult I knew who was crazy about the Red Wings and she could and did tell some amazing LUUUUKE stories. LUUUKE eventually retired as a player but stayed on to coach the Red Wings for a couple of seasons. Every time LUUUUKE walked on the field even as a coach, the crowd went wild.

Never before or ever since has there been such unified pandemonia at the ball park. His number 36 will never be worn by another Red Wing.

For some Rochesterian kids, Luke was one of the first black men that they had ever seen and he was beloved by all.

After leaving baseball, Luke returned to Cleveland. He went to work for Aircraft Alliance eventually becoming chief steward. On March 29, 1979, Luke was shot and killed while transporting $5,000 in union funds. Luke refused to turn over the armed robbers who approached him. They shot him twice.

Despite the tragic end to his life, Luke Easter still lives in the hearts of Rochester baseball fans.

My cousin Davey passed away several years ago. When I think of Davey, I think of Luke. I loved them both in different ways.

12 Steps

Rizz saw his daughters every other weekend. Laureen was seven years old and Lily was three. Laureen had been very helpful teaching Lily how to walk. Lily made great strides in her independence. She didn't mind when Laureen stopped holding her hand. Lily understood. Lily followed her sister everywhere but walked alone.

With his life unmanageable, Rizz had been twelve stepping it for a year, one day at a time. He liked to visit Ellison Park. In the middle of the park a series of twelve ancient steps led into the woods. Virgil always paused powerlessly at the steps and pondered their meaning figuratively as well as literally. The steps were very, very old but solid and reliable as Gibraltar.

One chilly day in early April, Rizz took the girls to the park. He showed them the steps. The girls were used to vengeful vigilance during their weekdays. They loved the park, especially Laureen.

"Laureen, honey, take Lily's hand; walk up those steps and take a look into the woods. I'll keep my eye on you from down here."

Laureen didn't need to be asked twice. She took Lily's hand. The two of them began the climb.

The climb up was slow going at first. These were BIG steps for little Lily. The pair paused after every step. Rizz applauded each advance.

After climbing step nine, Laureen grew impatient and bounded up the remaining three steps alone. She looked down at Virgil and Lily.

She disappeared into the woods.

Virgil watched her go, confident that she was adventurous and curious rather than negligent or non-caring.

By the time Lily reached the top step, Laureen had her view of the woods. She came out of the woods. She hugged Lily.

They looked down at their Dad for re-assurance. Rizz nodded parumapumpum.The girls waved.Laureen took Lily's hand.She had taken a look into the woods.She felt brave.She felt like a big sister.

They took the first two steps down together.

Laureen let go of Lily's hand.

Lily could handle it. Rizz was confident and proud.

Five minutes later, they were all on the ground looking up at the steps and less fearful of the woods.

Measuring the Pursuit of Perfection

A common bromide in the ever expanding universe of statistics states that,"if it can be measured it can be improved".

The classic example of this statement is the four minute mile. Roger Bannister proved that it was humanly possible to run a mile in less than four minutes. Since that day, hundreds of runners have improved upon and shattered that barrier. One of those runners was a Rochesterian named Dick Buerkle. Dick and I were members of the same parish and graduated from the same elementary school. Dick was one year my junior. We all were familiar with the sight of Dick running around our neighborhood but none of us suspected his greatness. He didn't start running track until he was a senior at Aquinas Institute but once he started in 1965, he kept running and running. He attended Villanova University.

On January 13, 1978, at the CYO Invitational held at the Cole Field he broke the indoor mile world record with a time of 3:54.93 He allegedly ate nine Oreos and two peanut butter jelly sandwiches only a few hours before the race. Dick is the only graduate from St. James parish to appear on the cover of Sports Illustrated. Inspired by Dick's achievements and training regimen, I took up running although most of my efforts were confined to training. I didn't run much but I ate a lot of Oreos and peanut butter sandwiches. Perhaps if I had added jelly to my sandwiches, I might have achieved more than I did in the Delta Kappa Greek games. My best effort was a farcical, sarcastic and sad two mile race during which I smoked a couple of cigarettes but yet finished the race within a half mile of the runner who finished second last in the event. Nobody even bothered to clock my effort but if they had, it could definitely be improved.

On the other hand "if it can be measured it can be improved" does not take into account the possibility of perfection. Perfection is possible, most notably in bowling and in golf. In bowling, a perfect game means twelve consecutive strikes in one game stretching from the first frame to the final frame. It is impossible to roll fewer balls and successfully complete the game. I've witnessed one perfect game in my life. When that kid rolled his twelfth strike, the crowd erupted. In this case, the crowd was me, my daughter and the proprieterix of the lanes. I had alerted the proprieterix after I noticed that the kid on the next alley had nine strikes in a row. The only people in the establishment at the time were the bowler and we three viewers. The kid buried the last three strikes with no emotion. We cheered. The kid was very calm. He immediately began his next game and threw yet another strike before he finally spared the second frame of the game at which point Mary and I left the building.

Although the lanes were empty, this did not diminish his achievement in my eyes. I had seen perfection! I'm still writing about it today.

In golf, a hole in one is perfect. It is impossible to put a ball into the hole in less than one swing unless you just carry the ball to the hole and drop it in without swinging which defeats the purpose of golf. Although I am not a good golfer, I have somehow struck a hole in one on two separate occasions. I was alone on the course on both occasions.

Here's what a hole in one feels like. You take your swing and the swing feels good. Part of the reason why the swing feels good is because you have kept your head down during the swing. When you look up maintaining your backswing, you see that the ball is heading towards the hole. You think, 'Damn that IS good'. You watch as the ball lands on the green, rolls a bit and then disappears from view. You approach the hole and with every step closer you wonder "Jeezuz, did that go in the cup". You get to the green. The ball is still invisible. You walk to the hole and there it is. It went in. You look around and realize there will be no crowd roar because there is no one else in sight. You pick up the ball. You put it in your bag. Gonna keep that ball.

Perfect.

A beautiful thing to see, even if you are the only one seeing it.

This perfection always takes me back to another feat of perfection that I witnessed with ten other guys, including Wild Bill, in my college days at Geneseo. We were always trying to come up with competitive measures for non-competitive situations. One of my dearest friends a guy named Dugie had set records in almost all events including the fastest apple ever eaten. There were problems with that record as it was difficult to establish a standard sized apple so any record would always have an asterisk. According to legend one attempt had gone terribly wrong, John McCormick attempted the record and took such a huge opening bite of a gigantic apple that his jaws locked and the apple had to be cut from his mouth while he was turning purple in suffocation.

We were living in the splendor of a brand new dormitory which featured a spacious lounge. The whole dorm would gather at the television three times a week in the lounge to watch "The Monkees"once and "Batman" twice but aside from those shows the lounge was usually empty even on Sundays before the NFL became a religion. Hard to imagine now that we've got teevees in every room that during the mid sixties there was only ONE teevee in an entire, state of the art dormitory. No computers nor teevee, we had to think of other ways to waste our time.

One of the "draws' to the lounge beside the teeveewas the Coke machine . I started wondering what would be the fastest time that a person could drop his dime into the machine, grab the subsequent Coke bottle, drink it and put it in the deposit case next to the machine. I set the standard as 12 seconds.

Eventually, word got around that a standard was in place so challengers began to emerge. John McCauchey thought that he would give it a shot. John was big guy whose distinguishing Coke idiosynchracy was that he liked to buy a bag of peanuts and pour that into his Coke before drinking. Someone speculated that if John skipped the peanuts part, he could match the standard no problem.

John decided to go for it.

He gathered a few people and went for the record. He dropped the dime, he got a pretty good drop time, around three seconds. He did well on his opening as well. Very quick but deliberate. A bad opening would destroy the effort.It had to be smooth. John grabbed the Coke bottle and chugged it. The time from the drop of the dime to the placing in the case was 7 seconds. Everybody cheered and praised the big man for his accomplishment. He had smashed the barrier.

Since it had been measured, it could be improved.

Later that week, Dugie got wind of the standard and thought he could challenge it. Most people thought that was impossible but few people at the time knew Dugie as well as I did. Dugie contended that it all depended on the drop and open time. If the dispenser produced a slow drop or the opening of the bottle was off the mark, then yes 7 seconds was impossible to beat but he thought he had a chance.

The moment came and it drew an audience of about a dozen guys with nothing better to do.

I can remember the attempt even more clearly than I can remember my holes in one.

Dugie, who was as big as McCauchey but whose avoirdupois was more magnificent stood before the machine in the posture of a gunfighter in a showdown at high noon. At the signal Dugie dropped the dime into the slot with an extra push and got a perfect drop. Less than second passed before the Coke appeared at the bottom of the machine. In one fluid, uninterrupted, upward motion, Dugie got a perfect 'open' and continuing that motion brought the bottle to his lips and hurled the contents down his throat before slamming the bottle into the case. Elapsed time between 3 or 4 seconds with the official time being recorded as 3 seconds.

The activity had been measured but was never improved. I don't think anyone even tried. For the rest of my time in that dorm, guys with nuthin' better to do would gather at the machine and tell the story of the perfect drop, the perfect opening and the unbeatable time.

3 freakin' seconds.

Perfection

Dugie went on to establish many more "records" at Geneseo before joining a band and splitting for the coast where he once beat Carlos Santana in a game of ping pong.

Memories of Mr Grin

It's too hot to walk before 7 PM. Our afternoon walks have become evening strolls. All of our walks tend to feature some sort of verbal essay questioning that we use as subject matter. The hotter the day, the more short answer the questioning becomes. Three days ago, in the relatively cool of the evening, the question appeared safely open ended.

Our responses wouldn't be held against us by each other.

Lynn asked "why do guys nickname other guys."

Good question.

Deserving of deliberation.

I thought about the nicknames that I had been given over the years and considered an examination of the reason for those nicknames as a response to Lynn.

Nah, that get's away from the question.

The real question is why did I give nicknames, particularly when I was a teacher? Why did I give more nicknames to boys than I did to girls.

I began to talk about Mr. Grin.

Mr. Grin was a nickname I gave to an eighth grade student named Rob.

Rob was a quiet, well mannered guy. He was neither jock nor genius; neither smart feller nor fart smeller He didn't want to be noticed so he went for invisibility which might have worked if it wasn't for his grin which I noticed due to its frequency and mystery. Mona Lisa has a smile....wouldn't call her expression a grin...likewise I wouldn't call Rob's grin a smile. A grin always has a trace of a sneer. Rob had that trace but tried to mask it with silent invisibility.

Invisible students tended to attract my attention.

I took it upon myself to remove the trace of sneer and increase Rob's visibility in the classroom. In a private conversation, I told him that I liked his grin. Hence forward I would call him Mr. Grin if I called on him and I when I did call on him with that nickname, I wanted it to be a sign of connection...an indication from the teacher that Rob wasn't an invisible boy...that Rob had a personality and opinion to go along with that personality. I wanted Rob to know that what he was doing was important, I wanted him to succeed and I would never quit on him.

I didn't put it like that. I just said "I like your grin Rob. I think Mr. Grin would make a great nickname.

Rob grinned in response.

I took that as a yes.

Very often over the course of the next year, I would ask an open ended question to the class. When nobody answered, I would ask "Mr. Grin what do you think?"

Rob would respond with his enigmatic grin while the class looked at him. I would then give my opinion of the question that I had asked and credit the opinion to Rob.

"Ah," I would nod. "Mr. Grin assures us that the Yankees will win."

Rob would grin in response to my response to his response which everybody took as agreement.

Rob was no longer invisible in class.

Rob became popular.

Often, I would ask a particular question of a particular person and that person might respond "I don't know. Ask Mr. Grin."

I would ask Rob. Rob would grin. I would interpret Rob's grin and shape his response to be the response to the question that I had asked. You can't fool Mr. Grin. Mr. Grin knows all the answers. The semi-sneer disappeared from Rob's grin; replaced with semi-confidence.

Close to confident .... not quite ....yet a hundred miles from arrogance or judgement.

All of a sudden, during my evening stroll with Lynn, Mr. Grin had appeared gently on my mind.

Mr. Grin had an older sister. I didn't realize that Doreen was Rob's sister. Eventually, Doreen got her degree in education and became a valued colleague of mine. That's when I found out about her kinship with Rob.

I retired. Doreen continued to teach. We became friends on Facebook.

Yesterday, a couple days after Rob's visit to my memory, I checked out Facebook and read this post from my ex-colleague and current FB friend Doreen,

"Can't let today go by without mentioning my brother's Heavenly birthday. Rob, my little brother, would have been 60 today! He's been gone since 2013. Rob was a warrior with external and internal wars. But he was MY brother. He was the baby who I first took care of! He was the one who would crawl into my bed as a scared little 6 year old at night. He would fix my brakes in exchange for chocolate chip cookies. He would stand up for me and my girls when times were hard. He would call me first when he needed help changing a dirty diaper. He would take my girls waterskiing and was proud of them when they got up and mastered the skill he loved. He would take me skiing when he knew I needed a diversion. All of these memories are mine. No one can take them from me. He was MY little brother. Good, bad, indifferent. Happy Birthday in Heaven Rob. I miss the old you more than anyone knows!"

I don't know what battles Rob fought along the way but I'm pretty sure that some sneers were involved as well as some well and ill placed defiance.

Yet, he had the power to come into my mind on a sunset walk. He was grinning at me even though now his grin was truly invisible. I grinned back. I let him know I was gonna write this story.

So I don't know why men give nicknames so readily to other men but I do know why I gave Mr. Grin his nickname. I liked him and I thought he liked the nickname.

Simple rilly.

A Christmas in Texas

I'm coming down from yet another moment of Christmas magic. Let me tell ya about it before I forget.

As you know, under the influence, memory and recommendation of Thornton Krell, wherever he is, I have become a long time fan of *Have Gun Will Travel*. Any fan of Have Gun Will Travel is also a fan of Richard Boone that paladin, that Knight without armor in a savage land.

Always of particular fascination are the episodes of HGWT that were directed by the man himself....Richard Boone, the terror of Stanford, the washed up hunter of the Last Dinosaur.

Today I was watching MeTv which specializes in showing teevee shows from the fifties. Actually, I was dipping into my taped collection of 22 episodes of HGWT. I have to be in a particularly nostalgic mood to dip into the collection as I have so much recorded sports and murder shows to watch on teevee and so little time between sleeping and reading.

I randomly fired up an episode entitled approximately Save Room for Strangers. That isn't the real title but it's about as close as I can come as I accidentally (and sadly) erased the episode after viewing it . My intention was to recap the story while re-watching it so that I could render all of the details exactly but since the sad erasure, I'm gonna have to go with my memory.

Save Room for Strangers begins with Paladin wearing a heavy jacket and riding into a small town on a freezing evening. He ties his horse up next to a saloon. Even while outside the saloon, Paladin can hear the raucous, drunken behavior going on in the inside.

When Paladin enters the saloon, he trips over the body of a drunken man who has blacked out while blocking out the swinging doors of the saloon. The place is completely packed. Paladin stops for a moment to check out the drunk in his way and in that instant he is approached by a prostitute eager to do business with our hero. Paladin rejects the advance of the blonde floozie named

Annie. He heads to the bar where he refuses some rotgut whiskey from an ornery, unwelcoming barkeep. Paladin is looking for a room but the barkeep, a guy named Jake, informs Paladin that the place is full and there is no room particularly for a stranger. Paladin is immediately wary but first things first.....he needs something warm to eat. Jake informs Paladin that the kitchen is closed, the only thing available is some stew, which "ain't too good but at least it's hot."

Paladin looks for an empty table and heads for it but he's beaten to the table by a blotto bearded bum who decides to tap dance on the table in his bare feet while the patrons gather around him, encouraging his ribald behavior.

Finally Paladin located the only other available table at which sits an older gentleman wearing a battered top hat who has a bunch of wrapped Christmas presents on the table. Paladin asks the old guy who the presents are for and Mr. Top Hat tells Paladin that the gifts are for himself....he buys and wraps them every year to give to his kids who have grown up and abandoned him just in case they miraculously show up which they haven't done in decades.

Paladin begins to slurp his stew when a young cowboy enters the bar and gets shoved into Paladin who spills the stew all over himself and Mr. Top Hat. Paladin reflexively goes for his gun but the young cowboy is quick to apologize.

Here's the first shock.

The cowboy is played by Duane Eddy. Duane Eddy is/was a guitarist who was at the time of the making of the episode going through a teen idol phase of his career. I had seen Duane live at a rock and roll show in Rochester in which I heard an electric guitar for the first time in my life, a sound that I'm sure changed my destiny. This was about the time that teen stars like Frankie Avalon, Fabian and Rick Nelson were getting movie and teevee gigs too bring in "the kids"

I was kid then now I'm more like the guy in the Top Hat except for the fact that my kids have stuck with me and I with them. Last week I was in Boston having Thanksgiving with one of my daughters and five of our grandchildren and the day after that I went with another daughter to pick out her Christmas tree.

My daughter is into vinyl these days and as we decorated her tree we went through her album collection which is mainly the remains of my album collection. We pulled out the first album that I ever bought which happened to be "The Twangs the Thang" by Duane Eddy on the Jamie label.

Oh where was I

Oh yeah

Duane needs a room but the bartender/owner tells Duane that he has no room.

Duane goes out into the freezing night and Paladin follows him. In Duane's stage is Duane's wife who is beginning to go into labor. Paladin recognizes the situation and assures Duane that he will get a room in the frontier dive.

He goes up to the owner and explains the situation to the unsympathetic barkeep who asks Paladin who the hell he thinks he is coming into this town and pushing everybody around. At this point Paladin takes out his famous business card....HAVE GUN WILL TRAVEL. The barkeep is intimidated and says he's got a stockroom in the back. Paladin, Duane and the very pregnant wife head for the stockroom which is tiny and filthy but the best anybody can do in this situation at that moment.

Once he gets the young couple into the stockroom, Paladin returns to the bar where he is again propositioned by yet another prostitute. He tries to locate the town doctor but is informed that the doctor is the guy blacked out by the door who once a year on Christmas comes into town, gets totally wasted and can not be revived no matter how much coffee gets poured into or onto him. He's a blackout blockout. Paladin wonders if there had never ever been a previous Christmas when the doctor was needed so desperately. The bartender said, "Yeah, Just once and the guy died."

Paladin fires his gun in the bar which gets everybody's attention. The reason Paladin had to use his gun was because another guy was trying to draw on him and Paladin had to shoot the cigar out of his mouth before throwing the guy over the blacked out doctor, through the swinging doors and into the freezing street.

Having gained the attention of the out of control joint, Paladin begins to describe the labor going on in the stockroom while asking for help and quoting from the bible. Another drunken bum walks up to Paladin and accuses Paladin of having his "halo on too tight" which almost causes another gunfight until the bum backs down.

Paladin now appeals to the womanhood of the two other prostitutes in the bar, including Annie who is getting her slender neck licked by yet another intoxicated townie.

The appeal works and Annie decides to go into the stockroom and help out even though "she doesn't know what she's doing."

Paladin returns to the bar and fetches some whiskey and the hot water. He comes into the stockroom where Duane's wife is into serious labor so he pours three or four shots direct from the bottle down her throat assuring her that this elixir will "help her with the pain."
He leaves the room for a minute and when he comes back in, the baby has been safely delivered. Annie is agog with wonder. She helped. Duane's wife is radiant. She promised him a son.

The riot outside the stockroom has quieted down. The town folk are embarrassed about their behavior. They take up a collection. The barkeep comes into the stock room and gives the money "not much" to the mother while Duane beams with pride while holding his newborn son delivered on Christmas Eve during the first dawning moments of Christmas Eve.

The Top Hat guy joyfully hands over his packages to the mother and the guy who questioned the tightness of Paladin's halo barges in with a huge Christmas tree.

Paladin smiles his odd smile. He heads for the door. On the way out, he takes one last look at the"doctor". The doctor has a blanket around him which

Paladin removes and puts over his own broad shoulders as he gets on his horse, apparently leaving his expensive jacket behind in exchange for the blanket. Paladin heads out of town when he sees a sign which identifies the town....Bethlehem Texas. The gunfighter nods in approval and rides away at which point I hit delete and started worrying that if I didn't run downstairs and start writing this recap, I wouldn't remember it.

Obviously I got to the keyboard in the saint nick of time.We opened our presents.Merry Christmas to all.

Fishing on the Genesee

We in Rochester live near the northern end of the Genesee River which starts in Pennsylvania and flows NORTHWARD until it reaches Lake Ontario at the port of Charlotte. The river cuts through the middle of downtown under the Susan B Anthony-Frederick Douglas Bridge. Rochester is proud of Anthony and Douglas In the winter it freezes over. Once upon a time, a deer got stranded on the ice and had to be euthanized even as hundreds of onlookers on the bridge watched in fascinated horror.

The lower portion of the Genesee River in Rochester offers some of the most exciting fishing in New York State. Each year the New York State Department of Environmental Conservation (NYSDEC) stocks over 155,000 chinook salmon, 22,100 rainbow trout (steelhead) and 22,000 coho salmon into Lake Ontario near the mouth of the Genesee River. Downstream of the lower falls near the Driving Park Avenue bridge, the fish population changes seasonally to reflect that of Lake Ontario, including species such as brown trout, rainbow trout (steelhead), coho salmon and chinook salmon.

The upper falls in Rochester attracts most of the attention. Only well informed fishermen are even aware of the fabulous angling near Driving Park. I spent 65 years in Rochester and only visited the salmon hatchery once. I've crossed the other bridges hundreds of times.

One man who knew about the hatchery was Arthur Shawcross. Arthur loved fishing and was a regular presence. Lots of people knew Art. Art was a big man...six feet tall and over 300 pounds.

Arthur was also a serial killer. His first known murders were in 1972 when he killed a young boy and a girl in his hometown of Watertown, New York. Under the terms of a plea bargain, Shawcross was allowed to plead guilty to one charge of manslaughter, for which he served 14 years of a 25-year sentence. He killed most of his victims in 1988 and 1989 after being paroled early which led to criticism of the justice system. A food service worker, Shawcross trawled the streets of Rochester in his girlfriend's 1984 sky blue

Dodge Omni (later using her blue-grey 1987 Chevy Celebrity), looking for sex workers to kill.

In the years of his murderous spree, Rochester was gripped in fear. Perhaps we would have been even more fearful had the victims not been sex workers.

When not fishing or mudering and cannibalizing, Shawcross was a familiar sight in the Monroe Avenue area of downtown Rochester. According to my son who went to school in the area, the bus driver pointed Shawcross out one day and warned the children to "stay away from that guy."

His killing spree finally ended in 1988

If you were a son or daughter of a WW2 veteran who lived in Rochester, it's likley that your first beer was a Genesee. The beer was brewed downtown.

My late friend Kevin's veteran father got a job at the Genesse Brewery right after the war. Kevin's father died early. When Kevin was working his way through colllege, he got hired by the brewery to load trucks in the night shift.

It was hard, manual labor but the pay was good. The fringe benefit was beer. Beer, fresh, cold Genny flowed through the water taps at all times. Kevin told me about this fringe benefit and invited me to share in it. If we were still drinking when the bars closed down, we could come up to the brewery and drink and bullshit to our hearts content.

One pre-determined night, when Al and I were still thirsty and the bars were closing, I took Kev up on his offer.

We arrived at the brewery at the designated spot. Kev met us and led us to the beer faucets. He gave us each a cup. My God, it was true. Endless, ice cold Genny beer.

We were drinking for about a half hour when the first off duty cops arrived.

Oh shit, this was too good to be true.We were gonna get busted.

The cops were younger guys, not much older than Al and me. They took off their hats. They walked over to the beer tap. They poured themselves some beer. Pretty soon there were twelve people gathered in the brewery....8 cops and four non-cops.

They wanted to know how we got there and how we got in. I explained about the invitation from my friend and Kev was gonna give us a lift home.

They all knew Kev.

Everything was cool

The atmosphere was very relaxed. I listened to cops tell cop stories for a few hours while Kev finished his shift. I asked the cop if they knew my uncle George. Damned right, they knew him. He was already a legend. I asked about my cousin Tommy, they all knew him as well and said he was gonna become the legendary Sandman. After his shift, Kev gave us a lift home.

I heard about a lot of weird shit goin' on by the river that didn't make the newspaper.

Over the rest of that summer we became semi-regulars at the brewery. We were part of the gang.

Twenty years later dead bodies began to pile up on the Genesee.

I was no longer living in the city.

I tried to imagine what the off duty cops were talking about when they partook at the Brewery as the murders mounted and the city started wondering what the hell the cops were doing?

The River flows

It flows to the Lake

Wherever that River Flows

It's not for Heaven's sake.

Yup. The Genesee River flows upward into a lake but it's not just any lake. It's a Great Lake. It's so great that we put the word Lake before the name of the lake. Lake Ontario..Lake Erie both shared by New York state and Canada.

Look at a map of the United States. The Great Lakes are an immediately recognizable splash of blue.

My personal favorite lake is Canandaigua which is one of the Finger Lakes. Nobody calls Canandaigua Lake Lake Canandaigua. It's not Great enough. No river flows into Canandaigua.

If you look again at the same map, you won't even see the Finger Lakes.

The Genesee River slows down in the winter when it becomes ice bound. Creatures get stranded on the ice and die. Debris freezes on the banks.
Remember the deer?

When a pair of discarded jeans was discovered near the river on December 31, 1989, containing an ID card for a girl named Felicia Stephens, police began an aerial search of the surrounding area. The local authorities sent out a helicopter to do some aerial fishing. On January 2, 1990, the helicopter spotted what appeared to be a naked female body lying on the ice surface of the river by a bridge in the forest. The body was not Felicia Stephens but that of missing sex worker June Cicero. She had also been mutilated post-mortem, as well as sawn practically in half.

Even more importantly, the helicopter spotted a man standing on the bridge next to a small van. He appeared to be either masturbating or urinating. Fortunately for the authorities, Shawcross had, as speculated, returned to the scene of one of his crimes to relive the pleasure of the attack. He was caught with his dick in his hand.

Shawcross got in his car and sped away. The copter got the plate.

The Genesee River Killer was at last on the hook.

Rochester can be a dark and dangerous town even minus Shawcross and Bianchi.

Ovid on Snoring

by Ovid Warren Peets

To begin with, I spend more time thinking about sleeping than I spend time thinking about any other subject. Some people might call that process insomnia.I call it another skirmish in the war between the sexes.

Snoring is the battle line. The only person who doesn't snore is the person who's awake. I am that person, awake and listening to my wife snore. The secret is to be the second one to sleep.

My wife Julia doesn't think that she snores. I didn't think that I snored until my wife mentioned it to me. Over time, the mentions grew more frequent and less gentle. Eventually, the mentions turned into motions and the motions turned into pokes and jabs. Ya know what really sucks? Being fast asleep….getting jabbed into wakefulness and upon awakening hearing this: "Stop snoring Ovid, God damn it."

Apparently I start to snore when I'm first falling asleep so when rudely interrupted my defense usually goes like this: "How could I be snoring, I wasn't even asleep" Even as I'm saying this, I'm coming to the realization that I must have been asleep because the poke woke me up.

"Well, you must have been asleep because you're snoring your ass off. Stop the goddamned snoring!"

"Hey, I know the difference between being awake and being asleep. If I were asleep now, this would be a nightmare but because I'm awake, it's just a pain in the ass."

"Yeah, well the next time you snore and wake me up, you're going out to the couch." For some reason, the reward of sleeping comfortably on the couch seems like some kind of punishment that must be resisted. So I try to fall back asleep and realize that I can't sleep. Furthermore, I must really be not sleeping because nobody is telling me to stop snoring.

Meanwhile, in this embryonic, insomniatic state.....Julia falls asleep and starts to snore. Her snoring is a good sign because that means she's actually asleep and it is now safe for me to go to sleep and not have to worry about snoring.

So I go through my usual thinking about sleeping and trying to figure out how to bring it on. Most of those methods are unclear to me now because instead of trying to fall asleep, I'm currently trying to stay awake but here are a couple of techniques that I think I use.

1) I recite and re-recite the Presidents of the United States in chronological order and then in reverse order. Madison always surprises me with how quickly he shows up chronologically and Rutherford B. Hayes surprises me with how clearly he arrives at all.

2) I try to think of people who I know who couldn't possibly have been thinking of me during this day. Then I think of the people that I always think of and try to estimate how many times I thought about them during the day. I've been told that we have 8 or 80 or 800 billion brain cells. I can't remember what the figure is (8 billion or 800 billion...what's the diff?) That's plenty of room to think about people. I figure that go through about 8 separate conscious thoughts per second not including what's disappearing into my subconscious. I might for example of 8 thoughts of Julia in one second.

I'm talking about brain cells igniting in nano seconds. I would guess that I think of my Julia 200,000 times a day, the Beatles 2000, Bob Dylan 1000, our dog Ranger 1000,Krell 50, MCC 30, Haylen 20 all the way down to the guy who was sitting on the sidewalk in Charlotte a couple of days ago....playing his guitar real good for free. I thought of him maybe 5 times today and pretty soon he will be in the memory cemetery only to be exhumed for an eighth of a second some night when I'm unable to sleep and am absolutely sure that he has not thought of me which, I'm pretty sure is and always will be the case.

200,000 thoughts a day takes about 22 minutes.

If I'm still awake, I start thinking about stories that I might write. This very story is a story I was thinking about writing last night shortly after I finished thinking about a guy who punched me in the mouth thirty years ago. By this time, it's usually about four in the morning. I've changed my position in bed at least five times and I'm starting to forget about the pain in my shoulder and then I start to catch a dream and run with it and lose it and re-catch it until I reluctantly wake up in an empty bed. Julia always gets up, a couple hours before me almost exactly at the moment that I start to get control of whatever dream I'm enjoying at the moment.

Usually, I "sleep" for maybe four hours a night. I come to the kitchen as the daily routine begins and ask Julia how she slept last night. She says, "Fine. How bout you? You didn't snore."

Come to think of it she hasn't snored much lately either.

Big Jim

Is there anything more profound and tragic than the humbling of a giant?

I'm talking about Big Jim.

Big Jim was a startling physical specimen at six foot four and a rippling 235 pounds. Big Jim had reflexes of lightning and the peripheral vision of a giant eagle. Big Jim had the eye hand co-ordination of a Krupa or a Rich. Big Jim was a great teammate whose joy in the game was an inspiration for all.When Big Jim came to bat, the third base coach backed up ten yards to try to avoid the laser shots ripping down the line. Baseball is one thing, survival another. Big Jim progressed through the minor leagues like a meteor. Pitchers learned early that it was impossible to throw a fastball past Big Jim. Many tried and many failed.

Next came Uncle Charley, the curveball. Uncle Charley separates the men from the boys. Big Jim murdered the curve ball.

In the field, Jim had a rocket for a throwing arm and enough speed to cover more than his share of left field. Big Jim destroyed the league in his last stop in Triple A ball. Clearly he was in the wrong league. The outlook of the home team always became more brilliant when Big Jim advanced to the plate.

While still a kid, Jim made it to the show where he immediately started to go yard.

If the ball was over the plate, fastball, sinker, curve, knuckler, slider, slurve or change up, Big Jim was ready willing and able. It didn't take long to realize that you couldn't get the ball past Big Jim even on the edges of the corners. It didn't take much longer for the big leaguers to discover the low outside curveball.

The discovery was accidental but inevitable.
Big Jim, like everybody else, had trouble hitting a ball that was far from the plate.

Everybody else learned not to swing at such an offering.
Big Jim was neither everybody or anybody.
He swung every time and missed almost always.
When he did make contact, it was usually a dribbler down the first base line.
The word spread. Throw Big Jim low outside curveballs.
Next thing you know, Big Jim was out of the show.

He returned to the league that he had just terrorized but his reputation and weakness preceded him. Big Jim had seen his last fast ball. Pretty soon, his weakness became evident to all of the people in the ballpark. This added to the drama of every Big Jim at bat. Everybody, including Jim, realized that he was more than capable of homering with every at bat. Everybody including Big Jim also knew that a strike out on an outside curve was far more likely.

Yet he persisted....going up to the plate over and over again and whiffing on the same pitch. He knew the problem. Everybody knew it but Big Jim couldn't resist the temptation. Over and over the giant waved at three pitches and took the walk of shame back to the dugout. All of those miraculous aptitudes wasted. Jim still remained a fan favorite so it took awhile for the booing to start but when it did, it was as humiliating as was the vulnerability itself.

Quickly Jim transmogrified from Hall of Famer to Freak of Shamer.

The nightmare increased as Jim was demoted, demoted, demoted until mercifully, he was released. No more outside curves. No more shots at the show or shots in the show. All that remained was the image of the giant trudging slowly back to the dugout holding onto his bat and his sanity. The story is that Big Jim like most of us failures, never learned to adjust or learned only after the opportunity has passed us by.That one glaring weakness...that one terrible secret that weakens and discourages us all.

The good news is that Jim started playing softball. In softball there are no outside curves. Big Jim went on to be a legend in softball but let's face it...Softball isn't the show.Not everybody makes it to the Show...that's why the Show is the Show.

As all Red Wing fans might have guessed by now, Big Jim's last name was Fuller. If I could have filled Fuller with the discipline to lay off the curve, Jim might have found fulfillment in the show.Even when we make it to the show, we gotta keep learning because only the Babe Ruths own the show and the show eventually deep sixes everybody including the Babe.So we find our level and do the best we can. Our failures are mostly personal in nature so we hide our weaknesses well until we are destroyed by them or gain some control over them.

Wherever we are, we are in our show. It's up to us to adjust or squander the gifts we were given on whatever irresistible temptations each of us face. Resist and layoff.

Women Drivers on Election Day

My Uncle George was a huge hulk of a man who dressed like a bum except when he was on the job. When George put on his cop uniform, he became a different man, everything buttoned down to the max and gleamingly clean. George was not a handsome man but again that impression changed when he put on the blue. His unusual facial features blended together to form an expression of contained ferocity mixed with unquestionable authority.

He walked the most dangerous beat in Rochester. The bad guys knew him and they left him alone. George did not return that favor. He carried a nightstick and a gun. He rarely if ever had to use them. His weapons lent the perception that they had been used many, many times. He was a legendary figure in the Bulls Head area off West Main near both St. Mary's hospital and Nick Tahou's. This is the area that became infamous after the unsolved Alphabet Murders of 1970-73 when thee little girls; Carmen Colon, Wanda Walkowys and Michell Maenza were kidnapped and murdered. Serial killer Bianchi lived in Rochester at that time and is still considered a suspect.

Off duty, George was a boyhood friend of my father as well as the husband of my mother's sister Rose. George could swear and yell like no other person I had ever known. He was always pissed off about something, second guessing somebody or defending somebody else. Fortunately for me, George was on my side.

George reserved his greatest bile for what he called "goddamned women drivers". I rode in a car with George maybe a dozen times growing up and every ride was punctuated with an outburst or five against a woman driver. Women drivers were comparatively rare in the early fifties. Men drove, goddamn it. Men knew where they were going and they weren't distracted by every goddamn thing that they passed plus knew the goddamned rules of the road.

I never could figure out what the woman driver whom George was swearing at had done that was wrong other then being a woman at the wheel. He wasn't a road rager.He never confronted anyone but he cussed them out within the privacy of his own car.

So I grew up with the idea that women were shitty drivers. If my mother and father were both in the car, my father would drive...no question. My father got banged up one time and he couldn't walk much less drive for months. My mother did all the driving. She was a great driver (better tan my father) although I'm sure that every so often there was a George type guy in the rear view who did not appreciate the fact that she was behind the wheel and wondering what the hell was wrong with the husband.

Let's skip ahead thirty five years.

When Lynn and I first started dating, I did most of the driving. I owned a messy Honda Civic...she owned a spotless, hot Pontiac Trans-Am. As we began to ride together in one car, the owner of the car did the driving. After a very short time it became evident that I was (how should I say this) a much better passenger than Lynn. Lynn was a bit of an Uncle George when I took the wheel. We were pretty close in driving skills but I enjoyed shotgun more than she did, plus she had a better sense of direction.

Skip ahead another thirty years.

Lynn does almost all of the driving now. She's a much better driver than I. She takes care of the maintenance of the Cadillac. We have one car and we own it. The car is meticulous. I never drive when Lynn is in the car. The last time I drove with Lynn as a passenger we both almost had heart attacks just backing out of my garage and into the street. When we got to the street, I stopped the car and handed her the keys.

I have a five mile radius in which I drive. Anything else Lynn is at the wheel.

I trust her completely.

So all of this takes me up to yesterday and then to now...election day. Tomorrow we'll know....Donald or Joe.

Yesterday I was on my solo four mile round trip journey to get milk and bring it home. I started thinking about Uncle George. I began to notice the women drivers around me. There were more women driving than men. I passed several cars where the woman driver had a male passenger.

I wondered what George would be saying if he were alive.

Yesterday Melania Trump held a super spreader event in our town. I'm gonna have to double mask it for the next few months. As I was heading away from the event I got a peek at the traffic flow heading towards the event. Almost all of the cars were being driven by men wearing red MAGA hats,

I couldn't wait to get out of that flow.

My home is in a suburb. Our suburb, on the border of Charlotte which is becoming increasingly a CARY (concentrated area of relocated Yankees). I am a white college educated male 65 and over. Trump doesn't reach out to my group too often as he sees that he won't get very far. He is reaching out, begging really, for my wife's vote...a white suburban woman. Trump can't understand why suburban women don't like him.

If he asked Lynn, she would explain in terms that would embarrass Uncle George. It's women who are driving this election....most specifically white suburban women. We are located in a swing state. If the CARYs of North Carolina prevail, driven by the white suburban women who are very used to driving than Trump will be out on his ass. It could all be decided right here in the Tarheel state. Right here in Mecklenburg County.

I don't know if white women can jump but they sure as hell can drive. Today they will prove it once and for all. Their vote will, once again, drive this country.

We'll know more tomorrow.

You go girls.

Buds With The Champ

Just North of Times Square and a little further uptown from Tin Pan Alley is where I met the Manassass Mauler, Jack Dempsey. Before Joe Louis, before Rocky Marciano, before Muhammad Ali and just before Gene Tunney, Jack Dempsey was the greatest heavyweight champ of all time.

I was seven years old but I knew all about Jack Dempsey. How he had won the title from Jess Willard who had won the title from Jack Johnson. I knew about Jack's slugfest with Luis Firpo, the Wild Bull of the Pampas when Jack was knocked clear out of the ring, helped back in by sportswriters and kayoed Luis moments later. I was familiar with the famous painting that captured Jack flying out of the ring.

I also knew that Jack was suspected of having loaded gloves when he destroyed Willard.

I knew a lot about boxing as I regularly read boththe PoliceGazette and Ring magazine when we went to visit my grandparents, which we did every weekend in Holcomb, New York...twenty miles from Rochester. Furthermore, I had watched the second Tunney/ Dempsey fight at least a dozen times on the nickelodeon that was on display at the George Eastman museum. We went to the Museum a lot and every time that we went I would turn the crank on the fight.

Tunney had shockingly outpointed Jack in their first battle. In their second fight, Tunney in 1927 was well ahead on points when Dempsey floored the champ. Jack stood over Gene waiting for him to get up so he could regain the title. He didn't go to the neutral corner. The ref pushed Jack back into the neutral corner before he started his count which gave the fallen champ a few precious seconds to recover and clear his head, Tunney beat the count, famously referred to as "the Long Count." He retreated for the duration of the fight and won a decision.

Gene Tunney would retire soon after the fight and become the first undefeated heavyweight champ.

Jack Dempsey remained the more popular figure but his boxing days were coming to an end. Eventually, he bought his restaurant in Manhattan called Jack Dempsey's on the bottom floor of the Brill building which subsequently became the home of musicians and songwriters ranging from Doc Pomus and Neil Sedaka to Burt Bachrach and Carol King to Benny Goodman and Tommy Dorsey.

This was my first trip to New York City. I was with my Dad. He knew his way around Manhattan. He asked me if I wanted to meet Jack Dempsey. I was stunned and asked "do you know him" my father said that everybody knew Jack."

We entered the restaurant and there in a corner booth, all by himself was the great man himself. My father walked right up to Jack and said, "Hello Champ."

Jack, said, "Hiya pal."

I didn't realize that Jack said that to everybody who approached him in his restaurant. My father introduced me to Jack and told the champ about my "expertise" on the Long Count because of my multiple viewings of the fight on the hand cranked nickelodian at the Eastman House. Jack was interested in my opinion and further interested in the filming of the fight.

I talked and talked. Jack nodded and laughed and winked at his "buddy" my Dad. I could have but thankfully didn't mention the loaded gloves. He shook my hand. He gave me an autograph.

He said "get some cheesecake."

My Dad got an order of cheesecake. I liked cake but I couldn't feature a cake made out of cheese.Dad finished up the cake and we left the restaurant, waving to Jack on the way out.

"So long, pal" said the Champ "stop back anytime."

My God, I was a friend of Jack Dempsey.

The restaurant closed down in 1974 but you can still see it in a scene from the Godfather.

Sports memorabilia was not a big thing in 1955.

I don't know what happened to Jack's autograph.

I became an even bigger boxing fanatic.

Why wouldn't I?

Jack Dempsey was my friend.

65 years later, I'm living in North Carolina having raised six children. I have 10 grandchildren. The grand kids are getting old enough now to hear this story although none of them have any idea who Jack Dempsey is or was.

Or Benny Goodman Or Tommy Dorsey

Or Tin Pan Alley

Jack Dempsey's restaurant is now a CVS.

They know what THAT is.

Three

We had a big party scheduled at my apartment on December 7th, 1969. We were tired of living in uncertainty. On that night, there would be a nationally televised draft lottery for service in Viet Nam. The purpose of the lottery was to lessen uncertainty. We had plenty of beer and high hopes that our numbers, based on our birthdays, would not be called until much later and in the meantime, we would drink and smoke.

In 1966, we had to take a draft test. The test was apparently intended to unearth those who entered college simply to avoid the draft. The night before the draft test, our band played until 2 in the morning at the M and B. By the time we finished up and got our gear out of the place it was pretty close to 3. The draft test was scheduled for 8 and we were warned that you better not be late.

So, hungover, I made my bleary way to the testing site which of course was packed. The test had 150 items. I guessed at most of them as did almost everybody else. I saw a lot of coin flipping going on and many a glance at the second hand of the clock. Depending on where the second hand was on the clock, we chose the multiple choice answers to questions we had no idea about. First quadrant A, second quadrant B, etc and if you had it down to two possibilities flip the coin.

My mind was foggy from the night before and at some point, I just wanted to get the whole thing over as best I could, get back to the dorm and crash.

We never got the results but someone somewhere had them.

A couple years later on the night of the lottery, we gathered at my apartment to learn our fate. By this time, I had graduated from college and had embarked on my teaching career.

They drew the first birthday and it was Sept 14th. Everybody cheered because no one at the party had been born on that day. The second birthday was drawn and once again, everybody cheered. They drew the third number and everybody cheered again. Everybody but me. The birthdate was December 30....my birthday.

I yelled out "God damn it."

I stormed into my bedroom. The party was over for me. Everybody left me to my thoughts.

I was number 3.

I was a goner.....just a question of when not if.

Needless to say my concept of long term career planning went down the drain.

I continued as best I could with my teaching job but I didn't take any shit from anybody.

I let my hair grow. I started a beard. I broke the rules. I took many risks in terms of instruction. Hell, if this was my last shot at teaching, I was gonna proceed the way I thought was right, not based on the traditions of teaching that proceeded me, the one's that I resented as a student. I became a non-traditional teacher who went over great with the kids but not so much with the administration.

Every day, I figured would be my last day. Three of my colleagues were drafted. I told them that I'd be seeing them soon. I was listening to a lot of Dylan. He knew what was going on. Days turned into weeks, weeks into months, months into years. Every day filled with more anxiety and more non-tradition.

In 1971 I got tenure after battling both my union and my building administrators. Tenure was almost a joke because it didn't protect me from the draft.

Finally around 1973, I figured that I was safe from Viet Nam but I still had administrators after my scalp. Meanwhile my cousin Tom's number had come up and many of my friends had enlisted because they knew that their numbers would come up soon. I opposed the war but not our warriors. I wasn't gonna enlist. I had important work to do if they let me do it.

My number never came up. Don't know why. I was prime meat. Then I remembered the draft test. Was it possible that I had scored high enough to be exempt?

I had a roomie at the time who attempted to claim that he was conscientious objector, which I'm sure he was. He told his draft board that he had only been in one fight in his life and he "immediately got pummeled." His application was turned down and he got drafted. He immediately took off to Canada. I kept waiting for somebody to show up at my apartment looking for "Bob" and finding me instead.

Nobody ever showed up.

I continued with my teaching career and somewhere along the line, my non-traditional ideas had become accepted and were now being used by other teachers around me as I moved on to even more non-traditional practices which ended up being imitated and accepted. I had seen a lot of bad teaching in my student life and I was determined not to do what they had done.

I was pretty fearless when it came to innovation.

I've never been able to figure out how I escaped.

I was talking to my cousin Tom about this subject a few months ago after he declared with great irony that the draft lottery was the only time he ever won anything...that "win" was being drafted.

I told him that the only reason I could think that I wasn't drafted was because I had done so well on the draft test which really made no sense to me based on my condition while taking the test.

Tom figured it out.

He figured that I didn't do so well on the test. He speculated that I had got such a low mark on the test that I was deemed too stupid to even be drafted. Hell, that might be true.

I was too stupid to fight in Viet Nam but smart enough to teach.

I believed that for awhile until I checked out the standards for exemption on the test. There were 150 items on the test and if you got 70 or more correct you earned a temporary exemption and if you got 80 or more correct that exemption became more than temporary.

It's all a memory now.
My friends made it back from Nam.
Bob has returned from Canada thanks to amnesty.
Still somewhere in the back of my mind, I am always number 3.
And the future continues to be uncertain.
Perhaps this is why God created Xanax.

Pink Elephants

The Disney company is applying some restrictions to several beloved cartoons including Dumbo and Peter Pan for insensitive racial portrayals. In Dumbo the problem comes with the singing crows and their leader Jim Crow, originally intended as a tribute to "blackface" entertainers still popular in 1941 when Dumbo was released.

As a child I had a more Catholic series of questions about Dumbo.

I was encouraged by my teachers to ask questions. Every once in awhile I'd innocently ask a startling question.

I was in first grade with Sister Denise, a kindly Sister of Mercy who had been my kindergarten teacher and who has presented me with my first degree; a prestigious MRB which stood for Master of the Rhythm Band.

I had recently seen the movie *Dumbo* and I had a couple of questions that were bothering me, particularly as I was learning more and more about sin in my catechism and wanted to avoid it at all costs. During religion class I raised my hand, explained that I had just seen Dumbo. I described the scene where *Dumbo* accidentally gets drunk and envisions pink elephants on parade.

"Sister, is drinking a sin and if it is, is it mortal or venial?"

Sisters of Mercy is an order that originated in Ireland so I'm sure now that Sister Denise had her experiences with drunken Irishmen.

Sister Denise tried to explain that it could range anywhere from a near occasion of sin to a venial to a mortal sin based upon subsequent behaviors. I understood but wasn't happy with the shading. I was a black or white, right or wrong kinda kid at the time.

"Sister, do you really see pink elephants when you drink too much?"

Sister Denise said that she didn't know from personal experience but that every person is different.

"Sister is it possible to see the pink elephants without committing a sin?"

Sister Denise said in the case of Dumbo, the drinking episode had been accidental so she didn't believe that Dumbo had sinned although other characters in the movie had sinned at different times by being unkind to Dumbo.

"Sister, what if you don't want to sin but you want to see the pink elephants on parade?"

Sister Denise said I shouldn't worry about that because I had a wonderful imagination.

I said "thank you Sister."

I was done with my questioning for that day.

I was afraid to say that I wanted to see the pink elephants as I came to the conclusion that if you wanted to see the pink elephants and set upon drinking for that purpose it was more likely a mortal sin than a venial sin.

I wondered about the pink elephants and sin for a long time, through communion and confirmation and graduation from St. James grammar school, through high school and college through my career, through my first marriage, through raising a family, through fifteen minutes of fame, through trauma, through fracture, through cancer.To some extent, after decades of vigorous experimentation I'm still wondering.

I've survived many visions but never pink elephants on parade.

Pretty sure they don't exist.

Flying Turtles? Maybe.

Check The Glyphic's On My Carapace

Lynn and I have located a great walk. It's a pond. Three times around the pond is a mile. We take this walk very frequently. When we have visitors, we take them for this walk. We call the place Turtle Pond because it is full of turtles. We've grown to recognize a few of them, one in particular. The last time we saw him, I tried to get into his head a little bit.

I'm a reptile for Christ sake. Do I look like an amphibian to you. Do I?

I got news for ya, I don't do metamorphosis. I am what I am. I'm not larva or any of that shit. I never become a tadpole.

Oh, I get it. You figure that because I don't look like a goddamned snake and crawl around on my belly that I can't be a reptile. I don't crawl. I walk around on my goddamned legs. I come with my own shell. I'm not some kind of newt who slimes around without a shell until all of a sudden a shell grows on my freakin' back. No way, I've got the shell from the first time I hit the land which is where I was born. The shell grows with me and tells the story of my life in glyphics on the carapace.

You hear me, I'm born on the land not in the effing water and I come out of an egg...an egg with a shell not that jelly ass larva crap that frogs slime heir way out of.And yeah, even though I spend a lot of time underwater, I'm not a goddamned fish. I can get around on land.

I must admit though. I am a little different from my reptile pals. They say I hibernated too long or picked out the wrong place for sunning and that's why my shell is all fucked up with the flaps and shit. I covered myself with too much mud trying to cool of on a day too hot for basking as long as I did because I was too vain to slide back into the pond with all the rest of 'em. Bullfrogshit.

One thing they don't know or they knew and forgot is that birds started out as reptiles so at one point one of our ancestors got the idea that it might be cool to fly around. When they got that idea, they decided to start growing wings. This process began with shell flaps and a million years later, they used their wings to get the hell out of the water except for some of em who still take an occasional dip. Believe me, it ain't easy to grow wings. Ya get a lotta shit from jealous assholes.

"Oh look at you," they say, "too good for the goddamned pond are ya. Tryin' to get the hell outta here?" Others just ignore me and pretend that I don't exist when they surface near me, they just turn around and dive back into the pond.

I can't help my heritage.

We were the ones who started the whole wing thing and truth be told, I am getting sick of this goddamned pond and I would like to fly. I know, it's impossible but you gotta start somewhere. I've already passed my flaps on to a couple of my babies and they'll pass them on to a couple of their sand then all of a sudden in the blink of a million goddamned years another one of us will emerge from the water and fly away.

Happy Jack

You ask me if I'm a turtle. You bet your sweet ass I am. Pass it on to your pal, McCallum.

Nearly A Miracle At Mildred's Barn

The woman who lives across the street from us told Lynn about an opportunity. The woman across the street is called Ko-Ko.

Ko-Ko had a friend who had lost her mind. Ko-Ko's friend who had gone cuckoo made the mistake of going nuts on QVC. As her insanity deepened, her purchases of junk from QVC increased. The proportion was direct.

Direct teevee.

Ko-Ko's insane friend was named Mildred. Nobody knew how nuts Mildred was.

She kept her condition well-hidden. Nobody knew how much crap she had packratted in the secluded country residence which she had inherited long ago from her wealthy parents. She kept her purchases as well hidden as her psychoses. All part of the same package.

One day, Mildred cracked. Kind strangers came to take her away. Ko-Ko was amongst the strangers. Mildred was going to need long-term care. Long term care requires long term bread. Going over the records, kind strangers discovered Mildred's country residence.

The kind strangers took a drive into the country. The kind strangers unlocked the door to Mildred's fortress of solitude. The kind strangers found thousands of unopened boxes. Most of them from QVC.The kind strangers realized that if they auctioned off these boxes, they might be able to come up with enough money to provide Mildred with the kind of long term care that she needed.

Mildred would be saved by the boxes that had led her to ruin.Before they could be auctioned ,however, the boxes had to be opened, priced and organized. The kind strangers who opened the boxes would have the first shot at buying the contents of the boxes the day before the auction of the boxes went public. Ko-Ko told Lynn about Mildred, the boxes and the auction.

Lynn agreed to help with the opening, pricing and cataloging of the boxes that Mildred bought from QVC while Mildred was losing her mind.

Lynn went over to Mildred's house.

Ko-Ko and five other women were in the process of discovering the contents of Mildred's broken dreams. Those fantasies were wrapped in boxes.

Unopened.

Lynn joined in the service. The women would open a box; look for the invoice inside the box; remove the object from the box; guesstimate a fair price for the contents of the box; organize the contents on various tables located within and throughout the barn; put the empty boxes in a big pile outside the barn and stash the contents of some of the boxes in a secret room in the main house.

The stashed items would be part of a closed sale that would occur the day before the other items went on sale.

If you stashed the item, you had first dibs on that item when the special pre-sale began. If you stashed it and could meet the price on the item, the item would be yours.

You knew that the price was fair. You were the one who had determined the price in the first place.

How reasonable can you get?

Not all of the items for sale were from QVC.

Not all of the boxes had never been opened.

I learned all of this from Lynn when she came home from her first day at Mildred's barn.Lynn said it reminded her a lot of Christmas. She also said that after one full day of opening, pricing and organizing, it had become obvious that they would need at least three more full days before they could finish After three days, they would be ready to set a date for the sale.and they would need a couple more people.

Lynn wanted to know if I wanted to help out.

I said, "I gotta see this".

Lynn asked Ko-Ko if I could join the team.

Ko-Ko said that Mildred needed all the help that she could get.

So Lynn and I jumped into the Sonata and headed for the country.

It's not a long drive from the suburbs to the country.

Within fifteen minutes we were pulling into the driveway of Mildred's country home. The barn door was open and most of the dreams had gotten out.

Ko-Ko and her compatriots were already hard at work as we approached. For an old fart like me, there's something fairly formidable about a group of six or seven middle aged women standing outside a barn each of them armed with box cutters. Ko-Ko greeted us warmly. She pointed over to a bunch of boxes that had just been hauled from the barn. Ko-Ko asked Lynn if she knew what to do.

Lynn knew what to do.

Ko-Ko handed her a box-cutter.

They try to keep me away from sharp objects so as Lynn headed to the sealed boxes from QVC, I headed towards a bunch of boxes that were unsealed and may or may not have been purchased from QVC.

The very first box I looked at came from a place called Projansky's. The box was circular. I opened the box and was astonished to see what was inside.....

A leopard skin pill-box hat.

I was under the impression that all the packages in Mildred's barn were up for grabs.

Wrong.

As soon as I discovered the leopard skin pill box hat, I called for Ko-Ko. "Ko-Ko look what I found in the first box that I opened. I've been looking for a leopard skin pill box hat for years" I knew that Ko-Ko was a religious woman. "Ko-Ko, I'd call finding this hat under these circumstances nothing short of a miracle"

Ko-Ko looked at me with a degree of sadness.

"Ice, that box had been previously opened. I don't know why it got put back with the unopened boxes. Out of all the boxes in this section of the barn, opened or unopened, this is the only box that has been not only claimed but reserved for another person. This box should not have been in that area. This is the only item that can not be claimed by you because it is the only item that has already been claimed by somebody else even before Mildred snapped. That somebody, if I remember, is named Julia. She's a cute little thing, barely five foot tall. She's involved in local theater. She was dressed like Scarlett O'Hara. She wanted the hat for wardrobe purposes in case they end up doing a production about the early sixties. She dropped by with her husband last night and picked it up."

Dayum.

What's the opposite of a miracle?

I'm very proud of my daughter Mary.

One of the things I really love about her is how willing she has been to accept the music of my generation. She's been listening to Dylan since she was a child.

By the time she was sweet little sixteen she's already seen Bobby in concert three times. And we listen to him in the car all the time. One of the CD's we've been listening to for quite awhile is *Blonde on Blonde*. Mary always liked the song *Leopard Skin Pill Box Hat*.

Knowing what I know about fashion trends, I'd been telling her for years that she would look great in a leopard skin pillbox hat.

Of course, she didn't know what the hell I was talking about other than it was part of a song on an album. Mary is involved in art. Her art teacher is also a big Dylan fan.

I'd been telling her for the whole semester that if we ever got a leopard skin pill box hat and she wore it to art class that her teacher would immediately say; " Hey I see you've got a brand new leopard skin pill box hat and I wonder how your head must feel under something like that"

Since I at the age of sixty, aside from photographs of Jackie Kennedy, had only seen one leopard skin pillbox hat in my entire life I sure as hell didn't think she would be seeing one much less wearing one to her art class so the whole image was just a father/daughter thing that we always share a laugh about.

Mary, Lynn and I saw Dylan at RIT live again about three months ago. The night before we went to see him, I researched the playlist from his most recent concert before the one we were going to attend.

Mary was with me when I did the research.

Before we started our research, we agreed that it would be great if he opened the show with Leopard Skin Pill-Box Hat.

Sure enough, of all of the hundreds of songs in Dylan's catalogue he had opened the show before the show we were attending with Leopard Skin Pill Box Hat,

We laughed.

We weren't surprised.

We were happy.

She told me that she considered Dylan and McCartney to be friends of hers.

I asked her why she liked Dylan.

She said "He knows what's going on".

The next night at the concert Dylan opened up with Maggie's Farm and didn't play Leopard Skin Pill Box Hat, even though a woman in the audience right up near the stage was wearing an actual leopard skin pill box hat and kept yelling "Leopard Skin" while the guy with her who was wearing a Lone Ranger type mask kept yelling out "Play meatball".

We noticed Dylan noticing the couple. He nodded at them but ignored their request. Pretty sure Dylan doesn't do requests. Ya never know what Dylan's gonna do.

We weren't disappointed.

I kept the ticket.

.

Bound And Gagged Guy

Unless you are a very secure person, don't come bound and gagged to a straight bar on Halloween night. Of course, you may not have a choice in the matter.

I saw a bound and gagged guy at such a bar many Octobers past.

At the time we arrived, the bound and gagged guy was sitting in his chair on the bandstand next to the keyboard player. Like most at the bar, I didn't notice him at first. He was just sitting there. Tommy Tron pointed him out to me "look at the bound and gagged guy on the stage."

Aside from the binding and the gagging, the bound and gagged guy looked remarkably normal. His clothes fit well and he was neatly dressed. Aside from being bound and gagged and wearing gloves, his normalcy bordered upon invisibility. In the midst of the raging party, bound and gagged guy, was a calming influence, sorta.

"How long has he been there", I asked Tommy Tron.

"He's been here since I got here but he's only been THERE for about ten minutes. Before that he was in the middle of the dance floor for quite awhile. At one point all the women in the place were dancing around him like native girls preparing a testosteronic sacrifice in the name of Andromedan revenge while the guys remained at their tables pounding and watching."

The dancing was furious that night and got even more so when Wild Bill walked in. I pointed out the bound and gagged guy to Bill. He nodded in approval. We began to drink and dance and bullshit and forgot about the bound and gagged guy.

When we looked up, he was no longer on the bandstand. Somebody had moved him atop the bar where he sat taking everything in and being taken in by anyone paying attention. The gag prevented him from drinking unlike the crowd clamoring around him.

The next time I saw him, about fifteen minutes later, he was seated in the middle of the mens room between the sinks, urinals and stalls. Everybody including me said, "hello, how's it goin" to the bound and gagged guy as we walked by to make our deposits. He nodded his head up and down, indicating that things were goin' great.

I went back to the table to join Tommy and Bill and Caroline and Lynn and Bruce and Kay. We drank and danced some more. Caroline disappeared for a moment and came back with the news that the bound and gagged guy was now sitting in the ladies room where once again he was the hub of an all female dancing, flashing wheel.

The night was nearing last call. The band announced last song as they carried bound and gagged guy onto the stage where he got a sitting ovation.

The band finished. The bar closed. Halloween was over. One of the best evah. We climbed into the taxi and pulled away. The last thing we saw as we departed was the bound and gagged guy....sitting in his chair in front of the bar. His hair was blowing in the wind.

God knows where his night went from there. The rest of us can only imagine..

Married 8 Times

Between us, my wife and I have been married eight times, six of those times to each other. We celebrated the most recent of our marriages yesterday on Veteran's Day. Let me 'splain.

Lynn and I had been married once before our first marriage together. Both of the folks that we had married prior had been married prior so in a way, Lynn and I have never been in a first marriage. We keep marrying people who are on their second marriage.

We met at a dance for Parents Without Partners one enchanted evening, July 11th 1987 to be exact. To us, that day will always be known as 7/11 a night when the pizza pie moon in the sky smacked us both in the eye. Yeah, that's amore. Two years and change later, we got married on the Field Of Dreams in Iowa. Everybody who knows us (and those who have read Full Filler) and millions of people who don't know us, saw our first wedding as it later achieved a certain amount of fame as the story was told on three major television networks.

I'll skip all of that for now. It's a story in itself.

When we got back from Iowa, nobody knew that we were married. We broke the good news gradually as we told our story to the people closest to us including our parents and our five children. We asked them to keep it on the low because we had a few more marriages to do.

Our second marriage took place at the Justice of the Peace office in the Irondequoit Town Hall. This was the place we might have gotten married earlier in the summer until we decided to give our relationship one more challenge by driving to Iowa and hoping to find a movie site called Field of Dreams which was either heaven or Iowa. The whole experience was so dream like that when we returned to New York, we decided to get married again in our home state just to make sure that the whole thing was real.

That was marriage number 2.

It was now time to let everybody in on our joyous secret. We rented the banquet hall in the Green Lantern in Fairport where we had met. We sent out invitations to our 11/11 wedding/reception.We needed someone to officiate the ceremony so we asked our great friend Bill Klein if he would do the honor. Bill is and remains a local legend for his radio work for WHAM, the local heart of gold. I had known Bill for a number of years. Every year he would visit my Cinematic Literacy class and talk movies.

We had a video tape of our actual marriage in Iowa. My idea was to have Bill call our invited guests to order in the hall. Lynn and I and our children would be in a side room waiting for his intro. Right after the intro, the seven of us marched into the hall. The four daughters; Erin, Kari, Amanda and Raegan in their blue wedding gowns and the son Beau boy in his spiffy tuxedo. We stood there for a moment and Bill gave the signal to play the video. The Green Lantern supplied us with the biggest video screen they could find. Huge portable video screens were a rarity in 1989. Our videotaped marriage hit the big screen and we lip synched our way through the vows once again to the amazement of our guests who were (for some unexplainable reason) expecting a "normal" wedding.

While all this was going on, Rooby Shoes the band that we had hired was setting up near the dance floor. The seven of us walked on the floor and the Band hit Blue Suede Shoes . Lynn and I had our first married dance on the exact same spot at which we had met two years before on 7/11/87. We signaled our guests to come out here on the floor and get to some dancin' which they did and the party was rockin' big time.

Our guests remarked about how cute the kids looked and how they'd never been at a "wedding" like this and wondered if it was a wedding or what the hell was it? They remarked that we looked like the Brady Bunch.We had hired the band for one hour and a deejay after that. One of my great memories is the deejay playing Rock Lobster and everybody getting down down down with the narwals and stingrays.

It was a fantastic day 32 years ago. I was and am a lucky man. Whatever choices I had made in my life to get me to the Green Lantern that July night must have been the right choices because I got to where I needed to be at the exact second that I needed to be there. Since that time, Lynn and I have had a production of our own....our daughter Mary. Mary is the child that the Dude might say has brought the whole room together as she is blood related to all in the "Brady Bunch" and both sides of our families.And the kids are allright.

Every day, I learn more about love and am enriched by the love that I have found.

(Bill Klein passed away suddenly a few years back. I was teaching a course at University of Rochester and once again Bill was coming in as a guest speaker. When I got to the University, they informed me that Bill had arrived earlier and had suffered a heart attack. They assured me that he was in the best possible of hands because the Strong Memorial Hospital, one of the nation's finest is affiliated with the U of R. I tried to teach the class and somehow made it through when someone came to inform me that Bill had passed away. I'm still in shock even as I write these words so Bill this one's for you)

A Sudden Loss of Balance

I'm old and I've lost my sense of balance.

I tend to forget that I'm old until that moment when having lost my sense of balance, I lose my actual balance.

I tripped over a deviously elevated slab of side walk a year ago in my daily walk with Lynn. I have a hard time keeping up with her in the first place as I tend to stop and smell the roses while she charges forward with cardio-vascular purpose. Lynn is six years younger than I so in my world she will never be old.

When you lose your balance after you've lost your sense, you're not going to recover from your stumble. You start lurching forward, out of control and desperately trying to find a safe place to crash. I was wearing a bandage on my right knee from a rug burn that I had suffered from an earler fall two days prior. That bandaged knee was the first part to hit the ground. I got my hands and arms out in front of me in time to save my nose.

There I was faceplanted in some guy's front yard.

Somehow, I managed to turn over and get into sitting position.

I could barely breathe.

Something happens to your breathing mechanisms during an old age fall.

So there I am gasping for breath. Lynn's asking me if I'm allright and I don't have the wind to answer one way or the other. Nothing is broken but the world is spinning and I can barely breathe.

She tries to help me up but I push her away.

I can't get up. I can't breathe.

After a few moments, Lynn reminds me that we're creating a "scene" and I better get up.

I try to get up on my own. I lose my balance again.

Another soft landing.
Another loss of breath.

Another cartoon in the scene.

Another pause filled with cold sweat.

Lynn tries to pull me up but legs are shot. I'm too heavy for her. We get about half way up and then bang, I'm down again after a pathetic, punchdrunk three step stumble.

Another breathless realization of the weight of my years and the gravity of the situation. I'm becoming an embarrassment. There is nothing "cool" about this situation.

Finally instead of trying to lift me, Lynn gets down on all fours and I use her body for leverage to pull myself onto my feet. This has happened a couple of times since. Now we know what to do. Lynn goes "table" and her support becomes literal.

We continue our walk.

I'm a hundred years older than I was when the walk started.

As I walked, I recalled an odd scene that I stumbled into five years earlier. I was approaching the green of the sixth hole at Champion Hills when I saw a man prone on the green. He had fallen on the green and could find no leverage to haul himself up. He had been there for at least 20 minutes and would have been there a lot longer if I hadn't come along. Although he had barely moved, he was covered with sweat and having trouble breathing.

Somehow, I was able to get the man on his feet and over to his golf cart. He assured me that he was allright and he puttered away.

I thought to myself "damn, I hope I never get that old."

Next week though, I hope to take back a few decades on that hundred years. I have a new hope. I'm gonna get my cataracts dissolved. Sometimes at this age, we get the sensation that our life and health is on a gradual decline until suddenly a crisis. It's nice to believe that something can improve and that something is a pretty big deal....vision.

In preparation for the procedure, I've been learning the art of eye dropping. I'm not good at it. I keep missing my eye and feeling the expensive eye drop roll down my cheek. I'm gonna get better at it. I'm gonna have a lot of practice in the next few weeks.
Maybe as my eyesight improves, my balance will improve and I'll become more skillful with the eyedropper. Perhaps my skill will peak at the moment that I'm dropping my last drop.

That's usually the way things go.

We'll see.

.

Seeking Second Sight Right

I don't mean to be flippant about cataract surgery and I surely didn't intend to alarm anyone. I'm not hospitalized.

Cataract surgery is becoming more and more routine. Many of my friends hearing about my surgery, wrote to tell me about their experience, every single one of them happy with not only the results but the procedure itself.

The day I had my first surgery, 24 other folks had the same surgery in the same operating room.

I had the cataract in my left eye dissolved this morning. The procedure was even less alarming than the procedure from the week before. Everyone who helped me was professional, informed, informative and good humored.

Let me go back to last week and give you some more details about the first procedure.

When the nurse called me from the waiting room, she guided me to room 3. I put those plastic coverings on my shoes and one of those stupid hats on my head. The attendant nurse asked me the usual set of questions about medications and allergies. When she finished she wanted to know if I had any questions....whenever that happens I always ask "What's the capitol of North Dakota?" She answered correctly and then said, "now for your IV."

I'm getting used to IV's now but this one hurt a little more than usual. She went for the hand rather than the arm. The arm is better. So once they had the IV inserted, I settled back for sedation. Earlier, the aneathesiologist had introduced himself to me. He said, "Just think of this surgery as an eye exam with benefits". I asked him what was the benefit? He told me the sedation.

Having been punctured, I was waiting for the "benefit" to kick in. I could feel myself growing drowsy and feeling relaxed. The groove was starting. I started to think about Dumbo and the pink elephants. The nurse invited Lynn into my room. Pretending to be stoned, I asked the attendants "who is this voman" which got lot less of a chuckle from everyone than I expected. Lynn at down and asked me how I was doing. I told her that I was feeling a little oaded but I suspected it would get better before the procedure. That's when Lynn noticed that the IV was not hooked up to a bag. She said, "You're not oaded at all, you just think you are."

A few minutes later, they wheeled me into the operating room. I could hear the doctor calling my name and telling everyone that I was in for a right eye cataract surgery and that I was allergic to penicillin. They instructed me to lay flat on the table and they removed my pillow. They threw in another series of eye drops. They put a breathing tube up my nose. I could feel slight pressure on my eye. They were talking about the instruments that they played in grammar school and the frustrations they had with those instruments.

I decided that I wouldn't join in the conversation even though I too had only reached second clarinet in my grammar school. Meanwhile, in my right eye which had been numbed by the eyedrops, I could see a light show occurring underwater. Kinda cool.

Then after about ten minutes, they rolled me out of the operation room to a recovery room, where I sat in the chair for maybe five minutes before they wheeled me out of the hospital where my wife was waiting with our new Buick. For the first time in many years, we were no longer driving our Cadillac. Yes my cataract had been dissolved and my Cadillac was also gone.

I was donning a dimpled see through eye shield protecting my right eye.

The next morning, we returned for a consultation with my surgeon about the procedure.

He took a look and seemed pleased. He wanted to know how the sedation worked at which point. I told him that I wasn't sure. I summarized him on his less than stellar career as a violinist career and since the last time I looked my IV wasn't connected to any bag. I also knew about the music careers of all the nurses in the room. I wondered where the hell was the sedation.

He explained that they gave it to me shortly after wheeling me into the OR. Wow that's some quick acting juice. The whole operation only took fifteen minutes which means the "juice" must have worked immediately even while I was hearing every word of every sentence yet the sedation was cleared out o: my system completety 10 minutes later when I sat down in my car.

But why quibble?

The vision in my operated on eye has improved dramatically. The difference in vision between that eye and my left eye is amazing and they tell me that, the vision will continue to improve every day. I can barely wait until tomorrow.

Better To See

Suddenly, I'm thirteen.

Thirteen with 60 additional years of experience.

.

My vision has already improved from 20/80to 20/20. They say I now have the vision of a thirteen year old. That wouldn't be ME at thirteen. I didn't realize how bad my vision was at 13 until I see what it's like now.

If I had this vision then, I might have lasted a couple more years in baseball.

Maybe even made the varsity. Maybe even started.

So, I'm starting now. It's beyond fantastic and they tell me it's only gonna get better as I become more accustomed to the light. Maybe this is a preview of the after life.

The left eye surgery was like the right except I can't recall what they were saying while they performed the operation. I can only recall a lot of laughter and good vibes in the room. When they wheeled me in, I asked if they had sedated me yet. The nurse said that she was just about to do so.

I guess she did but I remained awake and tried not to join in the laughter surrounding me. Once again, the bright lights and the sensation of water. Once again, I was leaving the OR after barely being in it. I'm getting used to this drill. Kinda wish I had another eye.

Now I get to put into practice my expertise in recovery. I'm already great at it. How do you improve on something that you're already great at. It's a tough question and something that I've never confronted before. In general, you have to work harder but in this case, I don't have to work at all. I'm very, very good at not working.

They fixed me up with another eye shield and off we went.We stopped at a grocery store. I went over to the bakery department and freaked out at the color and design of the baked goods. I'd never noticed the detail before. The baker asked if she could help me. I told her that I'm just looking but I'm looking in a way that I've never looked before. I explained that I was minus a cataract and plus a lens where the cataract used to be. She seemed happy to hear the news and appreciated the fact that I had a greater appreciation for the work that she had done as a result of the work that the surgeon had done on me which she could only imagine.

Here's the deal. First of all the cataract was gone. My sister in law is a nurse who has observed many a cataract surgery. She says the neatest part is when the cataract dissolves. In the place of the cataract is a brand new lens designed especially for me. Addition by subtraction followed by addition by addition.

I don't have to wear glasses anymore.

I've already freaked out several times today wondering where were my glasses before realizing that I didn't need them.

Teevee. Oh yeah. Best teevee ever.

Reading. Oh yeah. I don't have the book pressed to my nose anymore which means I can read sitting up and holding the book at a distance. This alone multiplies my exercise by two. This exact screen that I'm looking at right now is clearer than any computer screen that I've ever seen. Wouldn't it be nice if my thoughts and actions became clearer and kinder as a result to say nothing of the concept that even in my mid-seventies a condition can not only improve but continue to improve.

Even my balance is better as I lasted more than five seconds standing on one foot.

I'm very thankful as you can tell. I'm trying to figure out the allegory in all of this probably goes something like this...the more we see, the more we see there is to see.

Or to see or not to see is no longer the question. It's better to see.

Or the old faithful, it's possible to change without improving but impossible to improve without changing.

Maybe I've said that before.

.

Born to Recover

Most of us spend too much of our lifetimes trying to figure out what we're good at and when we kinda find it, we wish it was something else because the thing that we're good at is so easy that everybody must be good at it. So we spend too much of our time working on the things that we want to be good at even though the people who are naturally good at those things will always be better at those things no matter how hard we work even if they work only half as much as we do while we ignore what we should be doing etc.

I've tried on many hats and worn many a mask. It took me seventy plus years to discover something at which I'm really good. I'm great at recovering from cataract surgery. Here are some of the tasks that I have spent my lifetime mastering which describe the performance of RCS (recovering cataract surgery):

1) Do not lift anything or bend over. I have been practicing this for years. One of the fringe benefits of this skill is I don't even attempt to make a putt shorter than six feet because I can't reach down and take the ball out of the cup, if by some miracle it had sunk. Anything within six feet is a gimme. Furthermore if I happen to hit a longer putt to within 6 feet of the hole, I count that putt as if it went into the hole because it's close enough.

2) Do not strain. Since I'm not lifting anything, this concept is rather superfluous. I suppose that some folks think that strain is similar to stress. I don't stress either. I create stress in others. Perhaps strain is more physical than

stress as the strain to lift a huge amount of weight or the strain to evacuate some weight or some rented beer. Fuggedaboudid. I'm a naturally smooth mover. I'm no penguin whose pooping all over the place in an attempt to fly because the glaciers will soon be melting.

3) No vigorous exercise. Hey every once in awhile, I'll assume a slouching sitting position and maybe even stand up, that's about it. What's the point of moving when the earth is moving and television is bringing every thing to me. Sometimes, it's too much of a hassle to turn the teevee on by finding the right remote and figuring out which buttons to hit. That's when I pick up one of the books that I keep within arm's reach. I can read that book until it gets too dark in the room, at which point I've either got to open the blinds or turn on a light. Fuggedaboudid. I have the option of my Kindle. The kindle screen has a light of its own. I can turn the pages with a flick of my finger rather than having to go through the labor of turning the page in a book which involves a slight twisting ot the wrist.

4) No eye makeup....this is no great loss as you might imagine

Furthermore when in my position as RCS, I am entitled to the following conditions that are not always a given in the realm beyond the hospital, if I ever have to go to a hospital.

I have the right to have my pain managed. This is a good one because I've been trying to manage my own pain for years and sometimes that management has come in conflict with the law or the moral code.

I get quality care in a safe setting. Safety is as much a concern as freedom. In almost every other situation, I am petrified that my safety will suddenly become at risk. This is why I have become a recluse.

I know the names and the jobs of the people who are caring for me. This is so much better than the usual , "hey, you, Nurse Ratchett , WTF are you doing and why are you doing that."

I will be treated with respect, consideration and dignity. No more, "hey dummy, move your tired self outta the way before I sic my dung eating dog on ya."

I will be free from all forms of abuse, neglect, exploitation, harassment, discrimination and reprisal. I won't be sitting in a urine soaked nest like a second born eaglet somewhere begging for a glass of water from a "nurse" whose pissed off because I caught her on her phone sending a boob shot to her boyfriend.

I can complain without fear and have my complaints reviewed. I'm not a guy who complains a lot but usually when I do, it leads back to somebody accusing me of having caused the problem that I'm complaining about in the first place.

It's a pretty good deal and I'm excellent at all facets.
Now I've go to figure out how to make some money with my skill set.
I know....I'll become a consultant.

Good Vibes

Having survived prostate cancer, I know a thing or two about the process, at least MY process. Everybody has a different journey. I am full of gratitude that my journey went as smoothly as it did. I began writing on ABC tales the day that I was diagnosed when everything was up in the air. I can't help but think that sharing my story helped a little bit because I had so many people pulling for me from so far away. I didn't share my diagnosis outside of ABC for a few weeks when I knew more about the situation when I found that my case was TREATABLE.

The writing that I did during this period became a big part of *Full Filler.*

Sometimes, I go back in my writing and look at the lens through which I was viewing mortality in those first few weeks and I must admit that I am surprised at the equanimity I summoned during that waiting time which we all know is the hardest part.

I let me heart over rule my head. My heart sent messages of hope and gratitude to my brain which short circuited the potential high beta brain waves that my fear and anxiety was trying to amplify.

I could tell the difference between heart messages and brain messages.

In every fetus, the heart develops first. We keep thinking that our brains our running the show but that's because our brains control the microphone of our subvocalizations and always claim to be the boss....always striving to do or to solve. The heart is more concerned with "being" rather than "doing. Let's face it, no matter what we do, we still have to confront the blessed realm of our being. If our being is off kilter, it affects the momentum of what we do. To be or to do? To do or to be? Doobie Doobbie Doo.

I've just found out that one of my best friends is on the cancer journey. His road is different from mine and from all others who have embarked on that road. He had prostate surgery but his PSA count **increased** rather than decreased. I'm not gonna try to explain PSA other than to say that mine was at

16 before radiation and is now at .04. My friend was hoping to get that kinda report after the surgery but to his great surprise his PSA rose from 7 to 11 and they weren't using Theranos. His doctor was as shocked and disappointed as my friend with those numbers. His doctor suggested radiation until he discovered more news. The cancer had spread to the lymph nodes and the way prostate cancer develops, the lymph nodes are generally the first to be affected by the spread.

My friend has confided in me and now I'm confiding in you as very few of you know my friend so his confidentiality is secure. He's probably shared his secret with you few who do know him.

Meanwhile, I've been concentrating on my heart. The heart is where vibrations begin. The heart is full of love and faith. I'm too far away from my friend to share those healing vibes personally. I've come to believe that our vibes coincide with social distancing. The closer we get, the more our vibes can be received. Yet every heart message counts.

Our vibes, no matter how strong tend to mix with the vibes of our environment so I've been trying to keep my environment as healthy as I can while sending out invitations for others who have connected with me from a distance to connect with me once again with hope, faith and equanimity. Yeah, we are in the hands of the world but while we're here, if we pay attention to our hearts we can get the whole world in our hands momentarily and affect what we can.

Whatever happens is supposed to happen but guess what.... miracles do happen. It's common to see life as linear. At some point we learn about the non-linearity of existence and with the flight of so many black swans it becomes tempting to view the non-linearity as catastrophic which we think cushions our shock from whatever catastrophes await us. I am learning that life can be viewed as miraculously non-linear which helps to prepare me for and influence the power and frequency of the miracles that I observe every day which I can manifest even if I can't create.

The mere fact that you are reading this, if you have read this far, is helping you which helps the world which influences the vibes that are getting through to my friend.

Thank you for reading.

Bless your heart.

Dylan at RIT

Bob Dylan has turned 80. This is a review that I wrote about one of his performances at RIT.

Dylan failed last night to resolve one of my longest standing differences of opinion with my wife Lynn. Lynn is from the "Dylan is an icon of the sixties who writes great lyrics but who has a lousy voice and arrogant personality" point of view.

I'm from the "authentic cultural spokesperson whose unique voice and enigmatic personality are as inseparable from his lyrics as the lyrics are inseparable from the music and the message" point of view.

I resist "the icon from the sixties" point of view because it turns Dylan's timeless compositions into nostalgia acts. I agree with the "great lyrics" observation but always feel like Lynn is setting up the polite quid pro quo of devastating criticism with faint praise followed by the real message…"his voice sucks and he's an a-hole", which she unfailingly does.

I had seen Dylan perform live four times (including the amazing Rolling Thunder Review)before Lynn agreed to go with me to see him about ten years ago at the Finger Lakes Performance Center. That night, Dylan seemed angry at the audience and infuriated with his own songs, so his performance was brusque and furious. Lynn who believes that an entertainers first job is to entertain, (which means as the song goes to smile when they are low)was put off by the moody seemingly indulgent performance which fueled her original biases especially the A-Hole part.

"He never even talked to the audience. He never connected. Why didn't he at least tell a joke or something," Lynn wondered and would continue to wonder until last night.

I said "the guys not a comedian and he's not a let's all get together by the campfire and sing kumbaya type of guy. He is what he's always been which is exactly what he is at any particular moment and what he was that night was pissed off for whatever reason and that's good enough for me" and it was until last night.

Last night we took the tie-breaker with us, our thirteen year old daughter Mary. Point of reference, Mary attended her first concert of her young life a week before, Green Day at the Blue Cross Arena. She loved it. Mary plays guitar herself and blew us all away last week when she brought home the self-portrait in pencil she had been working on in her advanced art class.

Dylan played at a much smaller venue, one of my several alma maters, the Rochester Institute of Technology. The choice of venue in itself is interesting. Is Dylan playing to smaller houses because he seeks the intimacy of smaller crowds having exhausted himself on the stadium circuit or does he no longer have the drawing power to book larger spaces ?

The main reason we got the tickets in the first place was to expose Mary to Dylan as well as to RIT. We tried to get two tickets for just me and the Mare but since we had to buy a group of three minimum, Lynn went along for the ride.

Whatever, twenty minutes after the scheduled starting time of 8:00 at 8:22 to be precise the sound system crackled to life with a rapid fire minimalist introduction apparently pre-recorded by an invisible emcee featuring garbled clauses like "The poet laureate of rock music and his generation........thought to be washed up in the eighties....... His last two albums are two of the most critically acclaimed albums of his career thus the history of American recordings....the author of a currently best selling auto -biography.....Bob Dylan and his band".

Dylan came out in his black outfit with black Stetson. The members of his band, two guitarists a bass player and a drummer were also dressed in black, two of the four in cowboy hats kinda like Dylan's. Dylan went to the piano on the left side of the stage and the group broke into "Maggie's Farm".

Blistering.

Bitter.

Pertinent.

All of the elements of working on "Maggie's Farm" intact and primal
Lyrics mostly clear and decipherable. Off to a raucous start. Mary applauded
So did Lynn. I felt not only renewed but also partially redeemed.

Just before Dylan hit the stage, a friend of mine came over and told me that
he had researched the set list. There were fourteen songs plus an encore of two.
This would be a sixteen round contest. Round one was a winner.

My favorite fighters were guys like the Sugars Rays Robinson and Leonard,
Alexis Arguello, Jerry Quarry, George Chuvalo and of course Muhammad Ali.
As these guys got older, I used to count of each off their rounds one by one
hoping that somehow they'd win each round but with equal fervor that they
would at least survive the round. Then I get into the minutes per round, hoping
that somehow they could win ninety five seconds of each round and keeping
score in my mind as they neared the magic number of eight which would win
them a decision if they didn't get knocked out. I found myself using the same
accounting system with Zimmerman on this night.

Round two was "It's All Over Now, Baby Blue". Dylanologists remember
this song as the response Dylan used so many years ago when he was booed off
the stage at the Newport Folk festival for committing the unforgivable sin of
going electric. Since then, it's always been one of my favorites. An anthem I
use to chart my own changes and willingness to leave behind whatever is/was
no longer needed.Dylan remained to the side and guitar less as the first words
hit the air.

"You must leave now, take what you need, you think will last.
But whatever you wish to keep, you better grab it fast"

Unfortunately it sounded more like this

Ulleeenowuneeulas, whatchoo wishookeegrafaaaaaaaa.

Dylan hunched over the mike, growling, confronting the mike like a
gambler keeping his cards close to his vest because he's got such a bluff goin'

that if anybody sees the pasteboards he's screwed for the whole ante. I could see Lynn frowning and Mary following suit I could not give Dylan round two even though I wanted to.

Round three was another of my favorite songs, the haunting and magically melancholic Visions of Johanna whose first line is:

"Ain't it just like the night to play tricks when you're tryin' to be so quiet?"

The only word I could make out was night. Through the entire song, the only words I could understand were "Visions of Johanna" and I knew the song well.

For any of you like Mary and Lynn who don't know the actual words, let me quote the first verse as Dylan wrote and published . Read them and weep because last night they disappeared completely into incomprehensibility.

"Ain't it just like the night to play tricks when you're tryin' to be so quiet?
We sit here stranded, though we're all doin' our best to deny it
And Louise holds a handful of rain, temptin' you to defy it
Lights flicker from the opposite loft

In this room the heat pipes just cough

The country music station plays soft

But there's nothing, really nothing to turn off

Just Louise and her lover so entwined

And these visions of Johanna that conquer my mind"

Whoops, I made a mistake. I forgot that between "Baby Blue" and "Johanna", Dylan sang "Lonesome Day Blues". The fact that I forgot about it, tells me all I want to know about the effort.

Next came a song I won't forget for a long time, no matter how hard I try "Dignity", another one of my favorites. If Dignity is clarity than this rendering was particularly undignified. If Dignity is plunging into a compost pile and emerging as if from a Halloween hayride with the ghost of Aunt Helen then the effort had some saving grace. Once again Dylan's verbal articulation was puddle muddy and he continued to hover by the keyboard still not strapped in to his axe. I got the feeling that he might not be strumming' at all on this evening. Still when he gave his howling a break and hurled his oxygen into his harp, some of the magic returned. The band, minus one geetar was carrying the weight of this concert as if it had just pulled into Nazareth which seemed allright with everybody especially the integrationists amongst us who knew deep inside that there could be no segregation of lyrics and voice from music. The music in spite of the singer continued to soar even as the lyrics because of the poet continued to disappear.

At this point thirteen year old Mary turned to Lynn and commented "everything sounds the same". Lynn nodded in 'I told ya so' acquiescence. The show went on as it must.

I recognized "Tweedle Dum and Tweedle Dee" immediately which nudged it/them towards the win column even as it/they lurched and lumbered fitfully amidst the graceful thundering wonder of the musicians.

I grabbed Mary by the hand and with the approval of Lynn, we headed to the floor for a closer look. One of my weird aptitudes is my ability to wade through a crowd. When Dylan had played with Petty and the Dead at then Rich Stadium before a crowd thirty times this large, I had managed to work my way to the edge of the stage. The secret of getting through a crowd is knowing how to dance with it rather than shove against it. When ya dance the crowd dance, openings appear.

Of course, I was so much younger than I'm older than that now.

The closest we could get was about fifteen rows back as this crowd was much less fluid, hardly any dancing or even movement to make advancing through it amenable. A calm brick wall.

It was from here that we heard and saw Dylan sing three slower numbers in which he had more control of the lyrics as if he actually knew the words and was going to sing them. "Po' Boy", "High Water (For Charley Patton)" and "Girl Of The North Country". I could see Zimmy pretty well but Mary was being blocked by taller folks in front of her. I lifted my little girl up as high as I could for as long as I could so she might get a glimpse of the great man. With the way she's growing and the way I'm deteriorating physically, maybe that was the last time I'd lift her up like this. Made me kind of sad but kind of proud as well. While on my shoulders she spotted a girl wearing a leopard skin pill box hat.

I started to believe that maybe the reason we couldn't hear Dylan clearly for the first half-dozen songs was the fact that we couldn't see him. Ya know, that weird reflex that confronts us when we feel the need to shout at a blind man.

By the time Mary and I got back to Lynn, we were already learning the illusion behind that reflexive truth. I'm no longer a thin man but there was definitely something going on here and I didn't know what it was. I started wondering if Dylan did.

The last five songs of the show , "Stuck Inside Of Mobile With The Memphis Blues Again", "Ballad Of Hollis Brown", "Honest With Me", "Standing In The Doorway" and "Summer Days" proved to be a split decision. Three of the songs I was relatively unfamiliar with so I couldn't very well be disappointed with them. As a matter of fact one of the songs that I never heard before, Standing In The Doorway, sounded more familiar than most of the songs that I knew by heart based on the rate of decipherable words per lyric.

One of my favorite songs, "Stuck Inside Of Mobile With The Memphis Blues" Again was even more deconstructed than any of the previous numbers. I even resorted to whispering the chorus lyric into Mary's ear in the hopes of convincing her that these songs actually had words which meant I kept repeating "Oh Mama can this really be the end" over and over which I think is exactly what Mary was thinking when she was looking at Lynn and wishing she were somewhere else, wondering when the growling would cease. Of the final songs, "Summer Days" was by far the best. It sounded world class and indicated a rally in progress.

The band left the stage and I wondered if they would bother with an encore.I also wondered whether there was going to be enough applause to merit a return that could be anything more than hypocritical. Amazingly enough, the crowd didn't move and began to applaud some even igniting about two dozen of the traditional lighters. Sho nuff, it worked. The band re-appeared.

The encore consisted of "Like A Rolling Stone" and "All Along The Watchtower." These two turned out to be the best efforts of the evening. I later found out that the band had been encoring with these numbers through the entirety of the tour. It sounded like they had played them before and everybody knew the words and the music.

In the past when I've heard Dylan howl the anthemic "Like A Rolling Stone" he would stretch out the line "how does it feeeeeeel" and the audience would sing along with him. This time all but the required two e's were missing as was the audience participation. More stenography. Between the two numbers Dylan, as if sensing the tension between me and Lynn, did the unthinkable. He told a joke. The joke went like this, as he introduced one of the band members Dylan said . "He comes from Louisiana so he stretches rattlesnakes across the front of his car. Calls 'em windshieldvipers"

He introduced another band member by saying the guy was "so tough he shaves with a chain saw". Then a magnificent version of "All Along the Watchtower" prologued by what sounded like an electric version of Exodus turned everything over, under and upside down. Like all champs Zimmy came through in the end.

A little before the encore, I realized that I had been listening to the music through the ears of Mary and watching the performance through the eyes of Lynn. During Watchtower I watched and listened for myself and what I saw and heard was exactly what I wanted to see and hear other than the fact that Dylan never touched a guitar.

The concert reminded me of the Ali-Bonavena fight in which Ali looked listless and distracted throughout the fight until he finished off his clumsy, umbering foe with a sudden knockout in the final round which removed from he judges the task of ruling in favor of the clearly inferior fighter.

That's the task that the last song removed from my critique. I didn't have to rip Dylan any further. The final song of the encore gave me everything I could have wanted.

On the way back to the car Mary said, "I expected more" which pretty much sums up most people's feeling about Dylan even as we forget how much we already have.
Lynn said to Mary " I want you to keep this ticket stub because someday, you'll be telling someone that you saw Dylan and they're going to want proof". From Beatrice, that's high praise. I guess the joke worked and there are many here among us along the watch tower who think that life itself is but a joke.

As for me, well it had been ten years since the last time I was in the same room with Dylan. Ten years from now he'll be 73. I'll go again but I won't expect to get real close to the stage even though the crowd will be less than half a thousand. I suspect Mary will be amongst them. She might even be holding me up next time. Lynn and I will still be arguing.

Some times I'm a tick or two slow on the uptake. Sometimes I forget where I am and with whom I'm with wherever I am.
We in Rochester are fortunate to have the National Technical Institute for the Deaf as part of our Rochester Institute of Technology. RIT is where Bob Dylan played in the concert that I have just reviewed. When Dylan was leaving after completing his first fourteen songs, he paused in the middle of the stage raised his hands to chest level , palms out, fingers extended as if he were signaling "ten" while simultaneously wiping an invisible windshield using both hands.

From my distant seat, the gesture looked oddly quaint.

From where I sit now, I begin to understand. Dylan was using the universally accepted gesture of silent applause used by deaf folks, waving ten fingers. I bet the people in front of Dylan, part of the under whelming audible applause, were returning his gesture. The crowd on the floor nearest the stage and the performer were silently validating one another. A conversation was happening. Thus the non-hypocritical encore that followed.

Because we have so many deaf folks in Rochester, particularly in Henrietta, the community where RIT is located, I have become accustomed to interpreters speaking sign language at most large gatherings. At the time, I didn't think it was unusual that to the left of Dylan, off stage, a woman was interpreting the concert. As I've mentioned in this review, up until the moment that Dylan silently applauded, he positioned himself to the far left of the stage. In fact Dylan was as close to the interpreter on his left as he was to the lead guitar player on his right. If you count the interpreter as a member of the band, then there was Zimmy right smack dab in the middle of things. I make a practice whenever an interpreter is present to observe the sign language she is providing. I'm amazed at how quickly they can take complex ideas and instantaneously turn those into a lovely, commanding body language just beyond the reach of my intellect.

Now before me, I was watching a woman trying to signal lyrics like "You must leave now, take what you need, you think will last. But whatever you wish to keep, you better grab it fast" which as I mentioned in my review sounded more like this

"Ulleeenowuneeulas, whatchoo wishookeegrafaaaaaaaa".
Ulleeenowuneeulas, whatchoo wishookeegrafaaaaaaaa".

Imagine the problem of trying to turn THAT into sign and body language.

But by God, she was doing it. Maybe she had the written lyrics in front of her or maybe she was doing the best with what she thought she heard or maybe because she was so much closer to Zimmy she actually heard what none of the rest of the audience sitting in the seats could hear. Her interpretation sort of resembled a hula set to rock music. It was thing of beauty to observe, very sensual, very seductive.

I've heard it said that hula is all about the stories being told by the hands of the dancer and that some times the stories are so risqué that at the end of the dance, the dancer has to go and wash her hands out with soap. None of Dylan's yrics needed that kind of sanitization unless she was hearing something different than I was which she most assuredly was.

Later, Lynn commented that this was the first and only time that she ever wished that she were deaf and understood sign language. "I would have been spared Dylan's ghastly croaking and would have been able to understand the words."

Ouch.

I, of course, took it one step further in defense of Dylan. Is it possible that Dylan was actually singing in deaf speak. If you've ever listened to a deaf person speak, it has it's own unique sound and actually doesn't sound a whole lot different from

"Ulleeenowuneeulas, whatchoo wishookeegrafaaaaaaaa".

Could Dylan possibly be this aware and sensitive? Something had in fact happened there and until now I didn't know what, had Dylan known all along?

Why not. He's Dylan, I'm Rivers. There's a difference. Big difference.

I ran these ideas past Lynn who assured me that I was getting a little carried away. From Lynn, that's high praise.

Lynn had one further idea. Rochester is the home of Mitch Miller, the originator of the famous sing along with Mitch concept of fifties teevee. Mitch and his crew would sing a song and invite viewers to sing along by following a bouncing ball that danced over lyrics to the song which appeared at the bottom of the teevee screen. When Dylan performed at RIT he played in front of a backdrop upon which were projected different images during the show. Beatrice suggested that next time, the words of his lyrics should be projected on the screen with the bouncing ball so that everyone, not just the deaf could understand the words and sing along.

I think she's got something. I can see it now. Network teevee. Right After Desperate Housewives. Sing along with Bob Dylan. Might catch on.

You read it here first.

I took the advice that Lynn had given Mary. I put the ticket stub in my wallet and carried it to the end.

Outstanding Clickers

Decades ago, when students first started to comment on my photography and ask "How did you do that", I told them "once you have a camera and can say 1...2...3 and click: you're pretty much there."

Back then, I was considered a photographer because I had a camera with me more than 98% of the people. If somebody spontaneously combusted, I would probably be the only one who might catch the image for the simple reason that I was much more likely than most to have a camera.

I am from Rochester, after all. George Eastman was the guy who turned photography into a miracle that was available to the common person.

Another bit of advice I passed on was advice that was passed on to me. "Find a good place to stand".

That's what I did and once again, I thought I was pretty hot shit. I'm pretty good at standing, if I were a farmer I'd be outstanding in my field.

Sports Illustrated was a great inspiration to me. I was always in pursuit of that Sports Illustrated shot.

A month or two ago, Sports Illustrated was showing the best photos of the year.
Amazing of course.

Perhaps the most amazing photo was from the finish line at the Derby. I've always enjoyed the annual picture of the three year old champion charging for the roses. I've seen that image many times before.

This one was different because not only did it include the horses at the finish, it also included the crowd at the finish line.

500 people at least.

Every person in the picture had a camera.

Yeah, they might of have been cell phones but so what?

It's still a matter of;
   a) having a camera
   b) going one to three click at the right time
   c) and standing in the right place.

Simple rilly.

Matter of fact, it's too simple. The wonder of cell phone photography has made it so. Nowadays, if somebody spontaneously combusts, I can be pretty sure that somebody else will be there with a camera....maybe even Jem Masters who's always on the lookout for the sensational. As a result, I feel less obligated to get to the right place. For the last few months, the right place has been here at my keyboard typing away.

It's pretty clear that I'm morphing into a "writer" and away from "photographer". I'm gonna leave photography to my group of talented Rochester photographers which once again includes Ron, Guy, Cal, Robert and David Carry on fellas. You got this.

Are You A Turtle?

You didn't think I was going to leave y'all with an unreferenced allusion now did ya? Some of you close readers were wondering who the hell McCallum was and what was he doing resonating in the mind of a turtle whose shell was seemingly turning into wings and who challenged us all to check out his glyphics. McCallum is a college friend with whom I have shared many a beer and many a laugh. No matter how sad the occasion, McCallum had a way of looking at the humorous side or the positive side. I gave him the nickname Happy Jack after a character created by the Who in one of their pre-Tommy albums. In the song, it was impossible to stop Jack from being happy.

Happy Jack had a little bit of a stutter. He had come to Geneseo to major in their speech and hearing Dept. While he was overcoming his stutter, he joined our fraternity in the same pledge class as I. Naturally, as part of "hazing" the brothers were always making Happy recite impossible tongue twisters. I admired his good humor and humility. He's the kind of friend that you don't mind calling an asshole and don't mind in the slightest when he responds in kind.

Anyway, one night we were out drinking and Happy asked me if I was a turtle. (Before we go any further, let me repeat that question to y'all. Are you a turtle?)

I called Happy an asshole for asking me such a dumb question. He said that he would take that response as a no. I was kinda bothered by the question so I asked him why he asked me. He said that where he came from if someone asked you if you were a turtle and you knew what was happening, you proved your "turtledom" by answering "you bet your sweet as I am." and drink a beer. I wanted to know how to become a turtle. He said it was simple. He asked me if I was a turtle, I said, "you bet your sweet ass I am." I chugged a beer. "You're a turtle", he said and you retain your membership as long as whenever anyone asks you if you're a turtle you answer "you bet your sweet ass I am". The only people who will ask that question will be turtles themselves so there will always be at least one person who knows what your talking about. I asked Tim that question on his wedding day when he was offering a toast to his bride the beautiful Tiger. He bet his sweet ass that he was. I'm the only one who understood that allusion aside from whatever turtles were hidden at the reception pond that day.

Tiger McCallum

Begin Ending With Sad Finish

Raised Catholic, I came to believe that all pleasures were guilty therefore guilt itself was a pleasure. My life was full of pleasure...full of guilt.

Foolish I admit.

Which leads me to Foolish Pleasure

Which leads me to Ruffian

Which takes me back to 1975

To Belmont Park

With Wild Bill.

Foolish Pleasure was a great three year old bay. Pleasure had won the Kentucky Derby and come in second at the Preakness and the Stakes. Even though it was a standout season for The Fool, it left some folks disappointed that he wasn't able to win the Triple Crown....he was the favorite in all three races.

Meanwhile another three year old bay, a filly ran 10 races against other fillys and won them all, wire to wire, never giving up a lead... ahead all the way never getting any turf in her ferocious face.

So here we had the greatest filly of all time and a damned good male Derby winner. Ruffian and Foolish Pleasure.

Somebody said "let's see which one is better"

Somebody else said "Let's find out at Belmont."

A match race was put on the calendar.

July 7, 1975

I decided to make the trip from upstate to New York to Belmont...a trip of about 400 miles. Before I left, I called Wild Bill to see if he had any interest in going to the race. Did Rose Kennedy own a black dress? Of course he wanted to go.

We met at the racetrack. We threw down a twelve pack in the parking lot We were well lubricated and ready to roar along with another 50,000 folks when we finally entered the Park.

There were more women at Belmont that day than I had ever seen at a race track. Many of them were wearing buttons with a picture of Ruffian emblazoned with the word HER. Gotta admit, they kinda classed up the joint

Naturally Bill and I picked up similar buttons only a picture of Foolish Pleasure instead of Ruffian and with HIM instead of her.

Feminism was settling in and this race was taking on a metaphoric, symbolic meaning.

We flirted with the girls. We took the chauvinist stance, tongue through cheek.

"So this Ruffian is the best you got? This is your best ever? The Fool ain't our best. He's just one of the boys. He ain't no Secretariat. He's just a fool. And he's gonna beat your best with no problem."

The blonde in the bonnet spoke for most of the women in the crowd when she said, "You guys are full of shit. All you men are full of shit. You're gonna find out today."

Everybody was laughing and bullshitting with each other. It was a very pleasurable afternoon. Everybody was in a good mood. The governor was there. Pat Summerall was there once again.. 20 million people were tuned in on ABC.

We made our way down to the saddling area. Foolish Pleasure entered first. He was an impressive looking horse, not like Secretariat but handsome in his own bay way.

He walked around the paddock area as if he didn't have a care in the world.

Cool Dude.

And then came Ruffian...

I'd seen Secretariat in the same location. Secretariat was chestnut and looked like a horse. He looked more like a horse than any horse I've ever seen. He was the model for all horses to be compared with and he was incomparable.

And then came Ruffian. Ruffian was huge and pissed off. She stomped through the paddock as if she owned not only the paddock but the barn, the Park and New York city itself. She was shimmering black in color. Bay is too gentle a words. If Secretariat was a force of nature, Ruffian was a force of supernature with fury in her eyes and fire in her nostrils.Ruffian was fearsome and intimidating and once again...HUGE. The filly was more physically and metaphysictionally imposing than Foolish Pleasure.

I could imagine riding Secretariat. I didn't think he'd mind, same way with Foolish Pleasure. No way with Ruffian. If you've ever been out in a pasture on a dark starry night trying to lead a thoroughbred back into the barn, it can be frightening if you ain't a cowboy. Just thinking of Ruffian in the pasture in the moonlight was almost too much for my imagination.....

What would happen if Secretariat and Ruffian mated?
The possibilities were infinite but first there was the matter of the race.
They saddled up and headed through the tunnel to the track.

That moment of silence as horses travel to the track is one of my favorite memories. People in the saddling area have just had a close look and are still buzzing about the impressions as the horses enter that tunnel. There is a minute of silence as the horses pass through the tunnel before they emerge.

That's when the roar starts and the roar continues and grows while the orchestra plays The Sidewalks of New York.
East Side West Side All Around the Town.
Time to get to the stands.
Bill knows how to move in a crowd and so do I.
We dance with it instead of moving against it.
Somehow we were able to situate ourselves to the rail very close to the starting gate.

They loaded the horses in. We got a good look at the load. They lifted the gate. Ruffian still breathing fire brushed her shoulder against the side of the gate but the start was clean and they were off.

Ruffian had never been behind. We expected her to take an immediate lead and hope that Pleasure could make a stretch run. The start wasn't clean. The horses brushed shoulders. The brushed shoulder might have affected Ruffian's timing a little bit.

The Fool matched her stride for stride for the first hundred yards and as they headed side by side as one into the turn, Ruffian had finally got a nose in front All of us were waiting for the explosion.

We got two explosions at once.
It was the Fool who made the big move.

He blasted past Ruffian with a Secretariat like burst of energy and he left Ruffian in the dust. Everybody was watching the Fool as his lead increased and it became clear that he would win and win big; Secretariat big.

Then, with the race decided, the crowd began to look back to find Ruffian. Ruffian was stopped in her tracks. As she had tried to pull away from FP at the turn, her leg had snapped and exploded. Both sesamoids in her right ankle were shattered Her jockey tried to stop her but with that magnificent heart...Ruffian continued to race on with her shattered leg until she compounded the damage.

They brought the ambulance out and loaded the defeated bay. Surgeons operated on Ruffian right there at Belmont but during the surgery itself under enough drugs to knock out a five horses, she attempted to run while still on the table.

Of course none of us in the Park knew about the operation. All we knew was that the Fool had "won" the race and that Ruffian was badly, badly hurt.

All the joy
All the camaraderie
All the adrenaline

Vanished
As did the pleasure
As it was replaced once again by guilt.

It was as if we had been to a bull fight watching the marvelous bull being
tortured and murdered before our eyes as if we had been present at a hanging
and our passports had turned brown.

What kind of sport was horse racing anyway?

Bill and I didn't talk much about the race as we made our way to Babylon.
We knew we had witnessed something that we wished that we hadn't but was
significant in our continued bonding as friends.

Back at the track they put Ruffian to sleep.

They buried her in Belmont Park the next day with her nose pointed
towards the finish line.

Pleasure
Foolish and Guilty.

Mike's First Concert

I know for sure it was a Tuesday afternoon. I don't know if it was the first time I smoked weed, such moments are hard to pinpoint. Today is also a Tuesday afternoon. Today I found out that Ray Thomas, the flautist for the Moody Blues had passed away from prostate cancer. I know something about prostate cancer.
The beauty of metaphysiction is its ability to go flash forward and backward at the same time while flirting with the eternal and the imaginary.

The Tuesday afternoon that begins this story happened fifty years ago. I was shooting footage for a film that I was making in graduate school. My idea was to simply walk around and shoot whatever came into my lens on this Tuesday afternoon and call whatever came out "Tuesday Afternoon" I had shot enough weird footage so I was confident that within the images, I could find 10 solid minutes that would represent what a Tuesday afternoon looked and sounded like and that it would probably be interesting to watch in say 50 years so that I could clearly remember what fifty years ago looked and sounded like.

We were driving back to campus. We turned on an FM station. By this time I was an album guy and FM was the album station. I was trying to figure out what music I would use in the background of the film when on the radio came "Tuesday Afternoon". I had never heard anything like it before. When the song was over, the announcer said "that was Tuesday Afternoon by the Moody Blues from their new album Days of Future Passed"

Days of Future Passed might as well have been the name of my mindset on that Tuesday afternoon with *Tuesday Afternoon* playing. I hoped that I would see the Moody Blues in the Future and at that time, remember the past which would naturally include the moment that I was living that Tuesday afternoon in the present.

I knew the Moody Blues. I knew of their hit "Go Now" which I wasn't crazy about. I didn't know that the personnel of the band had changed and they had gone from THAT to THIS. Ray Thomas was in both versions, I learned ater.

Shocked, stoned and stunned by synchronicity, I became a Moody Blues
an. In other words, I too was a weirdo. At the time you had to be a little weird
o like the Blues. They were hanging with LSD guru Timothy Leary and proud
of it.

I couldn't believe that "drug music" could be so beautiful or that a simple
Tuesday afternoon could be so profound .

I had the music for my film.

I found my film in the music.

Now let's fast forward 15 years.

Every June, I felt as if I had given my absolute "all" to my profession and if
I wasn't exhausted on the last day of school, I hadn't given enough.

My first marriage was breaking up although I didn't realize it or perhaps
was denying the realization. I know I felt like I had a ton of bricks on my back.

The "famous" Mike had never been to a concert before and he loved the
Moody Blues. I invited Mike and a couple of friends to join my family at the
Moody Blues concert at the Canandaigua Performing Arts Center.

Mike accepted my invitation.

The night of the Moody Blues arrived. School had finished that morning.

I had purchased a dozen tickets for the show.

The day of the night of the Blues was very hot. I ran ten miles that
afternoon trying to lighten my load.

My brother, my sister, my wife, a few of our friends, my son Beau, Mike
and I made the short trip. We walked to the gates. I took out the tickets. I only

had eleven tickets. Everybody was looking at me. I counted the tickets only eleven again. I was going to have to exclude someone from the concert. I looked around at the faces. I knew I would exclude myself.

I looked at the tickets again. I counted the tickets. I looked at Mike. My marriage was falling apart. Mike was on his way to California. I had screwed up the tickets. I had ruined Mike's first concert. The eternal collided with the present. I had a choice to make. It was a much bigger choice than the concert. I was gonna need a guide to help me decide. I could feel the earth spinning. I said something incoherent to my brother. He looked at me with concern and said "whaaa?" I spoke again and once again sounded like Gregor Samsa when he tried to speak after his metamorphosis had turned him from a man into an insect. I started to stumble. The tickets fell out of my grasp. I looked directly into my son's eyes as the weight on my shoulders flew off and I fell in slow motion towards the ground. As I looked into his eyes, I realized that I was watching a son watch the death of his father. I wondered how this would affect him. I heard my wife scream "he didn't go to his physical!"

I hit the ground.

I knew I was dead.

When I opened my eyes some time later to see what heaven was like I saw two faces. One face was of a beautiful, elderly woman. I knew she was an angel. The other was Mike. This was Mike's first minute at his first concert. Both of them encouraged me to stay.

In the background Moody Blues music was playing.

They wanted to call an ambulance.

I didn't want that.

I wanted to go where the music was, where the angel was.

Somebody picked up the tickets and found all twelve.

We went inside the Shell and heard the Blues.

The angel had disappeared once it became clear that I was going to live.

The last time I saw her, she was listening to the show. The Blues may or may not have been playing Tuesday Afternoon when our eyes met.

Flash forward.

Today, Tuesday, I learned that Ray Thomas had died. Ray was 76 years old. I'm 71.
How could all of those future days have passed.

I hope Ray is with the angels.

That's a good place. I got a glimpse of it, my first but not my last.

Duck This

Whenever Daffy Duck hit the screen during 20 Cartoons, the audience went wild. Recently, the Cartoon Channel identified its ranking of the top 100 cartoons of all time. Rated as number one is the dark and despairing masterpiece by Charlie Jones entitled *Duck Amuck*.

Amuck begins innocently enough when Daffy Duck appears in a Scarlet Pimpernell/Three Musketeers costume but before any sword play, the background vista shifts to a mid_American rural scene. Daffy's musketeer outfit is clearly inappropriate in "Iowa" so he rushes out of frame and emerges dressed as a farmer at which point the vista immediately changes to Antarctica. Once again, Daffy rushes out of frame to emerge on skis which become immediately inappropriate as the Arctic scenery transmogrifies into a jungle paradise. Trying in vain to cope with the insanely evolving landscape, Daffy rushes out of frame again only to emerge in an Hawaiian grass skirt plucking on a ukulele at which point the environment disappears again.

Suddenly a terrifying eraser appears and removes Daffy completely from the scene until he emerges on a blank background as a singing cowboy only this time without sound. When the sound effects return, they are inappropriate (e.g. machine gun fire bursts from the guitar) until Daffy's voice returns along with a stick figure flat background without depth or color. Daffy complains and demands that color be added.

Color is added not only to the background but to the flummoxed fowl himself. Daffy is transformed into a grotesquerie recognizable only by his facial features. Daffy is unaware of his horrifying transfiguration until a mirror suddenly descends before him and the Duck is forced to confront his own mutilated, freakish image ala Winston Smith in 1984.

The horror, the horror is too much for the canard who immediately transforms into his former self only now dressed in a sailor's outfit. Confessing a life long desire to appear in a seafaring epic, Daffy seems satisfied until the background appears and Daffy finds himself standing ON the water. Daffy unable to walk on water descends into the deep until he miraculously emerges on an island in the distance, much like Turley Lura, from whence he calls for a closeup which reveals angry, bloodshot, frantic, disbelieving eyes.

Apparently as we are looking into Mr. Duck's pupils, a huge obsidian mass has fallen upon his head. Daffy struggles to recover some space and during this suffocating globulization, the Warner Brothers Ending logo appears prematurely. Daffy pushes the logo away and begins dancing against a suddenly white background. The sprockets of an imaginary projector running his very film fall out of synch resulting in a split of Daffy's personality between two frames neither one of which is in full focus on the screen.

As Daffy's personality unifies he becomes a fighter pilot flying through blue skies until a mountain is drawn on the immediate horizon into which Daffy and his plane immediately crash. Fortunately Daffy hits the silk in the nick of time but unfortunately, the parachute turns into an anvil and strikes Daffy in the head when he lands on the ground. After crushing Daffy's head, the anvil explodes like dynamite.

The camera pulls back from the perplexed, anvil crushed Duck to reveal a drawing board upon which all of the preceding chaos and catastrophe has been created. The artist is Bugs Bunny who turns to the camera and asks "Ain't I a Stinker?"

Whoa.

Absurdity is despair refusing to recognize the validity of anything including itself. Duck Amuck is a study in despair. A merciless universe is at the mercy of a non-sensical deity intent only upon obstacle creating and paradox, a big footed long eared deity who fully realizes his own malevolence and is amused by it.

On another level, Duck Amuck, offers caustic commentary on the relationship between artist and art, statue and sculptor, singer and song.

Finally Duck Amuck is reminiscent of Vonnegut at the zenith/nadir of his alienated idealist stage when in creation of *Breakfast of Champions*, Vonnegut creates a rupture between fiction and faction when he chooses to interrupt the

suicide of erstwhile car salesman Duane Hoover by bringing his omnipoten
author self into the scene not as a participant but as an observer. Of course, no
one recognizes the presence of the creator except for Kilgore Trout who comes
to the sudden suspicion that his own life may be nothing but another person's
imagination much like Ovid and Julia as they sat one Covid afternoon in
Birkdale in front of Big Daddy's.

Fortunately for Trout for Ovid for Julia or Paladin or Thornton Krell or Ice
Rivers and many others, the person imagining them wasn't Bugs Bunny. That
particular conundrum is saved for Daffy Duck.

Thus, Duck Amuck surpasses even Vonnegut in its visionary, surreal
chaotic desperate vision...a vision crystal clear to children everywhere.

Bringing Back the Rock Pile

I've made it back home from home.

My current home is in North Carolina. My home town state is New York.

When I grew up, I was blessed with grandparents, aunts, uncles, nieces, and nephews.

We visited one another often. I had a whole bunch of relatives on Wisconsin Street, just off of East Main, all of them were members of the Keenan family. My mother was the oldest of the four Keenan children. Wisconsin Street was one of my homes.

My grandmother and grandfather on my father's side lived in Holcomb, New York. My father's sister Martha, her husband Billy and their daughter Margaret also lived in the village. Holcomb was another of my homes.

Our family lived on Parsells Avenue in the 18th ward on the East Side of Rochester. Parsells was my first home. Before Martha and Billy moved to Holcomb, they too had lived on Parsells as had my grandparents before them.

My father's father bought some land on Canandaigua Lake in the 1930's and over the course of the next 30 years he built two cottages on that property. I was around for the building of the second cottage. We spent a lot of time in Canandaigua at the cottage and in the Lake. Canandaigua was yet another home for me. My parents let me bring friends with me when we went for weekends. My city friends grew to love the lake as well.

All four of the locations are distinct from one another. Although both Parsells and Wisconsin are city streets on the East side, Wisconsin Street was closer to the Main. Holcomb was a village. Canandaigua is a lake city. I had a different set of friends at each locale.

Now back to the home coming home.

My brother picked me up from the airport last week. He had bought and rebuilt a third house on Canandaigua Lake, next to the original two. I stayed at his house for the duration of my trip. Next door is my cousin Margaret who everyone has called Moonyeen since she was a child. Moon is 84 now. Her husband Corky lives with her. They married immediately after graduating from Holcomb High School. Holcomb High school no longer exists nor for that matter does Holcomb. Holcomb was absorbed by the larger town of East Bloomfield.

Corky and Moon have three children one of whom is my goddaughter. Lori also lives in Canandaigua but in the city not lakeside. Lori visits her Mom and Dad regularly and tries to intercede when her Dad starts one of his rants about driving. Corky only has one leg. He's had last rites a few times. His balance is shot. He's carrying a touch of dementia. He takes some spectacular falls. He insists that he can drive and that he's gonna get in that goddamned car and show everybody that he damned well can drive.

I was one of those gimmick Godfathers. I was only 12 myself so I imagine it was cute at the time. I hardly know Lori as she has moved around quite a bit and raised a family of her own. She has had a successful life which I tried to take credit for by claiming that my "godfathering style" was non interference and because I had left her alone, she had grownup correctly.

She got it.

She laughed

She thanked me for "not being there."

I assured her that it was no problem and I would continue to not be there.

That night, the remaining Keenans showed up. Tommy a retired cop who needs a walker to get around because of the bad knees he got chasing crooks around and Dotty, the youngest of the cousins who travels with her husband Jeff to Las Vegas very regularly now that they've become empty nesters. They were in Vegas just a few feet away from the target crowd when the sniper opened fire.

Dotty is the Keenan family historian.

Their brother Jimmy passed away in Covid season.

My sister Tears and her husband Larry also showed up. They live in Rochester, preserving the roots. They live on Shelford Road. Shelford Road is what Wisconsin Street becomes when it crosses into Irondequoit. Shelford and Wisconsin are the same street connected by a curve in the street called Wyand Crecent. After our family moved from Parsells we relocated to Wyand Crescent which is really an extension of Wisconsin Street where my mother grew up.

Neighborhood was a big deal back in those days.

Now many of us were together once again and perhaps for the last time for my "homecoming."

We touched a lot of bases together during this particular home run.

On the last day of my visit , I had one more goal on my homecoming bucket list, a dip into the waters of Crystal Beach. My brother had told me that he had a waterproof camera so I had a mission.

I wanted to take a picture of the "rock pile."

The rock pile has been in the same place for God knows how long. It's a bunch of large rocks gathered together in such a way that when you stand on them, your head is above water. If you step off the rock pile, the water is ten feet deep.

As soon as I was old enough, Vin took me out to the rock pile. I was scared to be in such deep water but Vin was near and he told me that I was safe.

I've repeated the process with my children.

A rocky rite of passage.

As far as I am aware, no one has ever seen the rock pile other than while experiencing it in/under the water. I decided to try and take a picture of it. reached its remembered location. I took a deep breath and dove down with Deke's camera.

There it was as it has always been.
Looking the same as it always does.
Silent and calm
Alone
No time had passed since the last time although it had been at least 10 years in above the surface time.
The rock pile was ready for its close up.
The rock pile has always been ready.

I didn't know how to use the new fangled camera. I surface dived and got near the rock pile. I clicked the camera button a couple of times before surfacing. I don't have glasses on when I swim and the cataracts are getting worse so I had no idea if the image was in focus, if the button I was hitting was the snap button or for that matter if the entire thing was actually happening as I have/had dreamed about this moment many times in my life and the camera never works in my dreams and I get back to look at the picture and there is nothing.

I swam back to shore.
I gave my brother the camera.
He asked me "Did you get it."

Like Mastin Thrust answered after catapult launching a paper mache boulder at a fake T rex when he was asked the same question in The Last Dinosaur, I had only one half-blind response.

"I don't know."

A few hours later I was on the plane and heading home from home.

This morning, as Jeff Bezos hurled himself into space at the cost of a few billion dollars, I received a photo message from my bro.

It's the picture of the rock pile
hat I have included here.
    Seen for the first time
    Out of the water
    I bring you back
    The rock pile
    And wish you all happy family
    And homes

Losing my Wallet

by Thornton Krell

Last month, my granddaughter Eva saw a woman right after the lady had been struck by a hit and run driver while jogging on Washington Street in Duxbury. Soon, other people began to crowd around this traumatizing sight.

The woman had been killed, her crumpled body on full display.

Soon it was discovered that the woman didn't have her wallet with her when she started her fatal run so for several hours after the body had been removed nobody had any idea who the victim was. She had no identity. A broken Jane Doe carted off in an ambulance.

This brings me to one of my greatest, secret fears; losing my wallet.

I am so afraid of losing my wallet that I never carry more than 20 bucks in my wallet at one time. I don't carry an ATM card or any credit cards because I'm scared to death of losing them. Whatever beer money I have, I carry in my pocket.

So, two nights ago, I lost my wallet. I was staying with the Peets, Ovid and Julia.

Everything was going perfectly. We were on our way to Birkdale Village for some music and ice cream. I got out of the shower and reached in my dresser to grab my wallet, fully expecting it to be there. It wasn't there.

Next began the furious search around the house to find the wallet. We had been all around Huntersville that day. We ate at a Lake Norman restaurant. We walked through the campus of Davidson University. We had a beer at our local Bistro, a place named Harvey's. I changed my clothes at least three times always feeling good about my wallet.

We checked all of those places to no avail. "Did anyone turn in a wallet today to lost and found." At the pool someone had in fact found a wallet and it was in lost and found. The lifeguard took me to it. It wasn't mine.

Mine was still gone.

My great fear had come true. I was in a state of panic. Everyone was concerned, not so much about the wallet...which had nothing in it....but rather about my propensity to brood and throw a black cloud over the rest of the visit.

I sat in my bedroom hyperventilating, two clicks away from a full fledged panic attack. I took many deep breaths and made up my mind that the lost wallet wasn't going to ruin the rest of the evening. To my amazement, I found that compartment and we proceeded to Birkdale. The compartment was my usual escape, comparing singers and bands. Elvis or Sinatra etc.

We arrived in the village. We listened to some music and had some ice cream.

While we were people watching in the village, it occurred to me that every single person that we saw had THEIR wallet. I was the only man without a wallet.

I had no identity.
I was nobody.
You know who else doesn't have a wallet.
Broken joggers
Victims of serial killers
Kids under the age of 12.
Those whose pockets had been picked.
Jane and John Doe
A bad crowd to be in for a "responsible" man.

The overwhelming humiliation of irresponsibility was calling and all I had to do was pick up the phone to ruin the night. I didn't pick up but the phone kept ringing.

When the worry phone is ringing, I start thinking about music and comparing bands.

Moody Blues or Pink Floyd. Allman Brothers or Dead or Band. Elvis or Sinatra.....Birds or Yardbirds.....Kinks or Costello...Animals or Zombies... GaGa or Madonna....Buddy Guy or Albert King....Jimi Hendrix or Neil Young.....James Brown or Bruce Springsteen....Yes or Genesis....Genesee Johnny or Blackjack Neelin...Clash or Ramones..... Johnny Cash or Garth Brooks.....Smokey Robinson or Lou Rawls...Aretha Franklin or Dionne Warwick....Frank Zappa or Jimi Hendrix....Beach Boys or Beatles....Heart or Dixie Chicks....Gene Vincent or Eddie Cochrane...Peter and Gordon or Jan and Dean.....Moody Blues or Who....Lynard Skynard or Marshall Tucker on and on.

If somehow a cop or a store owner asked me if I had my "license", I would have to say that I didn't. If they asked me why, I'd have to say that I had lost my wallet. We are so connected to our wallets that when we don't have them we begin to question our entire existence at least that's what the ringing phone was calling me to do.

Somehow the conversation drifted over to a discussion of the Sopranos.

I got a visual of Tony and asked myself "in this visual" does Tony have a wallet.

Of course Tony has his wallet. He's Tony Soprano. He ALWAYS has his wallet.
What kind of MAN, doesn't have his wallet.

RING, RING, RING went my unanswered inner phone.

Ronnettes or Supremes...Harry Belafonte or Neil Diamond.....Guns and Roses or Ramones....Tom Petty or Everly Brothers.....Johnny Mathis or Tony Bennet...Bobbwa or Adelle....Waylon or Willie.....Monkees or Rascals....Frankie Laine or Tex Ritter....Bobby Vee or Bobby Darin ....Glen Campbell or John Denver.....Four Tops or Four Seasons on and on.

We got through the night. I congratulated myself, whoever I was, which I wouldn't be able to prove if anybody asked me, on my composure based on the way that I was handling an overwhelming secret fear. My secret fear is that I am an irresponsible, immature, unfocused airhead, literally a loser.

We all have our secrets. Now you know mine. Without my wallet, I'm not Thornton Krell. I'm John Doe

I don't exist.

Shooting the Engineer

I keep shooting the engineer. He laughs and pulls his bullet ridden body of the linoleum tiles and says, "one more shot".

When I paginated my original, edited copy, it broke down to 700 pages. was expecting it to page out at around 190.

That's when the engineer rose from the dead for the fourth time and said "Whaddya think that you're Orson Welles or something this shit's way too long."

The son of a bitch started doing what he's always doing....revisiting.....revisioning, reflecting,.....line editing.......cutting....correcting, slashing, butchering

"You've got a million piece puzzle here and if any of the pieces are in the wrong place or if you have a few thousand pieces missing or if you have extra pieces from other puzzles mixed in with this one, then the whole thing becomes an unsolvable, phony mess."

He started slashing again.

That's when I grabbed his cleaver and slashed HIS ass.

"Maybe that's the end of your goddamned puzzle."

Then I shot the carcass a few more times to make sure

The son of a bitch immediately began to pull himself together although some of the pieces ended up in the wrong place and a couple of them were just plain gone.

I knew the book wasn't finished.

I knew the engineer would be back.

I knew what he was gonna say on his next reconstituted appearance.

What he says every time that I think I'm done with the book, whenever I'm ready to settle, whenever I think that nobody gives a shit anyway and that the whole thing is a waste of time pleading seductively for more time and more waste.

He's gonna say "one more shot".

Then we reflect.

Reflection always calms us down especially when we reflect upon downtown where the lights are much brighter. It's all about the light.

Then, finally we let go and get to the finish.

Fill Fuller

When I was a child and more susceptible to the invisible, I was told tha heaven and hell represented eternal reward or punishment. I asked "what is eternal?"

I thought I understood reward and punishment, Pretty sure that I over overstood sin and fire.

"Eternal is forever and ever and then on top of that another forever and another ever."

I tried to grasp eternity. Couldn't do it.

Still can't.

Same with God.

Hmmmmm

God is eternal.

Trying to grasp one is like trying to grasp the other and all of it is like trying to grasp the present moment which disappears the instant that we reach for it yet becomes immediately accessible a moment after that forever and ever or at least until we die, than the other thing takes over.

Each now moment is an atom in the infinite paradox of the eternal. When we enjoy the now, we enjoy a tiny bit of the eternal which means we get a glimpse of God within ourselves and suspect the eternal within each of us which is composed by the atoms of the moment.

It is our job, our destiny to fill each moment as fully as we are capable. Yet, let's face it most of our moments are occupied by the forgettable and we always orget when we're not paying full attention. We become so concentrated on the emporal that we lose sight of the eternal in our ongoing effort to measure our ives we imagine that the ruler rules or the scales dictate or the guy next door has a better car.

One of the many reasons that the Beatles were so spectacular is that when Paul and John were "full" of composing and or lead singing songs for their albums, they could call on George to fill fuller.

Something in the way fill fuller moves. Here comes Fill Fuller while my Fill Fuller gently weeps.

If you're still confused, imagine a stream cascading down a mountainside or glance at the accompanying images snapped by the great Ron Stochl or the upper falls tumbling into the Genessee as clicked by the magical Guy Coniglio or the visionary Robert Rondelli

Fill Fuller does at times resemble the two devouring snakes but at other times it resembles renewal, hope and indomitability.

So the challenge in our lives is to make more full the filler that defines our journeys. We do that by consciously filling fuller that filler. We become more aware of the paths leading up to whatever realizations we have collected. We all remember when we fell in love or when we broke our arm or went to our first ballgame or when we won the bet or when our parents died or are children born. Those moments stand out amidst the fog of the filler. As monumental as those moments are/were, they did not take place in a vacuum. We tend to remember where we were and who we were with but we tend to forget how we and they got there although sometimes we are reminded with music.These are the forgotten stories of our lives. We find ways to capture and express them, in my case with words that stay

It demands a constant conscious effort to more fully fill the filler. It demands struggle. It demands passion and suffering. It demands the loving of love. Humor takes care of itself and is present in every atom regardless of tears or laughter. It demands a sense of humility and guilt in the presence of the eternal. It demands appreciation for the paradox which embraces ambiguity. Humor is omnipresent when we are alert enough to seek it. It's our opportunity to shine as we all do when we remember to try and forget that we are trying.

It's our endeavor.

Our Forever endeavor.

Forever and ever.

Amen.

Photo by Guy Coniglio

Suddenly, it's too soon.

Most of the slings and arrows of life follow the same pattern. Gradual, gradual, gradual and then suddenly sudden.

Last week, we arrived in Boston for a meet the parents event. This time, we were the parents of Mary and we were meeting the parents of Jon.

Upon our arrival, we decided to take a walk along the river Charles, the muddy water made even more famous by the Standells as they sang about the city that they loved.

We started our walk at about 4:30 in the afternoon. The day was cool with the sunlight only occasionally peeking through the pouting cloud layer. Although leaves were aplenty, the peak season had already passed and left its memory on the ground. Early in the walk, we passed by a goose and he must have decided that we had some food or were a threat because suddenly all of the geese under his influence were out of the water and hot on our trail.

They followed us for fifty feet and must have come to the conclusion that we were neither threat nor food source as they slipped back into the river as suddenly as they had appeared.

By the time we got to our car, it was Five o'clock and the darkness was gathering around us.

As for Lynn and I, we are rarely out at night anymore. Our vision has diminished to such an extent that it's very difficult to drive at night. Driving is already the most dangerous activity that most of us engage in and it becomes an even bigger risk when ya can't see.

At home, our teevee schedule starts at 6:30 with David Muir, he of the perfect hair, who delivers us our dose of bad news every night. Then it's a flash through PBS news hour and then a fourteen minute zoom through Jeopardy. Next we're on the stream catching the big shows until it's 10 and we head for bed.

No time for night.

But here in Boston, after our walk we visited a tavern for burgers and beer The darkness descended. When we left the tavern an hour had passed in rea time but darkness was everywhere. Suddenly, I felt kinda drunk even though i was just one beer. Five hours had seemingly disappeared as the surrounding streets had taken on the aura of a midnight hour. I wasn't drunk, I was feeling midnight but if we hurried home we could still catch Muir and the bad news a 6:30 became 7;00.

Heading to Mary's mini-Cooper, I reminded myself of one of Yogi Berra's greatest observations, "It gets late awful early around here."

Same thing happens as we get older. The daylight surrenders with less graduality and the night arrives more suddenly. The more gradual, the less shocking is the sudden. I'll be 75 in two weeks. I'm beginning to learn these things in an end zone a couple hours before twilight.

The Reward

My oldest former students are approaching 70.
My youngest former students are turning 30.
I am in touch with many of them on Facebook.
I am in touch with none of my former teachers and I wish that I were.
Lynn is in touch with none of her former teachers
 She wonders why she or anybody else would be.
Here's the deal....all teachers good and bad
Remain in the lives of their students forever.
The butterfly and ripple effect.
When you ask someone to name their favorite subject
They will usually name a teacher to go along with that subject.
The seed is planted, interest activated
The influence is life long.
I learned from my bad teachers
How not to teach. How not to live
I put in practice what I learned from my good teachers
Every time that I make a right decision.
Learning what not to do from the bad
Learning what to do from the good
Even as I type these words.
Last week was Teacher's week
I heard from many of my students.
I treasured every shared memory
As they refreshed the power and the privilege
And the eternal reward of a career in education.
Stephen King's nightmare.
Some of those "kids"
Are reading this right now.
Good on ya
Don't do nuttin shtoopid.
Keep going, what you're doing is important
You will continue to succeed.

Re-Connecting with Mike

When Mike became a legend, I thought we would never meet again.

In 2014, I was delighted to add Mike to my list of Facebook friends. I wrote him a message and this is his response.

Hi Mr. Rivers

You wrote- 'I want to hear all about your life...' This line sort of freeze me up a bit and not sure how I would begin... Maybe I should start by saying that after all these years, I'm neither rich nor famous. But I'm doing mostly what I'm compelled to do, especially since 2000.

There were quite a few very difficult moments in time, but they happened to lie on the road I choose. Life from a material standpoint could have been much more comforting but I didn't find that they were the paths for me

The rewards that I've been blessed with don't necessarily translate to monetary means but in other forms that pertaining to the human spirit and I definitely feel very blessed with such.

Since leaving Rochester and heading to California, my goal has been to nurture and share film works that aim to express beautiful thoughts about this life on Earth. It was not my aim to work at the big studios like many of my classmates at CalArts, but then that was just exactly what I ended up when my college years came to an end...

In 1988, I began work at the Disney Studio and my production experiences began with 'The Little Mermaid'. It was very nice to be acquainted and gaining some insights into the film industry. It was just what I expected and I have no delusion even when the films I worked on were commercial successes.

I stayed there for 3 years and after Beauty and the Beast, I moved over to Warner Bros. at a time when animation suddenly become highly sought after by all the major Hollywood studios. For me, this is one way to grow artistically and not getting pigeon-toed into doing something the same forever.

There were many more features to followed, but the only one that I feel grateful to be part-of is The Iron Giant directed by Brad Bird. He's a wonderful director and definitely a very rare breed to find in such commercial enterprises.

In year 2000, a chance encounter allowed be to co-found a production company of my own and I began my indie feature entitled- 'My Little World'. I've been on this journey since, continuing and ongoing at moment... And so one may say- my tree hasn't bear fruit just yet

Also from 1994 to 2010, I became part time faculty at CalArts and giving classes relating to character animation. I thought this would be one nice way of sharing my creative experiences to the younger generations of artists. Many of my close friends today were once taking my classes over the years... and many new friendships are being forged in this same way and ongoing.

I'm very grateful for still keeping me in your thought (I have to say the content of this writing is definitely first of its kind in my life's journey).

In Vietnamese, there is a proverb 'When eating sweet fruits, do remember the ones who planted the trees'. I will always be grateful that our paths have crossed, for your always very supportive and encouragement at a time when a young person might need the most^^

Wishing you wonderful days and am definitely looking forward to learning the many interests in your universe through your postings here on Facebook
And in the End, the Truth Becomes Legend

After I posted Truth and Beauty on ABC tales I reluctantly sent Mike a copy of the story. Reluctant because I wanted the legend to be true. Mike responded and sure enough, the truth is as beautiful and wondrous as the legend and the perfect post script.

Hello Mr. Rivers,

WOW haha what an honor and I must say that I read most of your writing in extreme blushed condition... You have already prepped me with the *differences between truth, legend, fiction & faction... (Here, I remembered a moment in your book- the moment in the Eastman House theater I think)*

Memory often turns facts into larger-than-life legend, and in turn, more faction than true facts. I try to read your recollection from a 3rd person-point-of-view, learning about a person name 'Mike' in your story.

From this view, the story is fascinating and carries its own structure, with pieces of info that connect themselves into the grand ending, from beauty, to Kathy to Belle in Beauty & the Beast.

It was all very flattering and to this day, I still don't know how to behave when being flattered. It really is an honor for me to appear in your memory in such loving and delicate recollection as you have stated in the starting paragraph.

If I can make one wish, I wish the Disney facts can be more accurate. There are die-hard Disney fans that know all the facts on who did what; I worked on that film but I wasn't contributing in such deeper level creatively. I was credited as an animator in the Belle unit, but I wasn't the lead and didn't design that character.

Funny enough, the Lead Animator was James Baxter (very famous in the animation industry circle). He designed Belle after someone that he had a heart for at that time. Belle looked just like her. James had a Kathy and a beauty of his own.

Perhaps this particular part can be reworded in such a way that connects to the Kathy in your story, but from your perspective when you saw 'Beauty and the Beast' and recalling memory on Mike and Kathy that you once shepherded.

I don't have photographic memory of my past especially those early Henrietta days, and so it is always fascinating to learn how such moments in time were reflected especially, through the closer circle of friends and mentors that I crossed paths with.

I was surprised of your memory about Kathy. I did have a heart for a classmate named ___. But I thought no one knew that hahahaha She didn't know that for sure... I was extremely shy back then, especially with such social relations.

One fact that is completely true, beautiful, honest and elegant

'Mike is not famous. Mr. Rivers is FAMOUS!' It was true then, and still is now.

It's nice to be a legend in the mind of a legend.

Serenity is a Long Street

Lynn and I were cooling off on our front porch after a 3 mile walk. We were sipping on a bourbon inspired mixed drink. We noticed a family heading up the hill. Two young boys were racing each other up the hill, while the Mom and Dad lagged behind. The boy who was in the lead took a misstep and accidentally elbow dropped to the concrete, his brother tripped over the tumbler and took a knee dive of his own. Mom and Dad rushed to the crying boys. Mom lifted the son with the elbow scrape. Dad lifted the son with the skinned knee. We watched the whole thing happen as if it were in slow motion. By the time that the wounded parade got

to our house, Lynn had already gone to our fridge and grabbed a couple of popsicles. When they reached the sidewalk in front of our porch, Lynn said "that was quite a fall. Would the boys like a popsicle?"

The family stopped. The Mom said, "That would be nice."

Lynn came down the steps with popsicles already unwrapped and handed one to each crying child. The boys were taken by surprise. The wounded brothers accepted the popsicles and went right to work on them. They stopped crying. The parents thanked us. We chatted for a bit. As it turned out, the family lived on our street. Serenity is a long street. We went back to our drinks before heading inside for some reading, scrabble and teevee. It was yet another in a series of lovely days even as a deadly virus swirled around us. A week later Lynn was looking at our community web site. She noticed this entry and read it to me.

"It's so wonderful to live in a friendly diverse community like ours. Last week our boys were racing up Serenity hill when they took a spill one over the other. They got scraped up a little bit and they were crying. My husband and I picked them up and tried to calm them down and soothe their pain but it wasn't working. Then an older woman came out of one of the houses, carrying unwrapped popsicles which she offered to the boys. The boys took the popsicles and stopped crying as their pain eased. We chatted with the elderly couple who were so sweet and so kind. It's great to have neighbors like them."

Lynn finished reading the entry.

"Wow, Lynn, when did you get older and when did we become elderly, I asked with a smile". Lynn responded in kind, looking so young and beautiful.

After all the distance, and all the dreams, Lynn is still easing pain, including my own, while we continue to go the distance.

Who knew that the distance would lead to North Carolina, Huntersville, Birkdale, Vermillion and our young neighbors from up the street?

We like it here.

We grow older together. We appreciate the gift. We're only old once. There's still plenty of future to full fill and an eternal present to fill full.

Made in the USA
Middletown, DE
02 April 2024